Tina Nordström's Scandinavian Cooking
Simple Recipes for Home-Style Scandinavian Cuisine

Tina Nordström's Scandinavian Cooking

Simple Recipes for Home-Style Scandinavian Cuisine

Tina Nordström
Photography by Charlie Drevstam
Illustrations by Stina Wirsén
Translated by Veronica Choice

Skyhorse Publishing

Ramlösa Forever!

I WILL NEVER FORGET the day I held my first finished cookbook in my hands. It was like holding my newborn for the first time. I had a feeling of having made something that would last and live on forever. After that first book, things took off at lightning speed. I wrote a book a year for the next five years. Those first two books sold more than a million copies combined. Incredible to say the least! There were mile-long lines outside the bookstores where I was signing, and I remember sitting and writing "Merry Christmas from Tina" until my fingers were throbbing with pain.

My sixth "child" has taken some years to complete, but it's the most comprehensive book I have written yet. It's deliciously thick and sturdy, with its own distinct personality. It's not your typical, basic cookbook, although it does contain many classic recipes and foundations. Rather, I see it as a milestone. It contains the recipes I've carried with me and developed over the years; I consider it to be my foundation. Thus far, that is. Many of the flavors are from my childhood, but just as many come from other kitchens and traditions— even if I've given them my own interpretation. This book is a tasting key to my own kitchen!

The recipes for this book were written, tested, and photographed in a very special place. Ever since 2009, I've been renting this beautiful 19th century house at Ramlösa Park outside Helsingborg in the south of Sweden. This house is very special to me because I grew up in it as the child to a pair of restaurant owners! My current office is in my parents' old bedroom. From my office window, I can look out over Ramlösa Park, where I ran wild as a child, where I peed my pants, lost my teeth, fell in love, and broke up with boyfriends.

It's an important place for me, and not simply because my roots and my professional foundation are so incredibly entwined here (something I didn't fully realize until this book was photographed and completed). It's in this environment, on these worn-out wooden floors, that I renew my strength and energy. This somewhat ramshackle old house that holds so many memories for me ended up being the obvious backdrop for the photographs and the recipes for this book. I hope it has given this book a soul. This place makes me creative. This is where I have the people around me that I trust the most. Family and friends visit all the time, and I always have a pot of coffee brewing for anyone who shows up at my doorstep.

My parents, Gudrun and Björn Nordström, bought Ramlösa Tavern when I was a baby. Back in the day, fine ladies and gentlemen came to the springs at Ramlösa to drink straight from the source. My parents bought the tavern in 1974, and two years later, Mom and Dad acquired the Ramlösa Spring Hotel. It was an enormous investment. I was three years old at the time, and my brother, Peter, was five. There was a little pink house next to Ramlösa Tavern

Mom and Dad during one of their many events outside Ramlösa Spring Hotel, 1976.

Dad riding a horse in Ramlösa Park, 1976.

Mom with actress Anita Ekberg during her visit to Ramlösa, 1985.

RAMLÖSA WÄRDSHUS OCH BRUNNSHOTELLET

S. Brunnsvägen 70 — 253 67 HELSINGBORG
Tel. 042 – 29 62 57   Bankgiro 623 – 3365

Ramlösa 22/9-79

KÄRA GAMLA FRU NORDSTRÖM!

UNGA FRU NORDSTRÖM MED MAN
(DIN SON) BER OM VÅRT FÖRSENADE
TILLSTÅND ATT MEDFÖRA "BARNENA" PÅ
UTFLYKT TILL GÖTEBORG. SKULLE DU HA NÅGOT
ATT ERINRA MOT DETTA INSTÄLLER VI
GIVETVIS HELA UTFLYKTEN.
        VI BER OM SVAR OMGÅENDE
DÅ ALLT ÄR PACKAT O KLART.
        I HOPP OM DIN ÖDMJUKA
TILLÅTELSE TECKNAR VÄNLIGEN
            B.G. NORDSTRÖM m. BARN.

SVAR HAM
VÄMNAS PÅ BAKSIDAN

Har ingenting emot
denna som jag hoppas
trevliga ut färd med deka barn
men det är ju alltid bra att veta
dagen före eller så om barnen
i alla fall.

Ni behöver inte
deklarera edra privata angelägenheter
för mig, men barnen
vill jag gärna ha reda på var
dom är.

        Mycke nöje
önskar mor svärmor
o farmor.

My brother and I were almost always at Grandma and Grandpa's since Mom and Dad had to work almost all the time. Here are two letters, one written by my dad and the other by my grandma. The letter from Dad humbly asks if my brother and I may join him and my mother for an outing to Gothenburg with the family. My grandmother replies that it is okay for us to go but that next time she would appreciate if she could be notified earlier, not on the day of!

that once served as a makeshift cell for drunks who couldn't make it home after a night out; this was renovated, and my grandparents moved in. My grandfather worked the bar at the restaurant, kept track of the liquor inventory, and mixed the *Glögg* for Christmas. My grandmother was the epicenter of the family and the safe haven to which we kids ran for comfort. She was the one who helped us with our homework and the one to take us to gymnastics or soccer practice. And she was the one who cooked the most amazing day-to-day dishes. Sure, our dad's food was great, but that we considered to be more along the lines of "delicacies." Regular, everyday meals, such as green cabbage soup, and "custard," were grandma's territory.

The spring at Ramlösa is still active, and when you drink the water right by the rocks, it tastes like minerals and iron—almost like sucking on a nail. As a child, I used to play with the mineral deposits and wrote rust-colored messages on the walls.

When it's your job to stir up other people's appetites, it's important to guard your own. One way I do this—besides being in my favorite place on Earth—is to cook under the most simple of conditions. Many people are surprised when they see my professional kitchen and realize that it's as far from a sterile laboratory with cool machinery and shiny surfaces as you can get. There are no induction cooking ranges, large stainless steel kitchen appliances, or even a dishwasher. There is, however, an old electric stove and a tired, old bread maker. The coal filter fan makes noises, fuses blow, and the lighting could be better. But when I'm here, I do my best work, and this is where all my recipes for this book were created. I also have confidence that when I turn my recipes over to you, they'll work no matter what your kitchen looks like! If the recipe works in my Ramlösa kitchen, it will work in the most simplistic kitchen out there— because it's surely been tested in the direst of circumstances, just to guarantee that it will hold up under even the worst-case scenarios!

I truly hope that this book will be a staple tool in your kitchen, along with a great pepper mill and a really sharp knife. It should be placed right in the middle of the kitchen counter, it should be covered in sauce stains and embedded with thumbprints, and preferably some personal notations in the margins.

I also want this book to be as honest and true as possible. The pictures should exude the flavor of the dishes, and every item on the plate should be there for a reason. If the dish is brown, the picture should show it as brown. No fuss, but rather an honest book without any glitz.

It makes me happy to know that you are holding my book in your hands right at this moment, and I'm so proud that it's become such a substantial book to hold onto. I truly hope it will serve you well in your kitchen and that you find many new favorite recipes to cook often—because if this book ends up in the living room, I've failed completely!

Tina

One of my rust drawings offers a Ramlösa "Hello"!

My colleague, Benny Cederberg, and me planning the recipes for this book—perhaps making some changes and checking off what has already been photographed by Charlie Drevstam. We also do a lot of taste-testing!

Greens

Can you fall in love
with produce?
Can it love you
back?

Rutabaga = Candy for the Car Ride!

WHEN I WAS LITTLE, my grandparents gave me my own little plot of land where I could grow things. I was so incredibly proud of that little plot and started planning right away what I wanted to grow in it come spring. Carrots to the right and red beets to the left, and since I liked dill a lot, I had to have that there too.

I can still remember the taste of the first tender carrots that I pulled out of the soil. To be honest, I can't remember if the carrots were my grandmother's, my grandfather's, or mine, but the taste was definitely there. I just brushed off the dirt and took a bite. The idea that a little bit of dirt is good for the stomach applied even back then.

My mother's parents managed a dairy farm. It was in a beautiful location at Åsen in west Karup, with a spectacular view over Båstad. My aunt and my mother still live there today. I remember the smell of the hallways in their house— a little bit of cow and hay. The kitchen was pretty big, and the cabinets, which were once white, were well worn. I loved that kitchen and the white couch with its crocheted blanket that my grandfather always covered himself with to rest after dinner. To this day, it still hangs over our couch.

My grandmother's specialty was her crisp rolls. She would store her crisp rolls in the drawer at the bottom of the oven, where you generally keep your pans, so they would get drier

and drier each day. You had to
double dip them in juice in order
to make them soft enough to bite into. I especially loved the
darker edges.

Other fond memories are my grandmother's sago soup
and the teat-warm milk that Grandfather would let us sip
right there while he milked the cows. Warm and fatty, the
milk gently coated the interior of our mouths before the rich
drink slid down our throats and into our bellies. The warm,
sweet smell of the milk room was always special.

My grandparents also grew potatoes, carrots, lettuce, and
berries. My grandmother would make tea from blackcurrant
leaves and elderberry flowers. For my brother and me, it was
mostly fun and games at their house, of course, but the games
often included helping out around the farm. Like sowing
potatoes, for example. We sat in the back of the tractor with
our legs dangling above the ground, watching the seed
potatoes drop down the chute and on into the soil. The seed
potatoes were dropped in a chute from where we placed it
in a partition on its way down into the soil.

20

Another thing I will never forget is the rutabaga my grandmother gave us as a snack for the car ride home to Helsingborg. Today, if I gave my kids rutabaga as a snack, they'd look at me as if I were crazy, which is a shame, because I really liked the simple rutabaga and the sweet gesture from my grandmother.

Throughout my years as a chef, I've always been very fortunate. I've worked at restaurants where everyone knew what they were doing, and from them I accumulated a wealth of knowledge about the ingredients I use. You can, for example, peel or mash an artichoke, but when the petals are soft, you can either simply brush them or drag the rim of a spoon around the petals. Or you can easily roast  the artichoke in the oven with an unpeeled wedge of garlic. The sweetness of the artichoke becomes more pronounced when it's roasted and is almost caramelized.

Right now, we're not growing any vegetables in our garden because we simply don't have the time, but we do have wild cherry trees, four different kinds of grapes—two in our green houses and two located toward the southern end of the garden—as well as fig bushes and cherry,

apple, and plum trees. But I can't take credit for the berries, fruit trees, or grapes, since we moved into the former house of Christel Kvant, who is a great author and gardening expert from Helsingborg.

We've only cut down one apple tree since we moved in, and it was only because it was blocking a soccer goal. And just in case you're wondering: no, I don't preserve the berries and the fruit. We eat all of it right there and then. This year, we didn't get any apples because the kids stubbornly insisted on eating the unripe apples or using them as substitute golf balls.

I do dream of one day being able to weed among the asparagus, knees in the dirt, instead of being my kids' designated goalkeeper, or being able to grow my own tomatoes instead of buying them from the supermarket. You know, the old-fashioned way: seed, soil, and a little bit of sunshine and water! Somehow I always seem to forget that last part—even though I should be a natural jams and juices kind of girl—I never seem to succeed completely. I'm really good at sowing, but I'm not so good at watering, so the tomatoes usually end

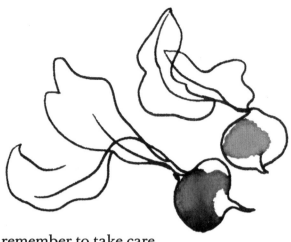

up falling to the ground before I even remember to take care of them. Once the kids start playing inside the green house, the grapes become just a distant memory, and the rhubarb is always overgrown before July is at an end.

But I guess there's no need to make things so complicated. Sowing spices and herbs doesn't really take that much time, and not much effort is necessary to water them and look after them. And it's such a joy to watch them grow! While my children are still young, sowing the herbs will probably be the only moments of "clog romance" I'll get. You know the feeling of putting on your "clogs" and walking out to your vegetable garden. I look for my scissors and walk out with a determined stride to the vegetable jungle to catch me some rosemary, dill, or sage. I love that feeling and I know I want more of that kind of living. But perhaps it'll take a few more years before I get there. . . . In the following chapter, you'll find all my favorite greens!

THINK LIKE TINA

BLANCHING

To blanch is to quickly boil a vegetable in un-salted water and then to cool it down in cold or ice water. Green vegetables or leaves can be blanched in club soda, since it naturally contains salt. This allows for the chlorophyll—meaning the green color—to be preserved within the vegetable.

BOIL SOME WATER

Vegetables should be boiled in "low" water (meaning water that just about covers the vegetables). When you *boil* vegetables—in comparison to when you *blanch* them—the water should contain salt, pepper, sugar, and either butter or a quality oil. You thereby create a nice broth at the same time, which you can store in the freezer and use for stews, soups, risotto, and sauces.

ROOT VEGETABLES
ARE NOT MARINE ANIMALS

If you want to prepare a meal by peeling the root vegetables beforehand, don't soak them in water until you're ready to cook with them. Instead, place the peeled root vegetables in a plastic bag and put them in the vegetable bin in the fridge. The exception is the Scorzonera, which oxidizes and turns dark very quickly. Put this in water with a few drops of fresh lemon juice to prevent the Scorzonera from changing colors. Potatoes should also be placed in water to prevent them from turning dark.

TREAT YOUR AVOCADO RIGHT

If you have a ripe avocado but you're not ready to eat it yet, you can place it in the fridge; this stops the ripening process. And if you have an unripe avocado that you want ripened faster, just place it in a bag with an apple or banana. These emit ethylene gas that speeds up the ripening process.

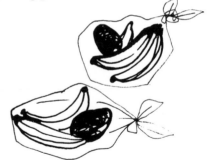

oldies but goldies

CHOOSE THE UGLY MUSHROOMS!

Pick the mushrooms that are a little shriveled. These have more flavor and contain less water, which makes them taste better. At restaurant school, I was taught to wash mushrooms in water and flour. The flour was used to carry the dirt and soil to the bottom of the flour bath. Back then this was absolutely necessary—in those days, horse manure was used as a mushroom substrate!

CUT THIN SLICES

When you need to cut your vegetables in really thin slices, use a vegetable slicer. Another word for vegetable slicer is a mandolin slicer.

KITCHEN FRENCH

Did you know that sauté is just a fancier way to say fry? And clarified butter is the same as melted butter? The meaning of *blanching* can be found on the previous page.

I BET YOU DIDN'T KNOW THIS!

If you have a hard time telling the difference between the *parsnip* and the *parsley root*, just remember that the parsnip's stalk-attachment retracts, whereas the parsley root's stalk stands up in a tip or peak.

The Scorzonera is also called poor man's asparagus since the flavor of Scorzonera is similar to that of mild asparagus.

In England, the rutabaga is called "Swede," and in the United States, it's called "rutabaga." Funnily enough, "rutabaga" is a twist on the Swedish word "rotabagge," which is what people in the southwest of Sweden call it!

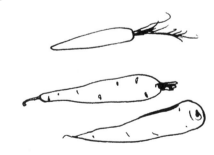

ROASTING FOR MORE FLAVOR

When you roast root vegetables, you concentrate their flavors. A boiled carrot actually has less "carrot flavor" than a roasted one.

1. Waldorf Salad

This classic salad always tastes the best at the Waldorf Astoria Hotel in New York City, where it originates. Other than this variation, that is! The dressing should be thick, not watery, and the ingredients for the salad should be dry. The dressing is meant to "glaze" the salad. A Waldorf salad is best enjoyed on its own, perhaps as an appetizer.

4 SERVINGS

½ celery root (celeriac)

3 celery stalks

2 firm pears

olive oil

*sea salt flakes, freshly ground white or
    black pepper*

DRESSING:

¾ cup (200 ml) walnuts

½ cup (100 ml) mayonnaise (see page 109)

½ cup (100 ml) heavy cream

1 tsp Worcestershire sauce

¼ tsp salt

DIRECTIONS:

1. Peel the celery root. Cut it first in slices and then into thin strips. Slice the celery stalks diagonally. Place the celeriac and celery in a pot of boiling water for about 30 seconds. Drain and rinse under cold water. Finish by drying the celeriac and celery on paper towels.
2. Preheat the oven to 425°F (220°C). Roast the walnuts in the oven. Taste a nut to make sure it has been fully roasted. Chop the walnuts.
3. Mix the rest of the ingredients for the dressing and stir the walnuts into the salad dressing mixture.
4. Slice the pears into thin slices with a cheese grater or mandolin. Arrange them flat on four small plates or on one large serving plate. Sprinkle some olive oil, salt and pepper on top of the pear slices—but be careful not to overdo it!
5. Add the celery and celeriac to the dressing mixture and pour on top of the pear slices. Serve immediately.

2. Endive Salad with Pear, Grapefruit, and Hazelnuts

Use grapefruit during the wintertime when it's in season and is cheapest. That way, there's a good reason to make this salad. Why not mix it with a little bit of cooked bulgur, wheat, or couscous to make it meatier? It's a perfect complement to a cheese platter, so leave out the grapes (and drink them instead!).

4 SERVINGS

1 orange

1 lemon

1 grapefruit

1 pear

2 endives

1 box watercress, garden cress, or fresh spinach

1¼ cups (150 g) roasted hazelnuts

CITRUS VINAIGRETTE:

⅓ cup (75 ml) olive oil

juice from the sliced citrus fruits above

½ shallot, finely chopped

½ tsp salt

¼ tsp freshly ground white or black pepper

DIRECTIONS:

1. Slice the orange, lemon, and grapefruit. Save the juices for the vinaigrette. Slice the pear into thin slices.
2. Mix the ingredients for the vinaigrette.
3. Rinse and separate the endive leaves. Place in a bowl with ice water (to remove some of the bitter flavor and make the leaves really crispy). Let dry on paper towels. Mix the leaves with the citrus fruits, pear, and cress, and place on a platter.
4. Drizzle the dressing on the salad, and top it off with the roasted hazelnuts.

3. Caesar Salad

This recipe originated in Mexico in the 1920s, and as with so many other classics, the salad was the successful result of a hasty burst of inspiration. Caesar Cardini was the man behind the recipe, and the dressing he created is just as good as a sauce to eat with steamed fish or roast beef.

4 SERVINGS
2 heads of Romaine lettuce

CAESAR DRESSING:
2 garlic cloves
2 egg yolks
7 sardine fillets
⅔ cup (150 ml) shredded Parmesan
½ lemon, zest and juice
⅔ cup (150 ml) olive oil
¼ tsp salt, ¼ tsp freshly ground white or black
  pepper

CROUTONS:
4 slices sourdough bread
2 tbsp olive oil
1 pinch salt

DIRECTIONS:
1. Preheat the oven to 400°F (200°C).
2. Mix the peeled garlic, egg yolks, and sardines until mixture is smooth. Add Parmesan, lemon juice, and zest. Mix for another couple of seconds. Add the oil, a little bit at a time, while stirring constantly. Add more oil if you want a thicker consistency. Add salt and pepper to taste.
3. Break the bread into large chunks. Drizzle with olive oil and then sprinkle some salt on top. Roast in the oven until golden brown, for about 4–6 minutes.
4. Rinse the lettuce and dry it with paper towels. Mix the lettuce and the dressing, and serve on a serving platter or individual plates. Top it off with the croutons. Serve the salad as is or with chicken, beef, or some delicious ham.

28

4. Cress Salad with Coconut and Lime

When I was younger, my mother would buy my brother and me each a coconut from time to time. It always took a long time to break into the coconut and even more time to eat it up—and the coconut would, unfortunately, dry out a little in the end.

Mirin is a sweet rice wine used in Japanese cooking. Consider this salad as an everyday salad. If you can't find large-leaf cress, just use fresh spinach and some garden cress instead.

4 SERVINGS
1 box watercress or baby spinach (approx. 2½ oz
  [70 g])
¾ cup (200 ml) thinly sliced coconut, fresh (use
  a potato peeler)
2 limes, peeled and thinly sliced

MIRIN VINAIGRETTE:
3 tbsp olive oil
2 tbsp mirin
1 tbsp Japanese soy sauce
1 tbsp freshly squeezed lime juice
freshly ground white or black pepper

DIRECTIONS:
1. Mix the ingredients for the vinaigrette.
2. Arrange the cress, coconut, and lime on plates and sprinkle the vinaigrette on top.
3. Serve with meatballs on any regular Wednesday.

ROASTED NUTS AND ALMONDS
Nuts and almonds are absolutely delicious when roasted. Roast them on a baking sheet in the oven at 425°F (220°C) for about 7–10 minutes.

2. 3.

4. 5.

5. Zucchini Salad with Sweet Peas in Lemon Vinaigrette Reduction

It's so easy to make a great salad! In this recipe the lemon vinaigrette reduction takes center stage—it's a super-vinaigrette that pairs well with many things. Compared to other vinaigrettes, it consists of more than just oil and vinegar.

4 SERVINGS
1 zucchini
approx. 9 oz (250 g) sweet peas
¾ cup (200 ml) fresh parsley
a pinch of sea salt

LEMON VINAIGRETTE REDUCTION:
⅔ cup (150 ml) water
1 tbsp honey
1 lemon, zest and juice
½ shallot, finely chopped
3 tbsp canola oil
salt and freshly ground white or black pepper

DIRECTIONS:
1. Cut the zucchini into thin slices with a vegetable mandolin or cheese grater. Slice the sweet peas into thin slivers. Combine the vegetables and parsley in a bowl, and sprinkle with salt. Mix carefully and put to the side.
2. Mix water, honey, lemon juice, and shallot in a pot, and let it simmer until the volume is reduced by half. Sprinkle with canola oil, and season with salt and pepper while stirring. Let the vinaigrette cool.
3. Dress the zucchini salad with the lemon vinaigrette, and pour onto plates.
4. Serve the salad as an accompaniment to barbecued pork during the summer.

6. Tomato and Buffalo Mozzarella Salad with Caramelized Butter and Basil

This dish is inspired by Copenhagen's really cool restaurant Paté (perhaps not so much "inspired" as I simply stole the whole recipe . . .). It uses only a few ingredients, but they're in perfect harmony, and the caramelized butter is addictive! A great dish to complement the cold cuts at that big party.

4 SERVINGS
3⅓ cups (600 g) tomatoes, preferably a mixed assortment
4 packages buffalo mozzarella cheese (each approx. 18 oz [125 g])
5 tbsp + 1 tsp (75 g) butter, preferably organic
½ lemon
1 bunch of basil
salt and freshly ground black pepper

DIRECTIONS:
1. Cut the tomatoes into slices or chunks. Chop the cheese into large chunks. Arrange the cheese and tomatoes on a plate.
2. Melt the butter in a frying pan.
3. Squeeze the lemon juice onto the butter and spoon the mixture on top of the tomatoes and cheese. Top the dish with fresh basil. Season with salt and pepper.
4. Serve immediately, either warm or at room temperature.

Super Tasty

CARAMELIZING BUTTER
Don't be afraid to melt the butter at high temperatures. The butter will first melt and then it will bubble up again; it's not until after it bubbles that the butter will start to caramelize. When it does, the salt will fall to the bottom of the pan and there will be a layer of golden brown butter on top.

6.

7. Thai Cabbage and Celery Salad

I created this salad when I was looking to update our regular Napa cabbage recipe (or Chinese cabbage as it is also known). Napa cabbage has fantastic qualities. It can be fried without getting soggy, and it's very crispy when eaten raw. This recipe is for all of you who don't think Napa cabbage belongs in the salad category. Eat this spicy Thai salad with some barbecued meat or fish. It tastes great with everything—even as the main dish.

4 SERVINGS
1 celery stalk
½ Napa cabbage
½ red chili
1 tbsp sesame oil
2 tbsp fish sauce
1 tbsp rice vinegar
1 tbsp mirin
chopped cashews (optional)

DIRECTIONS:
1. Cut the celery and the cabbage into thin slices. Core and shred the chili.
2. Heat a frying pan until it becomes really hot. Pour the sesame oil into the pan and flash-fry the celery, Napa cabbage, chili, and sesame seeds.
3. Add fish sauce, rice vinegar, and mirin. If you like, you can top the salad with some chopped cashews.

8. Cream-marinated Red Currant Salad

This cream dressing is beyond great! The fat from the cream and the acid from the lemon are perfect together. We often served this salad at the restaurant Petri Pumpa in Lund. Notice in the picture how the heads of lettuce should be cut to prevent them from imploding like a wet green lump when you "dress" them. It's a great side dish at barbecues. Eat it when you're longing for summer!

4 SERVINGS
2 heads of lettuce, leaf lettuce, for example
4½ oz (125 g) red currants or other red berries
CREAM DRESSING:
¾ cup (200 ml) heavy cream
3 tbsp freshly squeezed lemon juice
½ tbsp sugar
Salt, freshly ground white or black pepper

DIRECTIONS:
1. Rinse the lettuce and cut the heads in half.
2. Mix the ingredients for the dressing until it thickens slightly from the acid in the lemon juice. Season with salt and pepper.
3. Fold the lettuce and currants over in the dressing and set them on a plate.

Super Tasty

ADD BERRIES TO YOUR SALAD
Adding fresh, tart berries to your salad brings a lovely and refreshing touch.

9.

9. Kohlrabi Salad with Fennel, Mint, and Maple Syrup Vinaigrette

These flavors really get me going! With a few ingredients and some simple tricks, we can all be kings of our kitchens. From the supermarket, the mandolin slicer, also known as a vegetable slicer, will cost you about as much as a cup of coffee and a pastry, and it's definitely worth the investment. Make a big batch of the maple syrup vinaigrette. You can use it in many other salads too.

4 SERVINGS
2 kohlrabi
1 fennel
10–15 fresh mint leaves

MAPLE SYRUP VINAGRETTE:
1 lemon, zest + ½ lemon, juice
1½–2 tbsp maple syrup
3 tbsp olive oil
salt, freshly ground white or black pepper

DIRECTIONS:
1. Peel the kohlrabi if it has a thick skin. Clean the fennel. Thinly slice the kohlrabi and fennel with a mandolin. Place the slices in a plastic bag.
2. Mix the ingredients for the vinaigrette and pour it into the plastic bag. Tie the bag and gently massage the kohlrabi and fennel until they are soft.
3. Coarsely chop the mint leaves. Pour the salad onto a plate and spread the mint leaves on top of it.
4. Serve with any everyday dish you can think of!

10. Picnic Coleslaw

Doesn't it look great in that jar? Simple and tasty and without any mess! Put everything in the jar, close the lid, and just pop it in the fridge! It's a perfect gift to bring to any barbecue or summer potluck. And why not try it using different kinds of cabbage?

8 SERVINGS
1 small red onion
¼ savoy cabbage
¼ white cabbage
¼ red cabbage
1 endive
1 bunch parsley

MUSTARD DRESSING:
1½ tbsp Dijon mustard
2 tbsp red wine vinegar
1 egg yolk
1 garlic clove, finely chopped
¾ cup (200 ml) canola oil
1 tsp salt, freshly ground white or black pepper

DIRECTIONS:
1. Peel the red onion. Use a mandolin to thinly slice the cabbage, endive, and onion. Layer the ingredients with the parsley in a big glass jar.
2. Mix mustard, vinegar, egg yolk, and garlic and add the oil drop by drop while constantly whisking until the dressing thickens. Season with salt and pepper. Pour into a bottle and close the lid.
3. Pour the dressing into the glass jar. Shake the jar enough to coat all the ingredients in the dressing.
4. Serve the coleslaw with cold cuts and bread. It will last for one week in the fridge.

10.

11. Tomato Soup with Chili and Roasted Eggplant

This tomato soup is a great basic recipe that you can change up by just adding different things. The fun thing about eggplant is that although it can often lack flavor, if you roast it in the oven, it can really enhance the sweetness, and the texture turns smooth and silky. You can almost feel it tickle your throat as you take a bite. This is a solid and a somewhat spicy soup, with a bit of extra olive oil in it. The oil is used both for roasting and for enhancing the flavors of the soup.

4 SERVINGS

3 shallots
2 garlic cloves
½ red chili
10 tomatoes (approx. 2 lbs [1 kg])
3 twigs of fresh thyme (or ½ tbsp dried)
3½ tbsp (50 ml) high-quality olive oil
2 cups (500 ml) water
1 can whole tomatoes (approx. 14 oz [400 g])
½ lemon, juice
1 tsp sugar
2 tsp salt, freshly ground white or black pepper
Parmesan for serving

ROASTED EGGPLANT:

1 eggplant
olive oil for frying
salt, freshly ground white or black pepper
1 twig of fresh thyme

DIRECTIONS:

1. Peel and slice the shallots. Peel the garlic cloves and crush with the blade of the knife. Core and finely chop the chili.
2. Chop the tomatoes and fry lightly in olive oil. Add onion, garlic, chili, and thyme.
3. Add water, canned tomatoes with the juices, lemon juice, sugar, and salt. It might seem as though two teaspoons of salt is a bit much, but the acid in the tomatoes actually requires more salt. Let the soup simmer over medium heat for 15–20 minutes.
4. Preheat the oven to 425°F (220°C).
5. Peel the eggplant and cut it into long strips. Heat the olive oil in a pan and sauté the eggplant strips until golden brown. Season with salt and pepper, and place them on a baking sheet. Roast them in the oven for about 10 minutes.
6. Pour the roasted eggplant strips into a bowl, and mash them coarsely. Drizzle with olive oil and season with salt, pepper, and thyme.
7. Serve the soup hot, topped with roasted eggplants and shredded Parmesan.

PERFECT AS A SAUCE FOR PORK TENDERLOIN

This soup is perfect to pour over pork tenderloin. Put the pan in the oven at 300°F (150°C) for about 40 minutes.

12. Gazpacho

During my restaurant years, we used to run the gazpacho through the dough mixer, sometimes for hours. This was to make sure the ingredients got crushed together instead of just mixed. And it turned out so great! This recipe is for us everyday cooks who don't have giant 20-gallon dough mixers at home. Serve the gazpacho cold, at room temperature, or warm with a dollop of crème fraîche or fatty sour cream. It tastes better when it's been allowed to rest for a while, so prepare the soup the day before you plan to serve it.

8 SERVINGS

    2 cucumbers
    2 shallots
    2 garlic cloves
    4 slices white bread, without crusts
    6 ripe vine tomatoes
    1 red pepper + 1 orange pepper
    3½ tbsp (50 ml) olive oil
    3 tbsp red wine vinegar
    1 cup (250 ml) tomato juice
    ½ cup (100 ml) freshly chopped cilantro
    ½ lemon, juice
    4 dashes of red Tabasco
    1 tsp sugar
    1 tsp salt, freshly ground white or black pepper

DIRECTIONS:
1. Peel the cucumbers, shallots, and garlic cloves. Chop the cucumbers, onion, bread, tomatoes, and peppers into large chunks.
2. Mix olive oil, vinegar, tomato juice, cilantro, lemon juice, Tabasco sauce, and sugar for the marinade. Pour in the vegetables and let them marinate in the fridge for about two hours.
3. Mix it all together and season with salt and pepper.
4. Serve the soup with some fresh bread. Feel free to top it off with some seafood, such as crab, crawfish, or shrimp.

13. Jerusalem Artichoke Soup with Toast Greta

Your stomach will get a little bubbly from eating Jerusalem artichokes. Just so you know. This soup is so irresistible that it causes major problems in many restaurants because people can't get enough of it! The classic toast Greta—or beef Greta—was created by cook Lovisa Svanberg, who made it for Greta Odén, wife of the owner of City Hotel in Karlstad.

4 SERVINGS
JERUSALEM ARTICHOKE SOUP:
    3½ cups (600 g) Jerusalem artichokes
    1 yellow onion
    2 garlic cloves
    oil for sautéing
    ½ cup (100 ml) heavy cream
    1⅔ cup (400 ml) milk
    2½ cups (600 ml) water
    ½ lemon, juice
    1½ tsp salt, freshly ground white or black pepper
TOAST GRETA:
    9 oz (250 g) potatoes (3–4 regular sized)
    14 oz (400 g) beef tenderloin
    1 shallot
    butter for sautéing
    salt, freshly ground white or black pepper
    1 tbsp Dijon mustard
    ½ cup (100 ml) chopped parsley
    4 slices white bread

DIRECTIONS:
1. Peel and cut the artichokes into smaller pieces (if the skin is thin and light in color, you can just scrub them with a brush). Place the Jerusalem artichokes immediately in water, preferably with a little lemon juice so they don't change color. Peel and slice the onion and garlic.

2. Sauté the artichokes with the onion and garlic with a little bit of oil. Pour the cream, milk, water, lemon juice, and salt over the artichokes, and let simmer until they have softened, for about 15–30 minutes.

3. Mix the soup until it is smooth; use a hand blender right there in the pot. Season with some pepper.

4. Peel the potatoes. Cut the potatoes and the beef tenderloin into cubes. Peel and slice the onion. Sauté the potatoes in butter until golden brown. Add the beef and onion and continue sautéing until both potatoes and beef are thoroughly cooked. This all depends on how big you've made the cubes. Season with salt and pepper, and then stir in the mustard and parsley.

5. Toast the bread. Divide the Greta mix onto the slices and serve the toast right away with the hot soup.

14. Mushroom Soup with Goat Cheese and Thyme-infused Cream

Buy a more inexpensive goat cheese (the kind you can get in a long, prepackaged roll). It's perfect for this recipe. The cream on top is a little bit '80s style—but I like it and I'm sure you will too. This is a simple way to enhance a mushroom soup. The cheese provides a lot of flavor and makes the soup a little more "restaurant style"—in a good way.

4 SERVINGS
2 quarts (2 liters) mixed mushrooms
2 shallots
4 garlic cloves
7 oz (200 g) goat cheese
oil and butter for sautéing

2 cups (500 ml) water
¾ cup (200 ml) heavy cream
¾ cup (200 ml) milk
1 tsp freshly squeezed lemon juice
½ tsp sugar
1 tsp salt, freshly ground white or black pepper

THYME-INFUSED CREAM:
½ cup (100 ml) light whipping cream
2 twigs of fresh thyme
pinch of sea salt

DIRECTIONS:
1. Brush and clean the mushrooms.

2. Peel and slice the shallots thinly. Peel and crush the garlic cloves with a wide knife.

3. Sauté half of the mushrooms in oil with the onion and two of the garlic cloves. Add water, cream, milk, lemon juice, sugar, and salt. Simmer for about 10–15 minutes.

4. Crumble the cheese into the soup. Whisk until the cheese has melted into the soup and then remove the pot from the heat. Season with a little bit of pepper.

5. Sauté the rest of the mushrooms in butter and the last two garlic cloves. Season with salt and pepper. Distribute the sautéed mushrooms across four dishes. Pour the soup over the mushrooms and finish by adding a small dollop of the thyme-infused cream. Serve immediately.

CRUSHED GARLIC
If you're in a hurry, you don't have to finely chop the garlic. You can just crush the clove with the flat side of the knife blade and then sauté in butter or oil. The flavor will be just the same.

15.

15. Lebanese Lentil Soup

My daughter and I love lentils. The spice mix for this should be a little daring—something more than just salt and pepper. My little girl tells me that the flavor reminds her of tacos, which isn't entirely wrong since oregano is the only thing missing. . . . For those of you who consider lentils old and boring—think again! They're cheap and tasty and there are so many dishes to make with them. You can also serve this soup as a sauce for roast cod.

4 SERVINGS

1 yellow onion
4 garlic cloves
1¼ cups (300 ml) Beluga or Puy lentils
1 tsp ground cumin
1 tsp paprika
¼ tsp cayenne pepper
½ tsp salt
½ tsp freshly ground white or black pepper
2 tbsp olive oil
3 cups (750 ml) water
2 cups (500 ml) Del Monte tomato juice, or a
    similar variety (can be found in any supermarket)
½ lemon, juice
3½ tbsp freshly chopped parsley

DIRECTIONS:

1. Peel and finely chop the onion. Peel and thinly slice the garlic cloves.
2. Put onion, garlic, lentils, and dry spices into a pot. Pour some olive oil on top and let it all sizzle for a few minutes.
3. Add the water and the tomato juice and cover with a lid. Bring to a boil. Remove the lid and let the soup simmer for another 20 minutes—give or take a few minutes, depending on what kind of lentils you're using.
4. Season with freshly squeezed lemon juice and sprinkle parsley on top. Serve the soup hot with bread (for example, the Manitoba baguettes on page 268).

16. White Asparagus Soup with Bread and Salami

I'm almost too embarrassed to write this, but canned white asparagus is *outstanding* for this recipe! Anyone can make this soup. End of story.

4 SERVINGS

1 shallot
2 garlic cloves
olive oil
2 cans white asparagus with broth (each approx.
    12 oz [330 g])
1¼ cups (300 ml) heavy cream + 1⅔ cups (400 ml)
    milk
1 tsp salt
½ lemon, juice
approx. 8 slices salami
4 slices of bread, preferably ciabatta or another
    bread with a nice crust

DIRECTIONS:

1. Peel and finely chop the shallot. Peel the garlic and crush them with the blade of the knife. Fry the onion and garlic in olive oil.
2. Add the asparagus (whole or in pieces—it makes no difference, as the asparagus will dissolve quickly). Add the broth, heavy cream, milk, salt, and lemon juice. Let simmer for 10–15 minutes.
3. Mix the soup right in the pot with a hand mixer. Pour the soup into deep bowls. Top with some small chunks of bread and some "shredded" salami. Serve the soup hot. You can also pour the soup over a piece of fish before placing the delicious concoction in the oven.

NO CHEAP BREADS FOR SOUP

Fresh bread is really delicious with soup but make sure to choose good quality bread—preferably white bread. Good quality bread will keep its shape and crust when it's in the soup; cheap breads will just dissolve into mush.

46

16.

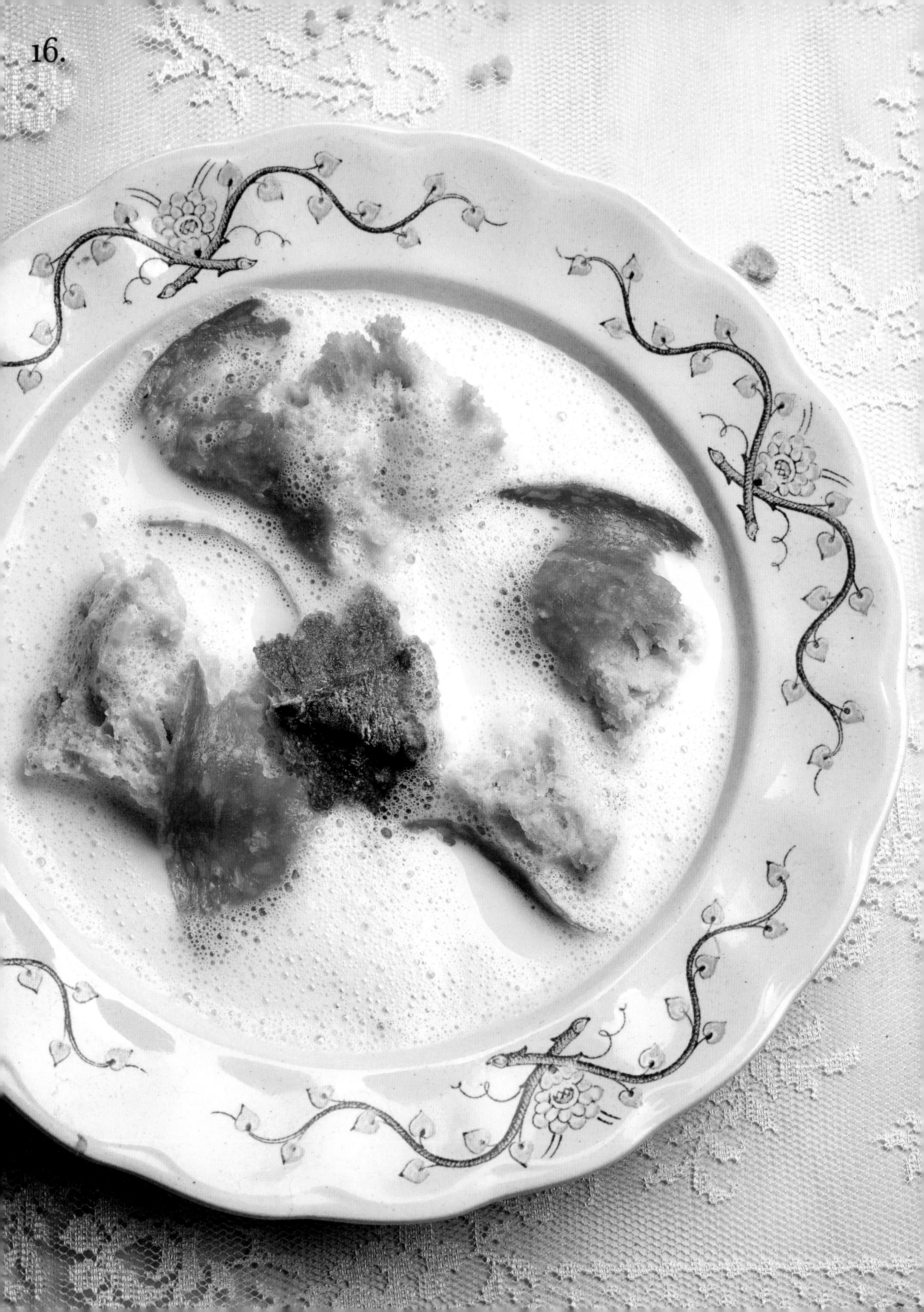

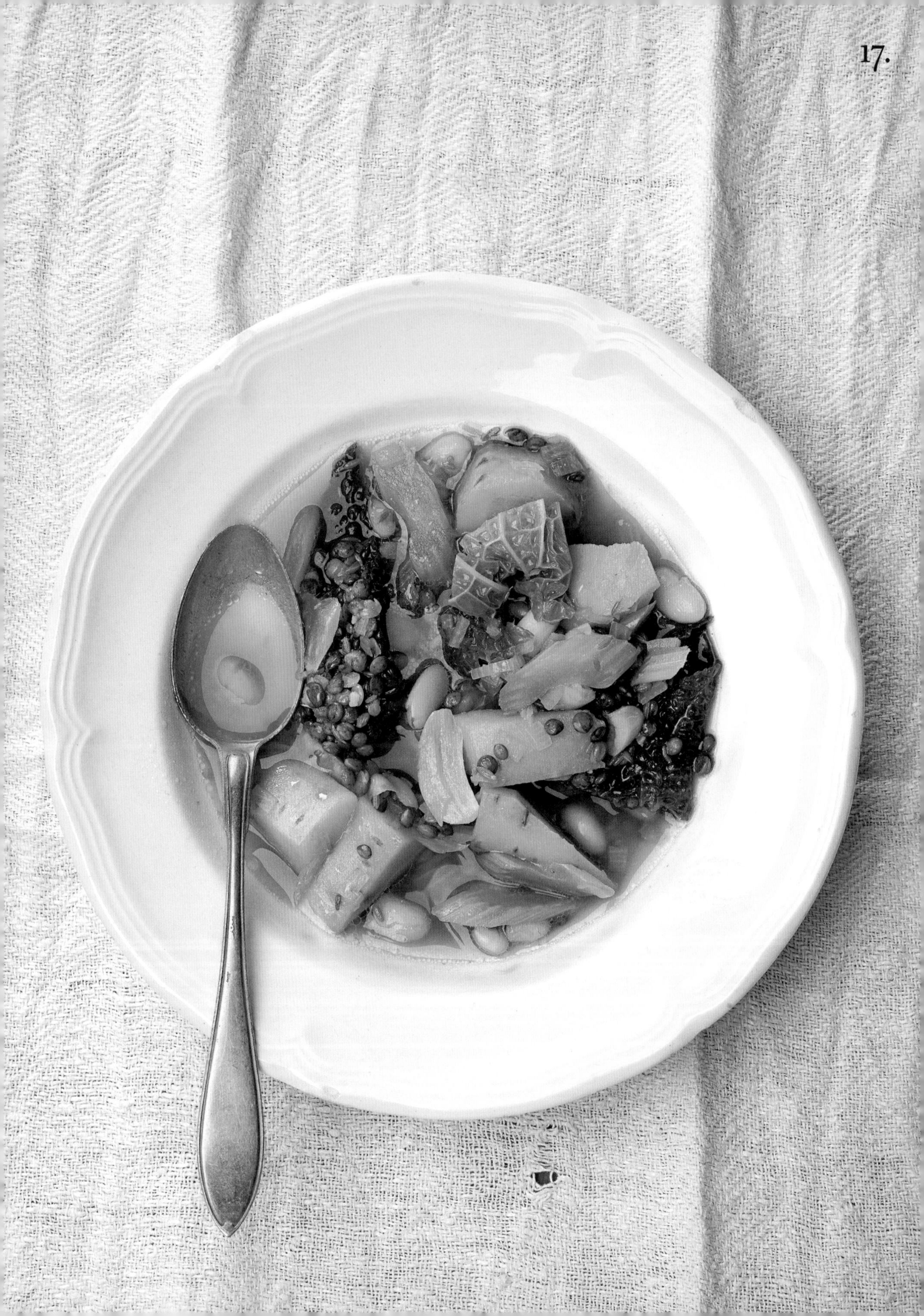

17.

17. Minestrone with White Beans, Saffron, and Cumin

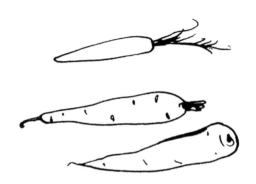

A fun soup that's also vegetarian. It's a simple concoction of saffron, cumin, and canned white beans with either beluga or puy lentils. You can turn the vegetarian soup into a hearty casserole by sautéing some sausages, slicing them into the soup, and simmering for a few minutes. It's up to you!

4 SERVINGS

1 carrot
1 parsnip
1 yellow onion
2 garlic cloves
2 celery stalks
2 tbsp olive oil
a pinch (½ g) of saffron (1 packet)
2 tsp whole or 1 tsp ground cumin
½ cup (100 ml) beluga or puy lentils
3 cups (700 ml) water
14 oz (400 g) canned white beans
1 tsp sea salt
freshly ground white or black pepper

DIRECTIONS:

1. Peel the carrot and parsnip and cut them into pieces. Peel the onion and garlic cloves. Finely chop the onion and crush the garlic cloves with the knife blade. Cut the celery diagonally as finely as possible.
2. Sauté the vegetables and onion in olive oil with saffron, cumin, and lentils. Pour water over the mixture and simmer under a closed lid until the lentils are soft. Add the white kidney beans (without their stock). Season with salt and pepper.
3. Serve the soup hot, perhaps with a slice of brie or a dollop of ricotta on top—and with a delicious slice of sourdough bread.

MY VEGETABLE STOCK

For soups, risotto, casseroles, and sauces where water is needed, you can substitute it with a flavorful homemade vegetable stock. You can also boil your vegetables in the stock, like in the cauliflower recipe on page 65.

1 parsnip, chopped
1 carrot, chopped
4–5 celery stalks, sliced
1 yellow onion, chopped
3 unpeeled garlic cloves in their skins, crushed
3–4 prunes
1 floret parsley and tarragon
3 star anises
4–5 crushed white peppercorns
½ tsp salt
water

DIRECTIONS:

Put all the vegetables and the onion into a pot with the prunes and spices. Cover everything with water and let it simmer for about an hour. Strain the stock and let it cool in the fridge.

18. Green Cabbage Soup

At school I always loved green cabbage soup because that always meant we would get pear ice cream for dessert. But nothing beats my grandmother's green cabbage soup with her delicious quenelles and egg. Nutmeg adds a nice flavor to the soup.

4 SERVINGS

4 cups (500 g) frozen chopped green cabbage
1 yellow onion
1 garlic clove
2 tbsp butter
½ –1 tsp ground nutmeg
1 tbsp flour
3⅓ cups (800 ml) water
1½ tsp salt
freshly ground white or black pepper
hardboiled eggs for serving (optional)

DIRECTIONS:

1. Defrost the cabbage.
2. Peel and finely chop the onion. Peel and crush the garlic. In a large pot, melt the butter and sauté the onion, garlic, and nutmeg.
3. Add the cabbage and sauté for a couple minutes more. Sprinkle the flour over the cabbage and pour the water on top. Let simmer for 20 minutes. Season with salt and pepper.
4. Serve the soup hot with a boiled egg on top (optional—boil the eggs for 4 minutes, page 93).

19. Potato and Leek Soup

Soup is total comfort food, easy on the stomach and makes you feel full. This is a simple potato and leek soup with a twist. The shrimp can be substituted with smoked ham if you prefer. As always, do what you please!

4 SERVINGS

14 oz (400 g) potatoes
1 small leek
3 garlic cloves
olive oil for sautéing
3⅓ cups (800 ml) water
½ tsp salt
freshly ground white or black pepper
3 dashes Tabasco (if you like it spicy)
2 big slices sourdough bread
5–7 oz (150–200 g) peeled shrimp

DIRECTIONS:

1. Peel the potatoes and cut them into pieces. Rinse the leek and cut it into pieces. Peel and finely chop the garlic.
2. Sauté the potatoes, leek, and garlic with a couple of tablespoons of olive oil. Add water and let it simmer until all the ingredients have softened, about 15 minutes.
3. Use a hand mixer right in the pot to blend the soup into a smooth consistency. Season with salt, pepper, and Tabasco. If you like your soup spicy, use red Tabasco, but if you're like me, use the green Tabasco, which is a bit milder.
4. Serve the soup in bowls with shrimp and pieces of sourdough on top. Finish it off by drizzling some olive oil on top. Serve right away.

20. Squash Soup with Quenelles

I made this soup during one of the tapings for my show in Vemdalen. It's a somewhat unusual soup with fun flavors. The great thing about Vemdalen is that, today, my husband and I own the place where we taped the program. At this very moment, I'm actually sitting in that house as the wind whines around the corners. Thank you blessed soup for bringing us here!

4 SERVINGS

9 oz (250 g) squash, either Muscat, Hokkaido, or butternut
1 yellow onion
4 garlic cloves
1 parsnip
olive oil for sautéing
1 can of coconut milk (14 oz/400 ml) + 1½ can of water
2 tsp salt
freshly ground white or black pepper
1 tbsp freshly squeezed lemon juice

QUENELLES:

14 oz (400 g) ground meat of your choice
3½ oz (100 g) cream cheese
½ tbsp green curry paste
1 tbsp pickled coriander, chopped (can be found among the Asian products in the supermarket)
1 tsp salt

DIRECTIONS:

1. Peel and core the squash. Cut the squash into large cubes. Peel the onion, garlic, and parsnip, and cut them into small pieces. There's no need to be pretty or even here! Flash fry everything in a large pan with some olive oil.

2. Add the coconut milk, water, and salt. Let simmer until the vegetables are soft; how long it takes will depend on how large the chunks are.

3. Mix the soup with a hand mixer right inside the pot. Season with pepper and lemon juice.

4. Mix the ground beef with the cream cheese, curry paste, pickled coriander, and salt. Shape the mixture into small balls. Place the quenelles gently into the soup and let them simmer for about 7–10 minutes.

5. Serve the soup hot with some fresh bread, and enjoy!

ROAST THE SEEDS

Save the seeds when you core the squash. They're really tasty when roasted and are delicious when sprinkled on top of a salad.

52

19.

20.

21. Frittata with Olives and Parsley

I often eat frittata with gravlax during the summer, perhaps with a dollop of sour cream and some freshly cut watercress. It's just as tasty chilled as it is warm, so why not prepare it a day in advance; cut it into slices, and serve as a side dish or with cold cuts with *Pa Amb Tomaquét* (see page 281). You'll have a delicious lunch using some really inexpensive ingredients.

4 SERVINGS

2 large baking potatoes or 4–5 small potatoes
1 yellow onion
butter and olive oil for sautéing
3 eggs
⅓ cup (100 ml) pitted and chopped green olives
1 bunch of parsley
salt, freshly ground white or black pepper

DIRECTIONS:

1. Heat the oven to 350°F (175°C).
2. Peel and thinly slice the potatoes and onions. Sauté them in butter and olive oil for a couple of minutes until they start to soften.
3. Crack the eggs into a bowl and whisk with a fork. Add olives, parsley, potatoes, and onions. Season with salt and pepper.
4. Fry the frittata on one side only in butter and olive oil (use a pan that can be placed in the oven). Put the pan in the oven for the last few minutes, and bake until the frittata has turned golden brown and is crispy. This will take about 25 minutes. Stick a knife into the frittata to make sure the potatoes are soft before removing it from the oven. Serve the frittata fried-side up.

22. Frittata with Green Peas, Basil, and Mascarpone

Super delicious with fried sausage—a simple dish made with love.

4 SERVINGS

1 sliced garlic clove
½ cup (100 ml) finely shredded leek
¼ tsp cayenne pepper
butter and olive oil for sautéing
4 eggs
½ tsp salt

GREEN PEA FILLING:

¾ cup (200 ml) defrosted frozen garden peas
3½ oz (100 g) mascarpone
3½ tbsp shredded Parmesan
1 bunch of basil
2 tbsp olive oil
1 shredded garlic clove
½ tsp salt

DIRECTIONS:

1. Mash the ingredients for the green pea filling coarsely with a fork.
2. In a frying pan, flash fry the garlic, leek, and cayenne pepper in butter and olive oil.
3. Crack the eggs into a bowl and whisk them quickly—not necessarily beautifully, just quickly. Season with salt. Pour the eggs into the frying pan along with the garlic and leek, and let the frittata cook for a few minutes.
4. Spread out the coarse pea mash onto the frittata and finish cooking the frittata.

23. Eggs en Cocotte

These eggs take me back to mornings at the Torekov campgrounds, when I would make this dish. This dish truly represents summer for me!

4 SERVINGS

soft butter for the ramekins
2½ oz (70 g) fresh spinach
1 garlic clove, finely chopped
olive oil for sautéing
salt, freshly ground white or black pepper
4 eggs
½ tsp chili powder
a pinch of sea salt

DIRECTIONS:

1. Preheat the oven to 300°F (150°C).
2. Flash fry the spinach and the garlic in oil. Season with salt and pepper. Divide the spinach evenly into each ramekin. Crack an egg into each ramekin.
3. Pour hot water onto a baking sheet so it's about half full. Place the ramekin on the baking sheet and bake in the oven for about 10–12 minutes, until the eggs have solidified on top.
4. Remove the ramekin. Season the eggs with chili powder and a pinch of sea salt. Serve right away.

24. Ratatouille with Egg

For me, this is the ultimate sailing food! It's perfect for when you have to cook something really quick on the boat. And there are hardly any dishes to be done afterward since everything is done right in the frying pan.

4 SERVINGS

4 eggs
salt
freshly ground white or black pepper

RATATOUILLE:

½ eggplant + ½ zucchini, chopped
1 red pepper + 1 yellow pepper, chopped
2 red spring onions, chopped + 3 garlic cloves, shredded
olive oil for sautéing
½ tsp ground cumin
1–2 tsp paprika powder
5 tomatoes
salt, freshly ground white or black pepper

DIRECTIONS:

1. Sauté vegetables, onion, and garlic for the ratatouille in a frying pan with oil. Add seasoning and tomatoes, and let it turn to a sauce, about 10 minutes. Season with salt and pepper.
2. Crack the eggs directly into the ratatouille. Cover with a lid and let the eggs cook at low heat. Season with salt and pepper.

25. Scrambled Eggs Deluxe

An act of love on my part. Perhaps it has a slightly higher fat content than regular scrambled eggs, but oh, so delicious!

4 SERVINGS

4 eggs
⅓ cup (75 ml) heavy cream
butter for frying
salt, freshly ground white or black pepper
1 bunch chives, finely chopped
Brioche or sourdough for serving

DIRECTIONS:

1. Whisk the eggs and heavy cream together with a fork. Melt the butter in a pan and add the egg mixture. Stir with a spatula at low heat for 2–3 minutes until the eggs start to get creamy and thicken. Season with salt, pepper, and finely-chopped chives.
2. Serve right away with toasted brioche or sourdough.

23.

24.

25.

26. Lemon-marinated Artichoke Hearts with Roasted Onion

A great summer meal. Swing by the store to pick up a jar of artichoke hearts and throw some onions on the grill. Most likely you'll have the rest of these ingredients at home. This tastes great with grilled fish and pairs nicely with sauces, like asparagus and lemon sauce (see page 107) or mayonnaise (see page 109). It's even great as a stand-alone vegetarian dish.

4 SERVINGS

2 yellow onions
1 can artichoke hearts (14 oz [400 g])
3 tbsp olive oil
1 lemon, zest and juice
1 tbsp fresh thyme (or 1½ tsp dried)
salt, freshly ground white or black pepper

DIRECTIONS:

1. Preheat the oven to 400°F (200°C).
2. Wrap the onions (unpeeled) in aluminum foil, and bake in the oven for about 1 hour—they're supposed to get really soft.
3. Divide the artichoke hearts and put them in a pot with oil, lemon juice, and thyme. Season with salt and pepper. Cook over low heat.
4. Move the onions to a plate and mash them with a fork. Place the artichoke hearts on top of the onions and drizzle the pan drippings on top.

HOLLANDAISE AND BÉARNAISE

The difference between hollandaise sauce and béarnaise sauce is the flavoring. Both are emulsions with egg as a base, but "Hollandaise" is made with lemon juice and water while "Béarnaise" is made with vinegar and spices.

27. Green and White Asparagus with Hollandaise Sauce

Asparagus with hollandaise sauce is good for all palates. If the sauce should accidentally "split," just remove the sauce from the heat and start over again with a new pot and a new egg yolk. Very gently, whisk the "split" sauce into the new egg yolk. If the sauce ends up too thick, just add a teaspoon of water or lemon juice.

4 SERVINGS

8 fingerling potatoes
1 bunch white asparagus + 1 bunch green asparagus
salt + a pinch of sugar
a few sprigs of dill for garnish

HOLLANDAISE SAUCE:

2 tbsp water
3 tbsp lemon juice
1 finely chopped shallot
3 egg yolks
2 sticks (200 g) butter, melted
salt, freshly ground white or black pepper
a few dashes of Worcestershire sauce

DIRECTIONS:

1. Boil the potatoes in salted water until they are soft. Drain the water and keep the potatoes hot under a closed lid. Boil the asparagus in lightly salted water with a pinch of sugar; they should be *al dente*, 3–4 minutes.
2. HOLLANDAISE SAUCE: Bring water to a boil with lemon juice and shallots. Boil until it is reduced to half its volume and then remove the pot from the burner. Whisk the egg yolks into the mixture. Continue to whisk over very low heat or over a water bath until the sauce turns thick and fluffy. Pour the warm butter gently into the mixture, dripping it in a little at a time while whisking. Make sure to keep the sauce at 125°F (50°C). Whisk until the sauce is thick. Season with salt, pepper, and Worcestershire sauce.
3. Split the potatoes length-wise. Place the asparagus and potatoes on a plate. Top with dill and serve the sauce on the side.

28. Oven-roasted Butternut Squash with Ricotta and Sage

A perfect "bring-to-the-office" dish. I actually ate it while writing recipes for this book. As you stare at the butternut squash in the veggie market, you find yourself asking, "How am I supposed to prepare this?" I can tell you that it doesn't get much easier than this. Try it—the butternut squash will become your friend for life.

4 SERVINGS
1 medium-sized butternut squash
3½ oz (100 g) high-quality blue cheese
4 tbsp ricotta cheese
½ lemon, juice
2 tbsp olive oil
2 tbsp maple syrup
2 stems of sage
salt, freshly ground white or black pepper

DIRECTIONS:
1. Preheat the oven to 400°F (200°C).
2. Split the butternut squash in half lengthwise and remove all the seeds. Place the two halves on a baking sheet.
3. Mix blue cheese and ricotta. Divide the mixture in half and press it onto the squash. Squeeze the lemon juice onto the squash, and drizzle with olive oil and maple syrup. Season with salt and pepper and a stem of sage for each squash.
4. Bake in the oven for 35–40 minutes until the cheese has turned golden brown.
5. Serve as side dish with roasted chicken or at a buffet-type dinner. It's always nice to set the two big squash halves right out on the table for guests to serve themselves from. It's a great social dish!

29. Cauliflower and Eggs with Béchamel Sauce

When I served this dish to my dad, his educated comment was, "Ah, cauliflower polonaise!" as the seasoned chef he is. Impressive indeed that he knows his kitchen-French so well! Serve the dish on its own so nothing can take the attention away from its glory.

4 SERVINGS
1 cauliflower
3–4 hardboiled eggs, chopped
1 bunch chives, finely chopped
BÉCHAMEL SAUCE:
½ shallot, finely chopped
butter for sautéing
2 tbsp flour
1¼ cups (300 ml) heavy cream
1¼ cups (300 ml) milk
salt, freshly ground white or black pepper

DIRECTIONS:
1. Remove the outer leaves from the cauliflower and cut off the bottom part of the stem. Boil the cauliflower in lightly salted water until it's soft; test the softness by poking it with a fork from time to time. When it's ready, you should be able to spike it with the fork with only minimal resistance.
2. In a pan with butter, sauté the onions for the béchamel sauce and sprinkle the flour on top. Add the heavy cream and the milk. Let it simmer for ten minutes while stirring. Season with salt and pepper.
3. Place the cauliflower on a plate and pour the sauce over it. Garnish with the chopped eggs and finely chopped chives. Serve the cauliflower on its own as a vegetarian dish.

29.

30. Apple-infused Beluga Lentils with Mint, Ginger, and Oven-roasted Yellow Tomatoes

This might not be the prettiest dish in the world, but ignore that because the taste will knock your socks off! Don't stir too much after you've added the tomatoes because if you do, you'll miss out on the delicious tomatoes bursting in your mouth! Beluga lentils taste great with just a little bit of sour cream, but they also complement fish and meat really well.

4 SERVINGS
    2 apples, for example, Macoun
    1¼ cups (300 ml) Beluga lentils
    1¼ cups (300 ml) apple juice
    ¾ cup (200 ml) water
    3½ tbsp Japanese soy sauce
    ½ tbsp brown sugar

OVEN-ROASTED YELLOW TOMATOES:
    approx. 9 oz (250 g) yellow cherry tomatoes
    1 tbsp olive oil
    2 garlic cloves
FOR SERVING:
    1 tbsp butter
    1 bunch of mint, freshly chopped
    1 tbsp shredded fresh ginger
    1 shallot, finely chopped

DIRECTIONS:
1. Preheat the oven to 425°F (220°C).
2. Peel and core the apples and chop them into pieces. Boil the lentils and the apples in apple juice, water, soy sauce, and brown sugar. Let the lentils and the stock reduce until the stock sticks to the lentils. Add the butter and fold the mint, ginger, and shallot into the mixture.
3. Place the tomatoes on a baking sheet. Drizzle with olive oil and season with salt and pepper. Peel and crush the garlic cloves and put them on the baking sheet. Roast in the oven for about 10 minutes.
4. Pour the lentils onto a plate. Place the roasted tomatoes on top and garnish with some fresh mint leaves. Serve hot with a tasty bread.

THE ROLLS ROYCE OF LENTILS
Beluga lentils are the best quality lentils. They're firm in texture and have a naturally nutty taste. It's a great ingredient that can be found in any supermarket. If by any chance, you can't find Beluga lentils, Puy lentils are a good second choice.

31. Asparagus Risotto with Marjoram

Here you go—a great standard risotto recipe (if you leave out the asparagus and marjoram). Use hot water instead of a cheap stock that contains too much sodium in it anyway. Or use homemade vegetable stock (see page 50) if you have some already made.

4 SERVINGS

2 shallots, finely chopped
1 bunch of marjoram
3½ tbsp olive oil
1⅔ cups (400 ml) Arborio rice
1¼ cups (300 ml) white wine
1 quart (1 liter) hot water (or homemade vegetable stock)
1 bunch green asparagus, cut into small pieces
1 cup (250 ml) freshly shredded Parmesan
salt, freshly ground white or black pepper

DIRECTIONS:

1. Sauté the onion and marjoram in olive oil until the onions are soft. Add the rice and cook until the kernels become slightly transparent. Add the wine and let it simmer until almost completely absorbed by the rice. Add water a little at a time (the rice absorbs the liquid), and let it simmer for 15 minutes.
2. Add the asparagus and let simmer for another 5 minutes. Fold the Parmesan into the mixture and season with salt and pepper. Serve the risotto right away.

WINES FOR RISOTTO

Wine is an important part in the risotto but if you don't have any available, you can use three parts water and one part lemon juice as a substitute. If you leave out the marjoram and asparagus and add an envelope (or a pinch) of saffron instead, it becomes a perfect side dish for the Ossobuco on page 198.

32. Ripasso Risotto with Red Beets

Risotto and Ripasso sound like they could mix harmoniously, and that's the case in this recipe. Ripasso is an Amarone wine that's light in flavor. It is a perfect match for the red beet juice that can be found at any health food store. This is a really luxurious risotto that can only be an expression of love to your guests.

4 SERVINGS

2 shallots, finely chopped
1 garlic clove, finely chopped
2 peeled red beets, cubed
3½ tbsp olive oil
1⅔ cups (400 ml) Arborio rice
2½ cups (600 ml) Ripasso wine
2 cups (500 ml) red beet juice
1 cup (250 ml) freshly shredded Parmesan
salt, freshly ground white or black pepper

DIRECTIONS:

1. Sauté onion, garlic, and red beets in olive oil until they turn soft. Add the rice and wait till it turns transparent.
2. Add half of the wine, and let it simmer until almost all the liquid has been absorbed by the rice. Add some red beet juice and alternate splashes of the wine and beet juice, as the rice absorbs the liquid. Let simmer for 15–20 minutes.
3. Fold the Parmesan into the risotto and season with salt and pepper. Serve the risotto right away, preferably with pan-fried corn-fed chicken.

33. Gnudi with Sage-roasted Tomatoes and Caramelized Butter

Gnudi is pronounced *njudi* and is an Italian "quick pasta"—at least, if you consider the small amount of work that goes into it—made from ricotta and durum wheat. There's no need for pasta machines or rolling pins—just a talent for making round little balls from dough.

4 SERVINGS

3½ oz (100 g) Parmesan, finely shredded
9 oz (250 g) ricotta cheese
a pinch of salt
freshly ground white or black pepper
4 cups (500 g) durum wheat flour
2 quarts (2 liters) water + 2–3 tsp salt

SAGE-ROASTED TOMATOES:

1 head of garlic
butter or oil for the pan
1 lb (500 g) mixed cherry tomatoes
a handful of fresh sage leaves
2 tbsp olive oil
½ lemon, juice
salt, freshly ground white or black pepper

CARAMELIZED BUTTER:

1 stick (100 g) butter

DIRECTIONS:

1. Stir the shredded Parmesan and ricotta together until it reaches a smooth consistency. Season with salt and pepper.
2. Cover the bottom of a pan with half of the durum wheat flour. Roll the cheese mixture into small balls and place them in the pan. Cover everything with the rest of the flour. It's vital that you cover the balls completely with flour because it's the flour that will form the shell of the finished gnudis. Let the pan stand in the fridge overnight covered with plastic wrap (for 24 hours would be even better) to let the gnudi dry really well.
3. Preheat the oven to 400°F (200°C).
4. Cut the garlic in half. Place tomatoes, garlic, and sage into a baking dish. Drizzle with olive oil and lemon juice. Roast the tomatoes in the oven until they're soft, for about 15 minutes. Remove the dish and lightly crush the tomatoes with a fork.
5. In a large pot, boil the water and salt. Carefully remove the gnudis from the pan and shake off any excess flour. Boil the gnudis for 2–3 minutes and remove them as soon as they float up to the surface.
6. In a pan, caramelize the butter. Set the tomatoes on a plate with the freshly cooked gnudis. Spoon the caramelized butter on top of the pasta and sprinkle some Parmesan on top.

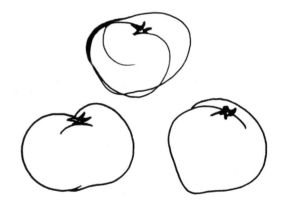

33

34. Tina's Potatoes Au Gratin

My most popular recipe! It would be impossible for me to write this book without including this recipe. Don't forget to add enough salt to the dish, because potatoes absorb a lot of salt. The level of saltiness in a perfect au gratin is meant to be felt far back in your palate.

8 SERVINGS

3 ⅓ lbs (1½ kg) peeled firm potatoes
½ leek
3 garlic cloves
olive oil
2 cups (500 ml) heavy cream
2 cups (500 ml) milk
1½–2 tsp salt
freshly ground white or black pepper

DIRECTIONS:

1. Preheat the oven to 350°F (180°C).
2. Shave the potatoes into thin slices, using a mandolin or a food processor. Rinse and shred the leek, and peel and crush the garlic.
3. Sauté the leek and garlic in olive oil until they get some color. Pour in the heavy cream and milk, and let the mixture simmer. Add the potatoes and season heavily with salt and pepper—since the potatoes absorb so much salt, you have to be heavy-handed here. Let the potatoes cook until the starch has been released and the mixture is thick and creamy. Don't forget that you have to stir the mixture continuously so it doesn't burn.
4. Pour the potatoes into a casserole dish. Bake the potatoes au gratin in the oven for 30–40 minutes. Test to see if the potatoes are ready by poking them with a fork. They should be soft.
5. Serve with beef tenderloin (see page 176).

35. Jackson Potatoes

I made this potato dish during a taping of "Power Meet" in Västerås while a group of local "raggare" (a Swedish rock-n-roll subculture) kept the mood lively with their chants and catcalls as they drove around the set in their classic American cars. It ended up being an awesome party dish that can be prepared the day before any event. Keep it vegetarian by leaving out the bacon.

4 SERVINGS

4 large potatoes (baking potatoes)
10 oz (280 g) bacon
1 red onion
1 bunch parsley, finely chopped
1 ⅓ cups (300 ml) aged cheese, grated
1 tbsp butter
2 tbsp canola oil
½ lemon, juice
salt, freshly ground white or black pepper

DIRECTIONS:

1. Preheat the oven to 400°F (200°C).
2. Wash the potatoes and poke them all over with a fork. (If you're short on time, you can microwave the potatoes for 15 minutes and finish the baking in the oven.) Place the potatoes in a baking dish or baking sheet and bake them until they're completely soft. Depending on the size of the potatoes, this should take about 1 hour.
3. Fry the bacon until crispy. Peel and slice the onion finely.
4. Remove the potatoes from the oven when they are soft. Split them in halves and carefully scrape the potatoes from their skins. Save the skins. Mix the potatoes with bacon, onion, finely chopped parsley, and half of the cheese. Add the butter and oil and stir the mixture. Season with salt and pepper.
5. Divide the potato mixture into the skins and sprinkle the rest of the cheese on top. Bake in the oven until the cheese has turned a lovely golden color.

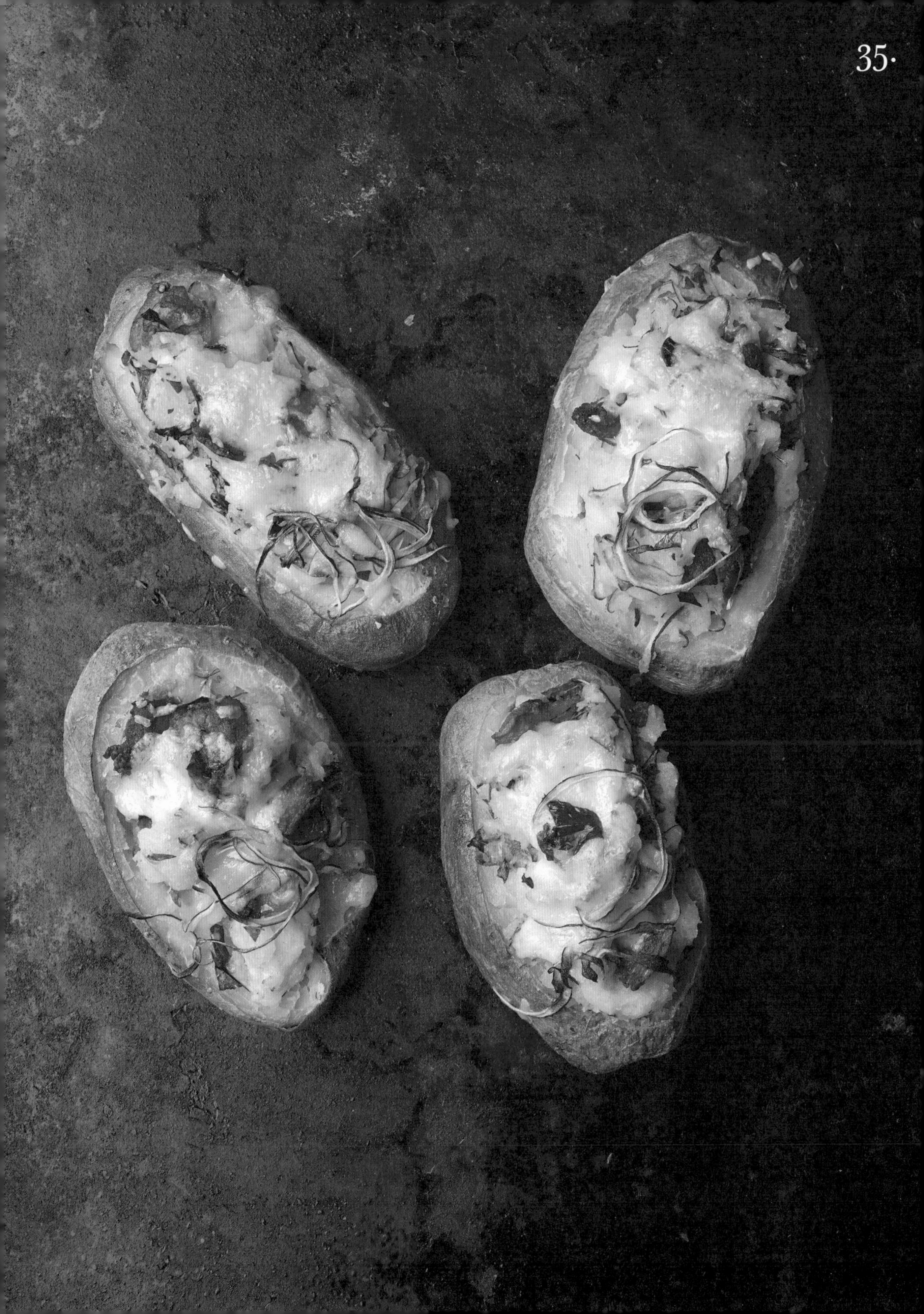

35

36. Garlic-roasted Root Vegetables and Hazelnuts with Lime Vinaigrette

A twist on regular roasted root vegetables. These can be served hot or cold, for many or for just a few. Perhaps pair this with the Sunday roast and a béarnaise sauce.

4 SERVINGS

2 black salsify roots
2 parsnips
2 parsley roots
½ celery root
5 apples, for example, McIntosh
1 head of garlic
⅔ cup (150 ml) water
½ cup (100 ml) olive oil
½ tsp salt, freshly ground white or black pepper
½ cup (100 ml) roasted hazelnuts (see page 28)

LIME VINAIGRETTE:

3½ tbsp olive oil
½ lemon, zest and juice
½ tsp salt

DIRECTIONS:

1. Preheat the oven to 450°F (230°C).
2. Peel the root vegetables and cut them into equal-sized pieces. Split the apples and the garlic down the middle. Rub a baking dish with the garlic halves and place the root vegetables, apples, and garlic in it. Season with salt and pepper. Drizzle with water and olive oil, and roast in the oven from 30–35 minutes.
3. Mix the ingredients for the vinaigrette.
4. Crush the hazelnuts lightly in a mortar. Fold the lime vinaigrette into the vegetable mix and sprinkle the hazelnuts on top. Serve as a vegetarian dish or as a side dish with meat or fish.

37. Mashed Root Vegetables with Apples and Oyster Mushrooms

This purely vegetarian dish is the easiest dish you can make. I'm not a vegetarian, but I still consider this as the main course whenever I serve it and any meat or fish as a side. Don't forget that the oyster mushrooms should be sautéed at high heat, as it's best with a crispy surface.

4 SERVINGS

½ celery root (10 oz [300 g])
½ rutabaga (14 oz [400 g])
1 parsnip
3 carrots
2 potatoes
1½ tsp salt
approx. 1¼ cups (300 ml) of the water from the cooked vegetables
1–2 tbsp butter
1 tsp salt
freshly ground white or black pepper

TOPPING:

2 apples, for example, Macoun, cut into small pieces
7 oz (200 g) oyster mushrooms
butter for sautéing
salt, freshly ground white or black pepper

DIRECTIONS:

1. Preheat the oven to 450°F (225°C).
2. Peel the root vegetables and potatoes, and cut into pieces. In a large pot with salted water, boil the root vegetables until soft. Mash them with 1¼ cups (300 ml) of the water they were boiled in. Stir in the butter in dollops and season with salt and pepper. Pour everything into a baking dish and bake for 3–5 minutes.
3. Sauté the apples and mushrooms in butter and season with salt and pepper.
4. Garnish the root mash with mushrooms and apples, and serve as a vegetarian dish on its own or as a side dish for grilled pork loin.

37

38. Dill Potatoes and Cumin Cheese in Puff Pastry

Finally I got a chance to create a covered pie—something I have been longing to do forever! My relationship with pies has not always been the best, and it's all because of the challenging egg royale. The usual egg and milk mixture is even worse than instant mashed potatoes. In this recipe, the eggs are mixed with cottage cheese and lots of cumin cheese and the results are outstanding. If you're feeling lazy, you can always leave out the puff pastry lid, but the dish does look a lot more professional with the lid, and it's not that difficult to make.

4 SERVINGS

PIE DOUGH:
1⅔ cups (400 ml) flour
3½ tbsp (50 g) butter
⅔ cup (150 ml) milk
2 tsp baking powder
½ tsp salt

FILLING:
14 oz (400 g) boiled small potatoes
1 red onion, finely chopped
1 bunch of dill (approx. ¾ cup [200 ml]), finely chopped
2 cups (500 ml) black chanterelles
butter for sautéing
9 oz (250 g) cottage cheese (or farmer's cheese)
1¼ cups (400 ml) aged cumin cheese, shredded
1 egg

PUFF PASTRY:
1 sheet frozen puff pastry
1 whisked egg

DIRECTIONS:
1. Preheat the oven to 400°F (200°C).
2. Mix all ingredients for the pie dough and knead until smooth.
3. Roll the dough out on a floured surface and lay it in a loaf pan so the dough hangs over the edges.
4. Cut the potatoes into large chunks and mix with red onion and chopped dill.
5. Sauté the black chanterelles in the butter and mix with the potatoes.
6. Mix the cottage cheese, cumin cheese, and egg. Combine the cheese mixture with the potatoes and chanterelles. Pour all of it into the pie form and cover it with the puff pastry lid (if you opt to make one). Glaze the lid with a whisked egg. Bake the pie in the oven for 35–40 minutes. You may need to cover it with aluminum foil after 15–20 minutes if the color is turning too dark.
7. Serve the pie hot or at a cooler temperature based on preference.

PERFECT PIE DOUGH
The simple pie dough used in this recipe works for any kind of pie, no matter what the filling is. You don't have to refrigerate it before using it, but rather smooth it out in the pan right away. The baking powder makes the dough crispy, and this means you need to use less butter compared to regular pie dough. Best of all—there's no need to pre-bake the dough. We just don't have time for such silly things!

Seafood

Why Is No One Biting?

FISH IS FAST FOOD—it's true, there's no other food that's easier to work with than fish. Toss on some lemon, salt, and pepper, and then into the oven it goes. The only challenge with fish is when it's still alive and swimming! You can't count on it, you can't trust it, and it's always MIA when you need it. It's almost like the fish knows when you're hoping for a great catch.

It's just like during a recording for an American show I was taping in Gothenburg. There we were, the whole team, with a kitchen set up on the beach, and we were all just waiting to catch something. The only thing we managed to get on the hook that day was a sorry little mackerel. A whole nation wanted us to catch something. . . . In Swedish, the letters T and V can also stand for "Tålmodigt Väntande" or "Patiently Waiting," which is exactly what we doing in abundance!

We were all out early in the morning with the boat fully loaded, camera equipment, kitchen equipment, TV host—yeah, pretty much everything we could possibly need. The mackerel swarms were supposed to be a bit off shore, so I got into position and started rehearsing my lines—all the while I threw out the hook, line, and sinker, as they call it in fishing terms. I've never really understood the colorful baits, and if I were a mackerel I would seriously have thought they

Dead

were crabs and made sure to stay far away from them! But enough of that. We basically sat there . . . waiting . . . with not a single mackerel in sight.

So what do you do when the whole program is banking on you catching a fish, and the hourly rate for the team on this boat is ticking away faster than a gypsy cab? Well, that's when you're grateful to learn something new. Such as, that you can't let a whole show go to ruin because of something beyond your control. The only thing for it was to start shopping for a mackerel that still had its head on. After we had scoured all the fish markets in the tiny village, we finally found a whole bag of frozen mackerels from the previous year.

We defrosted one little mackerel slowly on newspaper, carried it onto the boat, and carefully placed it on the hook. All we could do was keep our fingers crossed that the fish head wouldn't just fall off the body! Luckily, it stayed in place, and what you see on the screen is just acting.

I'm up front, giving my introduction, and—get a fish on the hook! I pull up the fish and shake the fishing rod to make it look like the fish is alive and splashing. I then put it in the bucket and say:

"Wow, look, it's truly alive . . ."

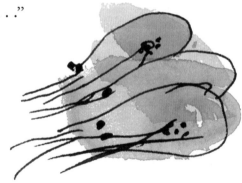

When it comes to cooking fish, many great home cooks have no self-confidence whatsoever. They're afraid to over-cook the fish and find it difficult to season and to pair with side dishes. If this is you, go ahead and try the recipes "Fish in Top Shape—Everyday in a Can" on pages 118–120. You simply cannot fail! Many people also get stuck trying one or two kinds of fish, and these are the only ones they use! This is a shame since there are so many types of fish to choose from in today's markets. Try to pan-fry a piece of sea bream and serve it with lemon-mashed potatoes. It's a delicious everyday meal. Another thing: you have to fail sometimes. Otherwise you'll never learn how to make it properly.

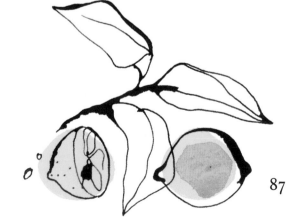

THINK LIKE TINA

HOW CAN I TELL IF THE FISH IS FRESH?

Fresh fish should smell fresh like the sea. It should have mucus on its eyes and moist, dark red gills.

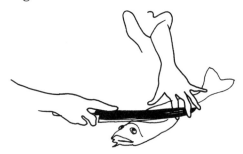

RIGOR MORTIS

The meat of the fish is always best before rigor mortis (the period of stiffness that occurs after death) sets in. The fish first turns stiff as a rod and then goes totally limp. After rigor mortis, decomposition begins and the enzymes start to break down.

RAW SALMON

If you plan on eating raw, wild salmon, the FDA recommends freezing it for up to seven days (or less depending on temperature). This doesn't apply to farmed salmon.

DON'T BOIL—JUST SIMMER

If you boil fish it will fall apart. This is why fish should *always* be simmered.

LOW OVEN TEMPERATURES ARE BEST

Baking fish in the oven at low temperatures gives the best results. At oven temperatures between 200°F (90°C) and 250°F (120°C), the fish releases the least amount of moisture and it stays nice and juicy.

WHEN IS THE FISH READY?

When cooking a whole fish, the temperature at the fish's core should be 130°F (55°C). If you cook a fillet, it should be between 118°F (48°C) and 125°F (52°C), except when it comes to salmon, which is fully cooked when between 113°F (45°C) and 118°F (48°C). These temperatures may be a little too exact for the everyday cook, but it can be a fun tidbit of knowledge for when you want to show off for your guests. Just use a regular kitchen thermometer to check the temperature so your fish is perfectly cooked.

LIGHTY SALTING THE FISH

Lightly salting the fish is done in part to bring out the taste but also to make the fish firmer in texture. Salt the fish at two tablespoons per pound for about twenty minutes.

BROIL THE FISH IN A PAN

Broiling usually refers to grilling over an open flame, but in this instance we're talking about broiling the fish in a frying pan—and preferably only on the side that has the skin still on it. This method works best with fatty fish.

TO FRY IN FAT OR NOT?

Fatty fish such as salmon and mackerel with skin can be broiled/pan-fried without fat. Less fatty fish, such as freshwater fish and cod, is best cooked with both butter and oil in the pan.

WHY FRY WITH BOTH BUTTER AND OIL IN THE PAN?

You see, the oil is there because it can handle higher temperatures, and the butter is used for its taste.

COOKING WITH LEMON JUICE

When you squeeze lemon juice over salmon, for example, the acid breaks down the proteins and the cooking process begins. You'll notice that the salmon turns a lighter shade. This is how ceviche is prepared.

WHEN IS SHELLFISH AT ITS BEST?

It's said that shellfish is at its best when the sea is at its coldest.

SHRIMP COCKTAIL WITH CRAB

Make your shrimp cocktail extra special by adding some fresh crab. Serve with asparagus and lemon sauce (see page 107) or green pea guacamole (see page 252).

39.

40.

41

39. Västervik Salad with *Boquerones* and Olives

This salad was named after the Swedish town Västervik, since this dish was created during a filming there. Perhaps the ingredients aren't very "Västervik," but I was inspired by the pier at Pepparängen, under the sunny skies. Yes, it does take some time to create the *boquerones*, but it's definitely worth it. If you're feeling a little lazy, you can just use regular sardines.

4 SERVINGS
  10 oz (300 g) new potatoes
  3½ oz (100 g) fresh haricot verts
  10 oz (300 g) mixed tomatoes
  1 shallot, finely chopped
  ½ cup (100 ml) kalamata olives
  16 boquerones (see page 143) or sardine fillets
  4 eggs, boiled for 4 minutes (see opposite page)
  salt, freshly ground white or black pepper
DRESSING:
  ⅓ cup olive oil
  1 tsp Dijon mustard
  1 tsp dry sherry or white wine (optional)
  1 tsp honey
  ½ lemon, juice
  1 tbsp water
  ¼ tsp salt
  freshly ground white or black pepper

DIRECTIONS:
1. Boil the potatoes in salted water. Add the haricot verts at the end of the cooking process and let them boil for a few minutes. Cut the tomatoes, potatoes, and haricot verts into various-sized pieces. Cut the eggs in half and put to the side.
2. Put all the ingredients for the dressing into a jar and close the lid. Shake vigorously. This is a great way to make and store dressing without any mess.
3. Drizzle the dressing on top of the tomatoes, potatoes, and haricot verts, and fold all of it around until every piece is coated with the dressing. Perhaps puncture some of the tomatoes and let the tomato juice mix with the dressing. Arrange the salad on individual plates or on a large serving platter. Add the egg halves and drizzle some more dressing on top. The salad tastes the best when the potatoes are still a little warm.

40. Shrimp Salad with Salted Cucumber and Lemon Mayo

A shrimp salad with Tore Wretman's signature Rhode Island dressing will *not* be found here! I like everything Tore has made . . . except for that sauce. It might be a bit of a challenge to make my own version of his classic, but I'm going to try. My shrimp salad has salted cucumber and, of course, mayo—although this mayo is a bit more acidic than most.

4 SERVINGS
  2½ lbs (1.2 kg) shrimp with shells (2¼ lbs [1 kg] peeled)
  ½ leek or a couple of spring onions
  lettuce of your choice
  4 eggs, boiled for 4 minutes (see opposite page)
LIGHTLY SALTED CUCUMBER:
  1 cucumber
  1 tsp salt
  1 tsp sugar
LEMON MAYO:
  1–2 tsp mustard
  2 egg yolks
  1 lemon, zest + 1 tbsp juice
  1¼ cups (300 ml) oil, (for example, canola oil)
  ¼ tsp salt
  freshly ground white or black pepper

DIRECTIONS:

1. Peel the shrimp and place them somewhere cold. You can save the shells and make shrimp bisque with sherry cream (see page 94).
2. Rinse the leek and slice it diagonally as thinly as you can.
3. Peel the cucumber and cut it into ½-inch (1 cm) thick slices. Place the slices in a plastic bag and pour in the salt and sugar. Shake and let the cucumber rest for 15 minutes at room temperature. If the cucumber becomes too salty, you can just rinse it under water.
4. Mix mustard, egg yolks, lemon juice, and zest. Drip a little bit of oil into the mixture at a time while whisking constantly. Season with salt and pepper.
5. Arrange the salad, shrimp, and eggs on a serving plate or on individual plates and drizzle the lemon mayo on top. Serve with some fresh bread.

41. Perfect Eggs with Fillings

Perfect as a quick lunch snack with some delicious fillings.

4 SERVINGS

8 eggs at room temperature

FILLINGS:

- *1 can of mackerel in tomato sauce*
- *¼ finely chopped cucumber with Kalles Kaviar spread*
- *stirred butter with sea salt*
- *smoked salmon with dill*

DIRECTIONS:

1. Place the eggs in a pot of cold water and let the water boil. Once the water begins to boil, the eggs should cook for exactly 4 minutes.
2. Drain the water and rinse the eggs in cold water until they cool down.
3. Cut the top off of each egg and garnish with any filling you like.

Super Tasty

GRANDMA'S PERFECT EGGS

My grandma was the best at boiling eggs. She always put the eggs in cold water, set it to a boil, and then boiled the eggs for exactly 4 minutes.

42. Shrimp Bisque with Sherry Cream

When I was young, my dad used to roast the shrimp shells at Ramlösa Tavern—and it stunk to high heaven! When we were supposed to actually *eat* the results of the roasted shells, I thought I would be sick to my stomach. I pledged never to eat anything remotely close to shrimp bisque ever in my life. It's wasn't until now that I've finally made peace with roasted shrimp shells.

4 SERVINGS

2¼ lbs (1 kg) shrimp
butter and oil for sautéing
1 tbsp tomato paste
½ tsp cayenne pepper
2 tsp paprika powder
1 yellow onion, chopped + 1 carrot, chopped
1 ½ quarts (1½ liters) water
1¼ cup (300 ml) crème fraîche (if this cannot be found, a fatty sour cream can be substituted)
salt, freshly ground white or black pepper

SHERRY CREAM:

½ cup (100 ml) heavy cream, whipped fairly firm
1 tsp sherry
a pinch of salt

DIRECTIONS:

1. Peel half of the shrimp.
2. Heat some of the butter and oil in a large pot. Add the tomato paste and the spices along with the unpeeled shrimp and the shells from the peeled shrimp. Sauté for about 10 minutes while stirring constantly to ensure that it does not burn. Add the water and let it simmer uncovered for about 20 minutes.
3. Mix the soup right in the pot with a hand blender. Strain the soup a little at a time by pressing it through a sieve with a spoon. This will take some time but the taste will be worth it in the end.
4. Let the bisque simmer once more in the pot and add the crème fraîche. Season with salt and pepper. Mix the heavy cream with sherry and salt.
5. Serve the bisque hot, garnished with some sherry cream and shrimp. Serve with some grissini (see page 269).

ROAST THE SHELLS

Be sure to thoroughly roast the shrimp shells, as they're what give the bisque its great flavor. Roasting the tomato paste is mostly for obtaining that lovely color, but it also makes some of that sticky tomato taste disappear.

MY SHRIMP STOCK

Bouillon or broth—this beloved child has many names. Many things that end up in soups make a great stock, such as the shrimp shells. Adding plenty of butter to the stock is a good chef trick. The butter will float to the surface and can then be skimmed off. This you can chill and use as a delicious shrimp butter, or when melted, you can drizzle it over soup or vegetables for extra flavor. Use the stock for fish soups or sauces for fish.

1 stick + 2 tbsp (150 g) butter
2 lbs (1 kg) frozen shrimp
1 tbsp tomato paste
1 fennel, chopped
¼ celeriac, chopped + 1 parsnip, chopped
2 yellow onions, chopped + 1 head of garlic, halved
3 bay leaves + 1 tsp thyme
5 black peppercorns
water
salt, freshly ground white or black pepper

DIRECTIONS:

In a pot, heat the butter and let it turn golden yellow. Add shrimp and tomato paste. Roast thoroughly. Add vegetables, onion, garlic, and spices, and cover it all with water. Let simmer for 20–25 minutes and season with salt and pepper.

42

43. Clam Chowder

Cockles (or saltwater clams) are also called Vongole clams or *Amandes des mer* in French. The meat of the elongated razor clam is also delicious, and you can even exchange the saltwater clams for sea mussels, if you like them better. Just make sure not to add them until the very end, as they should only cook for about five minutes. You will, of course, have to change the name of the soup to "sea mussel soup" if you do!

4 SERVINGS

3 tbsp (40 g) butter
1 head of garlic, halved
1 sprig of parsley
2 lbs (1 kg) saltwater clams or razor clams
¾ cup (200 ml) water
5 oz (150 g) bacon
1 large silver onion, finely chopped
2 garlic cloves, coarsely chopped
2 tbsp olive oil
2–3 bay leaves
17 oz (500 g) potatoes, cut in large pieces
3½ oz (100 g) celery root, cubed
½ fennel, in strips
¾ cup (200 ml) white wine
3 cups (700 ml) water
½ cup (100 ml) heavy cream + 1/2 cup (100 ml) crème fraîche (if this cannot be found, a fatty sour cream can be substituted)
¾ cup (200 ml) finely chopped parsley
½ tsp salt
¼ tsp freshly ground white or black pepper
lemon for serving

DIRECTIONS:

1. Heat the butter, garlic, parsley, clams, and ¾ cup (200 ml) water in a covered pot on medium heat for 2–3 minutes or until the clams open. Put the pot and its contents aside.
2. Fry the bacon, onion, and plenty of garlic in olive oil in another pot on low heat for about 10 minutes until the bacon is slightly crisp. Add bay leaves, potatoes, celery root, fennel, and wine. Let it simmer for 2–3 minutes. Add water, heavy cream, and crème fraîche, and let simmer for another 20–25 minutes until the potatoes begin to soften.
3. Add the clams with the stock to the soup and season with chopped parsley, salt, and pepper. Serve with a lemon wedge so guests can squeeze the fresh juice directly on top.

STRAIN AWAY THE GRIT

Saltwater clams can have a lot of sand and stones stuck inside, so make sure you strain the stock through a cloth. Or put the clams in cold water so they have a chance to "spit out" all the sand. Just stir and change the water a couple of times.

MY FISH STOCK

It's probably not every day you have a whole fish on your hands, but on the days when you do, it's good to know what to do with it. Homemade fish stock does wonders for fish soups and sauces. You basically exchange the amount of water in the recipe for your homemade stock. Freeze the stock and use it for both everyday meals and for special occasions.

2 lbs (1 kg) fish bones and heads, preferably from flatfish
1 yellow onion, sliced + 1 fennel, sliced
5–7 white peppercorns, coarsely crushed
2–3 sprigs parsley
2 sprigs fresh thyme (or ½ tsp dried)
3–4 bay leaves
water

DIRECTIONS:

Rinse bones and heads thoroughly in cold water. Place them in a big pot with onion, fennel, and spices. Add cold water until it almost covers everything and bring slowly to a boil. Skim thoroughly. Simmer for 10–15 minutes. Strain the stock and let it cool in the fridge.

44. Grilled Cod with Green Pea Pesto and Rough Potato Mash

I'm madly in love with this green pea pesto, but I can't take the credit for it. So I would like to extend a grateful thank you to Ebba Cederberg for creating this wonderful dish. Thanks Ebba!

4 SERVINGS

2 large cod fillets without skin (each approx. 14 oz [400 g])
a pinch of salt, freshly ground white or black pepper

GREEN PEA PESTO:

¾ cup (200 ml) frozen green peas, thawed
3½ tbsp cashews
1 handful of arugula (approx. 2 oz [50 g])
2 oz (50 g) parsley
½ cup (100 ml) shredded Parmesan or any aged hard cheese
5 drops of green Tabasco
3½ tbsp olive oil
a pinch of salt

COARSE POTATO MASH:

14 oz (400 g) firm potatoes
1 shallot, finely chopped
olive oil
1 tsp salt
½ tsp freshly ground white or black pepper
½ lemon, juice

DIRECTIONS:

1. Preheat the oven to 350°F (175°C).
2. Salt and pepper the cod and place the fillets on top of each other in a baking dish.
3. Mix the green peas, cashew nuts, arugula, parsley, Parmesan, and green Tabasco. Drizzle a little bit of olive oil on top. Season with a pinch of salt. Cover the fillets with the pea pesto and bake in the oven for 30–35 minutes.
4. While baking the fish, boil the potatoes in lightly salted water. When soft, drain the potatoes, and mash them together with the shallot and a little bit of oil. Season with some more salt, pepper, and the lemon juice.
5. Serve the cod right away with the potato mash.

Super Tasty

FRESH FISH TASTES THE BEST

Go ahead and get to the fish market to buy some fresh fish. Although it will probably cost a little bit more, fresh fish is so much tastier! The green pea pesto also works great with other fish or as a dip for vegetables or bread.

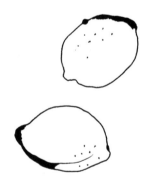

44

45. Baked Cod with Olive-braised Root Vegetables

Here two cold fillets are tied together to keep their shape and look elegant. Choosing frozen fish over fresh can be compared to using instant mashed potatoes! I try to use fresh fish as much as I can when the price is right.

4–6 SERVINGS

2 thick cod fillets from the middle of the fish, with skin (each approx. 18–21 oz [500–600 g])

1 bunch of thyme

5–6 bay leaves

2 tbsp olive oil

cooking string

sea salt, freshly ground white or black pepper

OLIVE-BRAISED ROOT VEGETABLES:

8 organic carrots

4 parsnips

3–4 sprigs of thyme

⅔ cup (150 ml) Kalamata olives with pits + some of its stock (approx. 3–4 tbsp)

3 garlic cloves

1¼ cup (300 ml) water

1¼ cup (300 ml) white wine

⅓ cup (75 ml) olive oil

freshly ground white or black pepper

DIRECTIONS:

1. Preheat the oven to 300°F (150°C).
2. Season the fillets with salt and pepper. Stack them one on top of the other with thyme and bay leaves in between. Top with more herbs and tie them together with cooking string. The skin should be facing out. Drizzle some olive oil on top and season with some more sea salt.
3. Place the fish in a baking dish and bake for about 50 minutes or until the core temperature is between 118°F (48°C) and 125°F (52°C) (if you are using a cooking thermometer).
4. Scrub and wash the root vegetables and cut them lengthwise. Place them in a pot, along with the thyme and olives. Add water, white wine, and 2–3 tablespoons olive oil. Boil under a closed lid until the vegetables are soft. Remove the vegetables from the stock, and reduce the stock until it is half its original volume.
5. Carefully mix the stock with 2–3 tablespoons olive oil and salt and freshly ground pepper. Plate the vegetables with the baked cod and spoon the stock on top of it.
6. This is best served with pressed potatoes and beurre blanc (see page 105).

46. Coconut Fish Stew with Water Chestnuts

Garam masala means literally "warm spice." This spice mix can vary and contain many different spices, but the basics are usually black pepper, chili pepper, coriander, cumin, cardamom, cinnamon, nutmeg, and cloves. It's very popular in the Indian kitchen and is added when the dish is almost finished.

4 SERVINGS

1¾ lbs (800 g) haddock or hake, in large chunks
1 stem lemongrass
½ cup (100 ml) finely sliced leek
1 can water chestnuts (approx. 5 oz [140 g])
1 tsp fresh ginger
2 tsp garam masala
1 tbsp olive oil
1 can coconut milk (14 oz [400 g])
1 tsp salt
1 lime, juice

DIRECTIONS:

1. Lightly pound the lemongrass with the handle of a knife to release the flavors. Sauté the leeks, drained water chestnuts, ginger, garam masala, and lemongrass in oil for 2 minutes.
2. Add the coconut milk and let simmer for 5–8 minutes.
3. Add the fish chunks and let simmer for another 6–7 minutes until the fish is cooked all the way through. Season with salt and lime juice.
4. Serve with rice (see page 236).

47. Miso-baked Snapper with Noodles

This beloved fish has many names: snapper, sea bream, gilthead. It's a great everyday fish that's becoming more and more popular in supermarkets. They live in the Atlantic Ocean and in the Mediterranean and are perfect for grilling. Make sure to salt liberally since the meat is really firm. And miso—what really is that? Well, it's just fermented soybeans.

4 SERVINGS

4 snapper fillets with skin (each approx. 5 oz [150 g])
1 box of noodles (approx. 5–6 oz [150 g])
4 cups (1 liter) vegetable strips (i.e., carrots, zucchini, red pepper, and leek)
olive oil for sautéing

MISO MARINADE:

3½ oz (100 g) miso paste
1 tbsp brown sugar
3 tbsp mirin
3 tbsp rice vinegar or saké
2 tbsp olive oil

DIRECTIONS:

1. Preheat the oven to 425°F (225°C).
2. Mix together the miso, brown sugar, mirin, and rice vinegar. Cover the fish fillets in 5–6 tbsp of the marinade (save the rest for later), and let them marinate for 20 minutes.
3. Place the fillets in a baking dish and bake for 8–10 minutes.
4. While the fillets are in the oven, boil the noodles according to the package instructions.
5. Flash fry the vegetables in olive oil. Drain the noodles and mix them with the vegetables. Season with a few tablespoons of the leftover marinade.
6. Plate the noodles, vegetables, and fish, and finish off by drizzling olive oil on top.

46.

47.

48. Herb-roasted Turbot with Beurre Blanc

This photo of the turbot was one of the first we took for this book. We had bought the most beautiful and expensive turbot in the store and roasted it in our "shitty" old oven (pardon my language!). And it turned out so damn tasty! Even at this stage in my life, having cooked so much fish, I'm still amazed by how easy it is to cook great-tasting fish. And when they try this sauce, your guests will be impressed—guaranteed. Try other flatfish as well, such as sole and flounder.

4 SERVINGS

1 whole turbot (approx. 1 lb [2–2½ kg])
olive oil for the pan
5–6 bay leaves
1 bunch of parsley
1 bunch of tarragon
1 bunch of thyme
7 tbsp (100 g) butter
sea salt
freshly ground white or black pepper

BEURRE BLANC:

1 shallot, finely chopped
butter and olive oil for sautéing
3½ tbsp white wine vinegar
3½ tbsp white wine
2–2⅔ sticks (250–300 g) butter, room temperature
salt, freshly ground white or black pepper
a pinch of sugar

DIRECTIONS:

1. Preheat the oven to 300°F (150°C).
2. Place the fish on a baking dish coated with oil. Score the fish straight down the middle and stuff it with herbs and dollops of butter. Sprinkle generously with sea salt and top with a few turns of the pepper mill.
3. Insert a thermometer close to the spine of the fish—at the thickest part. Place the pan in the oven and bake it for 45–60 minutes or until the core temperature is at 130°F (55°C) (if you are using a digital thermometer).
4. To make the sauce, fry the shallot in a pot with butter and oil. Add vinegar and white wine and bring to a boil. Reduce until only about 3 tablespoons remain. Add dollops of the room temperature butter while whisking constantly until the sauce turns smooth and silky. Season with salt, pepper, and a little bit of sugar.
5. Serve the fish with the sauce and almond potatoes that have been boiled with a large crown of dill in the pot.

Minced Fish—Several Dishes

I can't recall Mom, Dad, or Grandma ever mincing fish. No, this inspiration comes from our neighbors at number 28, who I visited every other day. This comes from one of those days when I stopped by, and dinner was pasta with canned fish balls in white sauce. . . . My reaction wasn't exactly negative, but more along the lines of, "What? Do people really eat this kind of stuff?" When I encounter things like this, I get inspired. So I decided to make minced fish that tastes better! With a food processor, mincing becomes a really quick process, too. And I'll never forget that time I made minced white fish from frozen pollock and cod, seasoned it with salt and pepper, and crumb-coated it with panko breadcrumbs. I pan-fried the minced fish in butter and served it with cucumber salad. The kids stuffed themselves until they couldn't stand up! Here is one of my so-called "basic recipes," which can be used as a base for anything by adding pretty much any spices and ingredients you like to create a completely new dish—just from using a simple, delicious fish to start. And for when you manage to catch plenty of fish on your hook, this fish mince can be used to make both fish burgers and quenelles.

49. Basic Fish Mince Recipe

It's important not to mix the ingredients for too long as this can cause the fat to separate from the mince and it will become mealy.

4 SERVINGS

7 oz (200 g) fresh salmon
7 oz (200 g) fresh cod, pike, or pollack fillets
½ tsp salt
1 tbsp mustard
1 egg white
⅔ cup (150 ml) heavy cream
freshly ground white or black pepper

DIRECTIONS:

1. Cut the fish into chunks and put them in a food processor. Add the other ingredients and mix at a high speed into a mince. Remember not to mix for too long.
2. Taste the mince—it should taste good (you can spit it out after tasting, if you like). Let the mince rest in the fridge for about 15 minutes.
3. Use the mince for fish burgers or quenelles— or why not make a nice fish pâté?

Super Tasty

FRESH FISH FOR MINCING

Fish mince is always best when you use fresh fish. When you use frozen fish, the mince gets a softer texture. The flavors are the same, though!

50. Quenelles in Asparagus and Lemon Sauce

Yet another great canned food that shouldn't be scoffed at! White asparagus is great in mixes and is perfect with these creamy quenelles.

4 SERVINGS

1 batch basic fish mince (see opposite side)
1 bunch of green asparagus
olive oil for sautéing
a pinch of salt

ASPARAGUS AND LEMON SAUCE:

1 shallot, finely chopped
1 garlic clove, finely chopped
olive oil for sautéing
¾ cup (200 ml) heavy cream
1 jar of white asparagus with stock (approx.
  11 oz [330 g])
½ cup (100 ml) milk
½ lemon, juice
salt, freshly ground white or black pepper

DIRECTIONS:

1. To make the sauce, fry the shallot and garlic in a pot with olive oil. Add the heavy cream and the asparagus with the stock and let simmer for 8–10 minutes. Add the milk and mix the sauce with a hand mixer (right inside the pot) until smooth.
2. Shape the mince into quenelles using two tablespoons. Dip the spoons in water every so often to make sure the mince will release each and every time. Place the quenelles in the sauce and let them simmer at low heat for about 5 minutes. Remove the pot from the stove and let it rest for another 5 minutes.
3. Cut the green asparagus into pieces (you can also peel them, if you prefer), and fry them in a pan with olive oil and a pinch of salt for 2–3 minutes.
4. Serve the quenelles with the sauce and top it off with the asparagus pieces.

49.

49.

50.

51.

51. Fish Patties with Roasted Mini Peppers and Mayo

Panko breadcrumbs are a must for this and can be found in well-stocked supermarkets or an Asian grocery. Panko breadcrumbs make things taste so much better and lighter compared to regular breadcrumbs.

4 SERVINGS

1 batch of basic fish mince (see page 107)
½ leek, finely chopped
7 oz (200 g) peeled shrimp, chopped
½ chili pepper, finely chopped
1 lemon, zest
butter and oil for sautéing
1¼ cups (300 ml) panko breadcrumbs

ROASTED MINI PEPPERS:

16 mini peppers
2 tbsp olive oil
1½ tbsp sea salt
freshly ground white or black pepper

MAYONNAISE:

1 egg yolk
1 tbsp spicy brown mustard
¾ cup (200 ml) canola oil
1 lemon, zest
1 garlic clove, shredded
¼ tsp salt
¼ tsp freshly ground white or black pepper

FOR GARNISH:

1 bunch cilantro, coarsely chopped
chopped pulp from 1 lemon
1 garlic clove, shredded
1 head of lettuce, for example, Romaine

DIRECTIONS:

1. Preheat the oven to 525°F (275°C).
2. Place the whole peppers on a baking sheet. Drizzle with olive oil and season with salt and pepper. Roast the peppers in the oven for about 10 minutes, until they are golden brown or almost black.
3. Mix the ingredients for the fish burgers in a bowl. Form the mixture into small patties. Pour panko breadcrumbs on a plate and coat the patties completely. Pan-fry the burgers in butter over medium heat for 3–4 minutes on each side until they turn golden brown.
4. Mix the egg yolk and mustard for the mayonnaise. Drizzle in the oil, a little bit at a time, until the mayonnaise thickens. Season with lemon zest, garlic, salt, and pepper.
5. Mix cilantro, lemon, and garlic in a bowl.
6. Plate the roasted peppers with the fish patties. Garnish with lettuce and the lemon and cilantro mix. Serve the mayonnaise on the side.

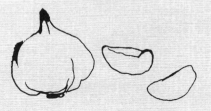

52. Pan-fried Mustard Herring with Restaurant-style Mashed Potatoes and Cognac Lingonberries

I met my husband during a time when I was quite heavy and had round cheeks like a balloon about to burst. It was all due to these restaurant-style mashed potatoes. The recipe was created by a famous French chef, Joël Robuchon, and we used his recipe every single day when I worked at the restaurant Kattegatt in Torekov. A beloved old recipe . . .

4 SERVINGS

12 herring fillets (approx. 17 oz [500 g])
3 tbsp coarse-grain sweet mustard
3½ tbsp chopped dill
salt, freshly ground white or black pepper
butter and oil for sautéing
rye flour for breading

COGNAC LINGONBERRIES:

8 oz (225 g) lingonberries, fresh or frozen (or cranberries)
⅔ cup (150 ml) sugar
3½ tbsp cognac

RESTAURANT-STYLE MASHED POTATOES:

1 lb (500 g) peeled, mealy potatoes
1 stick + 2½ tbsp (150 g) butter, room temperature
½ cup (100 ml) heavy cream
salt, freshly ground white or black pepper

DIRECTIONS:

1. Mix the lingonberries with sugar and cognac. Cover with plastic wrap and let it rest at room temperature for 1–2 days until the sugar has melted. Add more sugar or cognac if needed.
2. Boil the potatoes in lightly salted water. Press the potatoes in a potato ricer and stir in the room-temperature butter. Add heavy cream and season with salt and pepper.
3. Cut off the herring fins and spread out the fillets. Spread mustard on top. Sprinkle with dill, and season each fillet with salt and pepper. Fold them back up lengthwise. Pour rye flour onto a plate and coat the fillets with the flour. Pan-fry the fillets in butter for 4–5 minutes on each side until they turn golden brown and crispy.
4. Serve right away with mashed potatoes and cognac lingonberries.

Super Tasty

LINGONBERRIES

Don't stir the lingonberries or cranberries too much; instead, let the sugar melt slowly. The best thing to do is to mix everything the night before and cover the bowl in plastic wrap. Then, just let it sit on the kitchen counter. If you're the forgetful kind—just like me—you can also heat them in a pot, carefully, to make sure they stay intact. If you don't have any fresh lingonberries, you can also flavor store-bought lingonberry preserves with some cognac and lemon zest.

52.

53. Flounder Fish 'n' Chips with Remoulade Sauce

At Cirkus Maximum in Östhammar, I was cooking with a pregnant belly beside journalist Pelle Westman. I was preparing fish 'n' chips served up on newspaper—just the way it's meant to be served. This utterly British dish is like a Swedish shrimp salad sandwich . . . it can turn out so incredibly delicious or it can be an absolute disaster. If you have the right touch and clean oil in the fryer, I promise you it will turn out great.

4 SERVINGS
8 flounder fillets (approx. 1⅓ lbs [600 g])
salt, freshly ground white or black pepper
4 eggs
¾ cup (200 ml) cornstarch
2 cups (½ liter) corn oil for frying
parsley sprigs

REMOULADE SAUCE:
½ cup (100 ml) pickles
3 tbsp finely sliced leek
½ cup (100 ml) mayonnaise (see page 109)
¾ cup (200 ml) crème fraîche (or sour cream)
1½ tbsp curry powder
sea salt
freshly ground white or black pepper
freshly squeezed lemon juice
1 tbsp shredded fresh horseradish

FOR SERVING:
lemon wedges

DIRECTIONS:

1. Chop the pickles for the sauce. Rinse the leek and slice it thinly. Mix the pickles, leek, mayo, and crème fraîche (or sour cream) in a bowl. Stir in the curry powder. Season the sauce with salt and pepper and a little bit of lemon juice. Finish it off with the shredded fresh horseradish. If you don't want to use store-bought mayonnaise, you can make your own using the recipe on page 109.

2. Whisk the eggs and cornstarch until you have a smooth batter. Heat plenty of oil in a pot (read more about deep frying on page 248). Season the flounder fillets with salt and pepper. First dip them in the batter, and then place them in the hot oil for 3–4 minutes until they curl and turn golden brown. Dip the parsley sprigs into the batter and fry them quickly.

3. Serve with remoulade sauce and lemon wedges—perhaps even cut them like the Russian lemon (see page 188). This, of course, tastes great with crispy french fries. And go for it—serve it on a sheet of newspaper!

54. Fish Braid in Champagne Sauce à la the '80s

When I grew up in the '80s, this dish was typical of the food my dad made in the restaurant. Dollops of whipped cream in soups, pressed potatoes, and beef tenderloin "black and white." Today, I'm happy to have been a restaurant child, but back in those days I didn't know what a gift it was! My brother and I preferred to stay with my grandmother and grandfather, where we were served regular food instead of strange luxuries we didn't even like. Time to bring out your old braiding techniques, because we're making a fish braid! And add the champagne sauce to your favorites, because it's great with any type of fish. It's just a fancier type of white wine sauce.

4 SERVINGS
14 oz (400 g) salmon fillet
14 oz (400 g) flounder fillet
CHAMPAGNE SAUCE:
2 shallots
6 white peppercorns
1 tbsp butter
¾ cup (200 ml) dry white wine
¾ cup (200 ml) fish stock or water
3½ tbsp + 3½ tbsp sparkling white wine
¾ cup (200 ml) heavy cream
½ tsp salt
2 tsp freshly squeezed lemon juice
freshly ground white or black pepper
FOR GARNISH:
5 oz (150 g) sweet peas
3 oz (80 g) salmon roe
1 small bunch of chives
FOR SERVING:
pressed potatoes

DIRECTIONS:
1. Preheat the oven to 275°F (130°C).
2. Cut the fish fillets lengthwise into thick strips. Braid the fish into four braids. Put them on lightly buttered parchment paper and bake in the oven for about 10 minutes.
3. Peel and thinly slice the onion. Crush the peppercorn. Fry the onion and the peppercorns in butter. Add white wine, stock, and 3½ tbsp sparkling wine and reduce to half its volume. Add the cream and let it reduce some more until the sauce becomes nice and creamy. Sift the sauce through a sieve. Season with salt, pepper, and lemon juice. Keep the sauce hot until ready to serve.
4. Heat the sweet peas gently in a pot with a few tablespoons of the sauce. Pour the peas onto four plates and place one fish braid on each plate. Garnish with salmon roe and chives.
5. Add another 3½ tbsp of sparkling wine to the sauce and make it frothier by mixing with a hand mixer right in the pot.
6. Serve the fish braid right away with the champagne sauce and pressed potatoes. Don't forget a large dollop of butter on top of the pressed potatoes, along with salt and freshly ground pepper.

54

55. Pickled Char with Salsa Verde

Now I'm going to tell you about a sauce that is really diverse—almost like a chameleon that changes its appearance faster than Clark Kent becomes Superman. One day he's lying down (I'm sure it's a he) on a spoon with Mrs. Flounder, and the next day he's playing billiards with the best quality sirloin steak. I'm talking about a sauce called salsa verde in Italian and Spanish, and it works with everything, even tacos (see page 248), and is a great summer sidekick. Here, the sauce is accompanied by char, but don't let that limit you. You can forget about the fish and enjoy the sauce. . . . No, all jokes aside, I do think the pickled char deserves its own recognition, as it is a simple fish that's very easy to find culinary success with.

4 SERVINGS
2 char fillets (each approx. 14 oz [400 g])
BRINE FOR PICKLING:
4 cups (1 liter) water
3½ tbsp salt
1½ tbsp sugar
SALSA VERDE:
1 bunch parsley
1 bunch tarragon
1 bunch mint
1¾ oz (50 g) spinach
2 tbsp capers
2 garlic cloves
2 tbsp Dijon mustard
1½ tbsp water
½ cup (100 ml) olive oil
a pinch of salt
freshly ground white or black pepper

FOR GARNISH:
1 lemon
1 bunch of parsley, coarsely chopped
2 tbsp olive oil
2 heads of lettuce

DIRECTIONS:
1. Place the fish fillets in a casserole dish or something similar. Boil water, salt, and sugar into a brine. Pour it over the fish and cover the pan quickly with plastic wrap.
2. While preparing the brine, make the sauce by mixing all the ingredients, except the olive oil, with a hand mixer. The mixture should be smooth. Add the oil in drops until the sauce thickens and season with salt and pepper. Put the sauce in the fridge.
3. Peel the lemon. Cut the pulp into nice fillets, and then chop them into small cubes. Mix the lemon pulp with parsley and olive oil.
4. Split the heads of lettuce down the middle and "dress" (spoon over) the lemon and parsley mixture on top.
5. Remove the char from the brine and remove the skin. Plate the fish with salsa verde and salad.

Super Tasty

SOMETHING NEW FROM LEFTOVERS
Make a salad from yesterday's cold potatoes and salsa verde—a great side dish for some cold slices of roast beef.

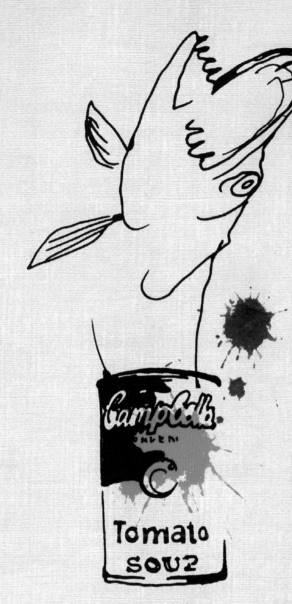

In Top Shape—Everyday in a Can

Time for some product placement and canned nostalgia! Many consider fish casserole a more advanced level of cooking, and probably not something to be made on a regular weekday. But on the weekdays we need shortcuts, and I have plenty of shortcuts in my kitchen! Fish casserole is healthy and tasty, but best of all, it cooks itself in the oven. I'll show you how you can turn fresh or frozen fish into simple and tasty everyday food, just by using Campbell's canned soups. I love simple and great solutions, and this is why I don't think there's anything wrong with canned sauces and soups (as long as they taste good). And that's what I like about Campbell's. Using their soups for anything and everything is not only a tasty option, but also a smart one. So stop closing the kitchen curtains when you open a can of soup! It's cool to use half-finished products, if you do it the right way. Stock up on some soups and add anything from salmon to cod, mackerel to flounder. And just think about what a lovely stack of soups you'll have in the pantry.

56. Flounder in Lobster Au Gratin with Broccoli and Zucchini

I made this casserole once during a downpour at Marstrand during a taping for my TV show with Tomas Tengby. It has almost been ten years since then, but I still make this dish once a week, either on a weekday or on a Saturday. And remember this: if the Fussy Family comes to visit, it's perfectly okay to say that you made the lobster soup from scratch.

4 SERVINGS

8 flounder fillets
1 can of Campbell's lobster soup
½ can milk, water, or heavy cream
1 zucchini
1 head of broccoli
2 crushed cloves of garlic
olive oil for sautéing
salt, freshly ground white or black pepper
¾ cup (200 ml) heavy cream + 1 egg yolk

DIRECTIONS:

1. Preheat the oven to 475°F (250°C).
2. Season the fillets with salt and pepper and roll them up so the skin is on the inside. Put the rolls in a baking dish.
3. Slice the zucchini and broccoli stems. Break the broccoli head into small pieces. Sauté the vegetables and garlic in a pan with olive oil for a few minutes. Season with salt and pepper.
4. Pour the vegetables into the pan with the fish. Mix the soup with half a can of milk, water, or heavy cream and pour it over the vegetables and fish. Bake in the oven for about 10 minutes.
5. Whisk the heavy cream and stir in the egg yolk. Dollop the whipped cream onto the baked fish. Bake in the oven for another 5 minutes. Serve with pressed potatoes or rice (see page 236).

57. Cod in Asparagus Au Gratin with Sweet Peas and Lemon

I love making casseroles with heavy cream because it tastes so much better. If you buy fresh cod, be sure to have it cleaned and filleted for you at the fish counter so it will be free of bones.

4 SERVINGS

1½ lbs (700 g) cod fillets
1 can of Campbell's asparagus soup
½ can milk, water, or heavy cream
1 leek
5⅓ oz (150 g) sweet peas
1 bunch of green asparagus
olive oil for sautéing
salt, freshly ground white or black pepper
1 lemon
1 bunch of dill or chervil

DIRECTIONS:

1. Preheat the oven to 475°F (250°C). Clean the cod fillets by removing the small bones attached to the thickest part of the fillets. This will make the fillet open up, and it will look like a pair of pants. Put the fish in a baking fish and squeeze lemon on top. Season with salt and pepper.
2. Clean the leek and sweet peas and cut into smaller pieces. Cut off the bottom part of the asparagus and throw it away; chop up the rest of the stem. Sauté the vegetables in a pan with olive oil, salt, and pepper. Pour the vegetables into the pan.
3. Mix the soup with milk, water, or heavy cream and pour it over the fish and vegetables. Bake in the oven for 20 minutes.
4. Garnish with fresh dill or chervil and serve with rice (see page 236).

56.

57.

58.

59.

58. Salmon and Hake Casserole with Mushrooms and Cauliflower

Just use salmon by itself if you can't find hake—nobody will berate you for it! At least I won't.

4 SERVINGS

11 oz (300 g) salmon fillets
11 oz (300 g) hake fillets
1 can Campbell's mushroom soup
½ can milk, water, or heavy cream
4 cups (1 liter) mixed mushrooms
½ cauliflower head
1 bunch tarragon, freshly chopped
olive oil for sautéing
salt, freshly ground white or black pepper
3½ oz (100 g) shredded cheese

DIRECTIONS:

1. Preheat the oven to 475°F (250°C).
2. Cut the fish into two-inch (5 cm) cubes. Clean the mushrooms. Break the cauliflower into small florets. Chop the tarragon coarsely. Flash-fry the mushrooms, cauliflower, and tarragon in a pan with a bit of oil. Season with salt and pepper.
3. Place the fish cubes in a baking dish along with the vegetables.
4. Mix the soup with milk, water, or heavy cream. Pour the soup into the oven pan and sprinkle shredded cheese on top. Bake in the oven for 10–12 minutes. Serve right away with pressed potatoes.

59. Tomato-baked Mackerel with Fennel and Parsley

If you use smoked mackerel, the casserole will taste like warm mackerel in tomato sauce—a favorite dish in Sweden. You don't need to dilute the soup for this, but rather use it as is.

4 SERVINGS

4 mackerel fillets
1 can of Campbell's tomato soup
½ fennel
2 celery stalks
olive oil for sautéing
salt, freshly ground white or black pepper
1 bunch of parsley, coarsely chopped
1 tbsp breadcrumbs
2 tbsp (25 g) butter

DIRECTIONS:

1. Preheat the oven to 475°F (250°C).
2. Score the skin of the mackerel. Clean and slice the fennel and celery. Sauté the vegetables and parsley in a little bit of olive oil for a few minutes. Season with salt and pepper.
3. Place the fish in an oven pan with the greens on top and then spoon the tomato soup over it. Sprinkle some breadcrumbs on top and dollop the butter onto the fish. Bake in the oven for 10–12 minutes. Serve right away with some delicious rice (see page 236).

FIRMER FROZEN FISH

It's always a good idea to salt the fish if it has been frozen and then let it rest for about fifteen minutes before working with it. That way, the fish won't release as much liquid during the cooking process and will be firmer in texture.

60.

61

60. Smoked Salmon with Creamy Dill Potatoes

I love this classic. Super easy to prepare since you buy the fish pre-made. Anyone can boil potatoes and make sauce. . . . Let's go! Keep in mind that milk burns easily. If your sauce does burn, just throw it out and start over. Heat the smoked salmon in a bit of foil in the oven or on the grill.

4 SERVINGS

4 pieces of smoked salmon (each approx. 5 oz [150 g])

CREAMY DILL POTATOES:

1 lb (500 g) potatoes with skin
½ silver onion
2 tbsp butter
2 tbsp flour
1¼ cups (300 ml) milk
a pinch of salt
freshly ground white or black pepper
1 bunch of dill

DIRECTIONS:

1. Boil potatoes until soft in lightly salted water.
2. Peel and finely chop the onion. Sauté it in butter until the onion turns soft. Stir in the flour and add milk, a little bit at a time, while stirring. Bring to a boil. Season with salt and white or black pepper.
3. Drain the water from the potatoes and cut them into halves. Place them in the hot sauce. Coarsely chop the dill and sprinkle it on top.
4. Serve the creamy dill potatoes with the smoked salmon.

61. Salmon with New Potatoes and Caviar Crème

This is a perfect summer food made from leftovers. Depending on where you live, new potatoes can be called "early potatoes," but they're all the same. Just crush yesterday's leftover cold potatoes with a fork and add Kalles Kaviar and cream—so incredibly delicious! Kalles Kaviar spread is an everyday, spreadable caviar that can be found at IKEA. You can also make this dish without the salmon and just eat it as is, perhaps with some hard-boiled eggs cut into halves. If so, you can also omit the cheese and place it in the oven. It's a perfect "I-have-nothing-at-home dish." Lightly salted cucumber (see page 252) goes really well with it.

4 SERVINGS

14 oz (400 g) boiled potatoes
1⅓ lbs (600 g) salmon fillets, without skin
¾ cup (200 ml) heavy cream
½ tube Kalles Kaviar spread (3 oz [85 g])
freshly ground white or black pepper
⅓ cup (100 ml) shredded aged cheese

DIRECTIONS:

1. Preheat the oven to 425°F (225°C).
2. Place the boiled potatoes in a baking dish and press them with a fork.
3. Cut the salmon into 1-inch (2 cm) thick slices, and layer the slices and the potatoes in the pan.
4. Whisk the heavy cream and flavor it with caviar. Season with pepper. Spread out the caviar crème in the pan so it covers the fish and potatoes. Sprinkle shredded cheese on top and bake in the oven for 15 minutes.
5. Serve the dish as a quick appetizer or prepare it when a neighbor shows up hungry.

62. Salmon with Warm Citrus-and Onion Vinaigrette

Serve this dish as an appetizer or as a main course with boiled potatoes. The salmon becomes a little sweet in flavor because of the onion. It's really simple to make and tastes great!

4 SERVINGS

14 oz (400 g) fresh salmon fillet
1 large shallot
½ red onion
3 limes
2 tbsp honey
½ cup (100 ml) olive oil
a pinch of salt
a pinch of white or black pepper

DIRECTIONS:

1. Peel and finely chop the onions. Flash-fry them in a pan with a little bit of oil until they turn soft.
2. Zest one lime and squeeze the juice out of all three. Add both juice and zest to the pan with the onion. Add honey and olive oil. Bring to a boil and let simmer until the vinaigrette thickens slightly.
3. Slice the salmon as thin as you can and divide the slices onto four plates. Season with salt and pepper. Pour the warm vinaigrette on top of the raw salmon and serve right away.

DIFFERENT WAYS TO CUT SALMON

If you want extra thin slices, place the salmon in the freezer for a short period because this makes it easier to cut the salmon really thin. Or you can just forget the traditional way of cutting salmon diagonally and simply cut it straight down as if you were slicing bread. Just be sure it doesn't have any skin still attached before you do.

63. Salmon with Warm Grapes and Capers

I had this salmon dish with my colleague Benny at La Boqueria in Barcelona. The grapes were close to bursting. We gurgled and snacked while trying to figure this recipe out, and this is what we came up with. The grape brine with capers is also delicious when eaten chilled with some cold cuts.

4 SERVINGS

14 oz (400 g) fresh salmon fillet
2 shallots, finely chopped
3½ tbsp olive oil
2 tbsp white balsamic vinegar
1 cup (250 ml) seedless green grapes
2 tbsp capers
a pinch of sea salt
a pinch of freshly ground white or black pepper

DIRECTIONS:

1. Place the onions in a warm pot with olive oil and white balsamic vinegar. Add grapes and capers and let simmer for seven minutes, until the grapes have turned soft and juicy. Cover the pot if you want to speed up the process.
2. Slice the salmon as thinly as possible and divide the slices onto four individual plates. Season with salt and pepper and spread out the warm grapes over the raw salmon. Serve right away.

62

64. Lemon and Pepper Gravlax

Making gravlax is easy, because it makes itself. It's both fun and simple, and you really can't go wrong. If you just make sure to roll the salmon around in the spices once in a while, keeping your hands clean and the salmon cold, you'll be successful, I promise!

4–6 SERVINGS

3⅓ lbs (1½ kg) salmon fillet, with skin
5 bay leaves (preferably fresh)
2 tbsp whole white pepper
3 lemons
½ cup (100 ml) sea salt
½ cup (100 ml) coarsely chopped dill

DIRECTIONS:

1. Grind the bay leaves and white pepper in a mortar. Wash and cut the lemon into thin slices.
2. Mix the sugar, salt, and dill with the ground bay leaves and white pepper. Rub the salmon with the spice mix and then cover the whole fish with lemon slices. Let it rest at room temperature until the mixture begins to melt; it takes about an hour.
3. Place the salmon in the fridge covered in plastic wrap and preferably under a little bit of pressure. Let it rest for at least twenty-four hours.
4. Cut the salmon either diagonally or straight down (like a loaf of bread) into thin slices. Serve as a main dish with creamy dill potatoes (see page 124) or at a buffet.

SEARED GRAVLAX

Flash-fry a thicker piece of gravlax in a pan without any oil for 20 seconds per side. Serve with artichoke cream (see page 292).

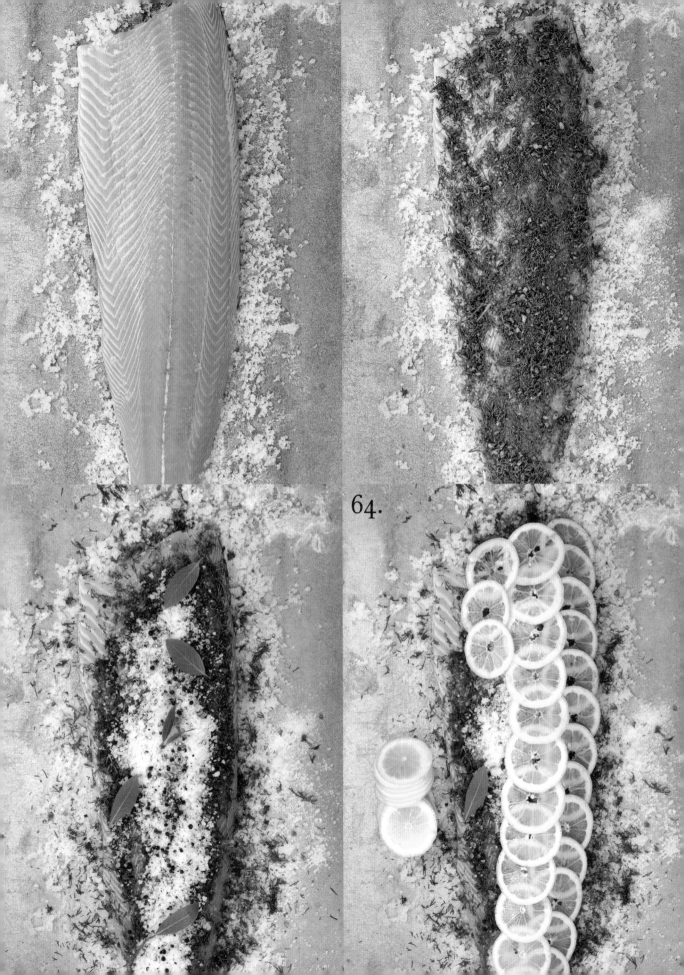

64.

still alive...

A Net Full of Mussels—Four Fabulous Recipes

Blue mussels are festive, delicious, useful, and best of all, they're cheap. They cook really quickly as well. Serve them steamed; au gratin; seasoned with chili, lime, and coconut milk; or seasoned with cinnamon and cardamom. Try a number of flavors so you can have a reason to eat mussels more often!

It's important that the mussels be alive, and you can confirm this by tapping on the open mussels. The ones that close their lids can be eaten; the ones that don't should be thrown away. The best season for mussels is the spring, before they start their mating season. It's said that you shouldn't eat shellfish during months that don't have the letter "R" in their name. Here are my favorite blue mussel recipes. So for those of you who have only cooked these in white wine, see how easy it is to vary the flavors and be inspired to try something new!

65. White Wine Poached Mussels with Fennel and Garlic

This is a weekend classic at my house to pair with a cocktail or glass of wine. I put the mussels in a big bowl and serve them with some tasty bread and a stack of napkins. And then we dive in!

4 SERVINGS

  1 net of blue mussels (approx. 2 lbs [1 kg])
  2 shallots, finely chopped
  3 garlic cloves, finely chopped
  ½ fennel, cut into strips
  olive oil for sautéing
  ¾ cup (200 ml) dry white wine or water
  ¾ cup (200 ml) heavy cream
  1 tsp salt
  ½ cup (100 ml) parsley

DIRECTIONS:

1. Rinse and scrub the mussels and remove the beards. Throw away any open mussels that don't close when you tap on them.
2. Fry the onions, garlic, and fennel in a large pot with oil. Pour the mussels into the pot and flash-fry them over high heat for a few minutes. Add the wine (or water) and the heavy cream. Let the mussels cook for about five minutes under closed lid. Shake the pot once or twice during the cooking process. Season with salt and pepper.
3. Chop the parsley. Plate the mussels and sprinkle the parsley on top. Serve immediately.

66. Mussels in Chili and Lime Coconut Milk

Really creamy and tasty! The coconut milk with the lime leaves almost turns this dish into the Tom kha gai soup (see page 232) served on the beaches in Thailand.

4 SERVINGS

  1 net of blue mussels (approx. 2 lbs [1 kg])
  1 large red onion, finely chopped
  3 garlic cloves, finely chopped
  olive oil for sautéing
  1 red chili, cored and cut into strips
  5 lime leaves
  1 can coconut milk (14 oz [400 ml])
  approx. ½ cup (100 ml) water
  1 tsp salt
  1 bunch of cilantro, finely chopped

DIRECTIONS:

1. Rinse and scrub the mussels and remove the beards. Throw away any open mussels that don't close when you tap on them.
2. Fry the onion and garlic in a large pot with oil until soft. Add chili, lime leaves, and mussels and sauté over high heat for 1–2 minutes.
3. Add the coconut milk and water, and bring to a boil. Let simmer under a closed lid for about five minutes until they open. Shake the pot once or twice during the cooking process. Season with salt and stir the fresh cilantro into the pot. Serve right away.

 65.

 66.

67.

68.

67. Spicy Mussels with Tomato and Lime

Here's a dish with plenty of spices that I hope will inspire you to try mussels spiced with your own favorite seasonings.

4 SERVINGS

1 net of blue mussels (approx. 2 lbs [1 kg])
2 shallots, thinly sliced
3 garlic cloves, finely chopped
olive oil for sautéing
1 cinnamon stick
1 tsp ground cardamom
1 tsp ground fennel
1 tsp whole mustard seeds
1 can crushed tomatoes (approx. 14 oz [400 g])
¾ cup (200 ml) water
1 lime
1 tsp salt
some tasty bread for serving

DIRECTIONS:

1. Rinse and scrub the mussels and remove the beards. Throw away any open mussels that don't close when you tap them.
2. Fry the onions and garlic in a large pot with oil. Mix all the spices and let it all fry for a minute. Add the mussels, tomatoes, and the water, and gently shake the pot. Let simmer under a closed lid for about five minutes.
3. Squeeze the fresh lime over the mussels and season with salt. Pour the mussels into a deep bowl and serve right away with some bread.

68. Oven-baked Mussels with Chili and Tarragon

So incredibly delicious! Keep in mind that it's important to use white bread for this dish, because it absorbs liquid so well. Sourdough, for example, won't soak up as much and will retain its chewiness—something that won't work for this dish. Great for a quick snack.

4 SERVINGS

1 net of blue mussels (approx. 2 lbs [1 kg])
½ cup (100 ml) water
1 slice of white bread
5 tbsp + 1 tsp (75 g) butter, room temperature
2 tsp Sambal Oelek
1 lime, zest
2 tbsp chopped fresh tarragon
a pinch of salt
1 garlic clove, pressed

DIRECTIONS:

1. Preheat the oven to 525°F (275°C).
2. Rinse and scrub the mussels and remove the beards. Throw away any open mussels that don't close when you tap them.
3. Place the mussels in a large pot with the water. Bring to a boil and let simmer under a closed lid for about five minutes. Release each mussel from its shell. Return the freed mussel to one half of the shell and place in a baking dish. Save the stock and use it for fish soup or for the champagne sauce on page 114.
4. Tear apart the white bread and mix it with butter, Sambal Oelek, lime zest, tarragon, and salt. Press the garlic into the pan. Scoop the mixture onto the mussels. If you plan to refrigerate and cook later, you can prepare up until this step.
5. Bake the gratin in the upper part of the oven for 3–5 minutes. Serve right away.

69. Pasta with Mozzarella, Tuna, and Caramelized Lemon

You get what you pay for. The more expensive canned tuna is usually caught with a fishing rod and is preserved in olive oil in whole fillets. Sustainable fishing is good for everyone and guarantees that there's no dolphin meat in there!

4 SERVINGS

14 oz (400 g) pasta, for example, bucatini
¾ cup (200 ml) dark bread, preferably
*   sourdough, in chunks*
1 lemon
½ red onion, finely chopped
2 garlic cloves, shredded
2 cans tuna fish in oil (each approx. 7 oz [200 g])
2 bags of mozzarella cheese (each approx.
*   4½ oz [125 g])*
3 tbsp olive oil
salt, freshly ground white or black pepper

DIRECTIONS:

1. Boil the pasta according to the directions on the packaging and drain the water.
2. At the same time, toast the bread in the oven at 425°F (225°C) or in a frying pan with a little bit of olive oil. Put to the side.
3. Split the lemon and fry it in a hot pan until it turns golden brown and has been caramelized by the fruit sugar. Put the lemon to the side.
4. Pour the drained pasta into the pan and stir in the red onion, garlic, and some of the oil from the tuna fish cans.
5. Pour the pasta onto a serving platter. Spread out small pieces of the tuna fish, mozzarella, and bread on top of the pasta. Season with salt and pepper and squeeze the caramelized lemon on top. Serve right away.

70. Everyday Paella with Salmon, Shrimp, Cauliflower, and Tomatoes

You can add whatever you want to this dish. Mussels, smoked ham, whatever you like. . . .

4 SERVINGS

2 carrots
1 red onion
2 garlic cloves
½ head of cauliflower
3 tbsp olive oil
1¼ cups (300 ml) Arborio rice
a pinch (1/2 g) of saffron
½ tsp chili powder
2 tsp paprika powder
14 oz (400 g) cherry tomatoes
2½ cups (600 ml) boiling water
1½ tsp salt, freshly ground white or black pepper
1¼ cups (300 ml) peeled shrimp
3½ oz (100 g) smoked salmon, in pieces
1 bunch chives, finely chopped

DIRECTIONS:

1. Peel the carrots and red onion. Cut them into small pieces. Peel and crush the garlic. Separate the cauliflower into small florets.
2. Sauté the vegetables and the onion in a heavy-bottomed pot with olive oil. Add the rice and the spices and sauté for another couple of minutes.
3. Add the tomatoes and the hot water and let simmer over low heat for about twenty minutes while stirring constantly. It is ready when the liquid has almost been completely absorbed and the rice is *al dente* (meaning that it still has some resistance when you bite into it). Season with salt and pepper, and fold the shrimp and salmon into the rice. Top with some chives.
4. Serve with some fresh bread and a glass of dry sherry.

70.

71.

71. Seafood Lasagna with Spinach and Chanterelles

I had to have a seafood lasagna recipe in this book and it had to be a great one. If you choose inexpensive, canned seafood, this dish is perfect for a weekday. Or you can omit the seafood completely and use chanterelles for a vegetarian version.

4 SERVINGS

  2 yellow onions
  1 garlic clove
  11 oz (300 g) chanterelles
  3 tbsp (70g) butter
  14 oz (400 g) shrimp in brine (net weight)
  14 oz (400 g) crawfish in brine (net weight)
  9 oz (250 g) frozen spinach
  salt, freshly ground white pepper
  a pinch of sugar
  ground nutmeg
  7 oz (200 g) fresh lasagna noodles
BÉCHAMEL SAUCE:
  butter
  2 tsp flour
  1¼ cups (300 ml) heavy cream
  1¼ cups (300 ml) milk
  salt, freshly ground white or black pepper

DIRECTIONS:

1. Preheat the oven to 400°F (200°C).
2. Melt the butter for the béchamel sauce in a thick-bottomed pot. Add the flour and let it sauté for a short while. Add heavy cream and milk, a little bit at a time. Let simmer while stirring. Season with salt and pepper.
3. Peel and finely chop the onion. Peel and crush the garlic. Sauté half of the onion with the garlic and the chanterelles in 2 tablespoons of the butter. Remove the pan from the heat. Set aside 2 tablespoons of the chanterelles for garnish, and then add the shrimp and crawfish to the mixture. Season with salt and pepper.
4. Sauté the rest of the onion with the spinach and 1 tbsp of butter. Season with salt, pepper, and some ground nutmeg.
5. Layer the lasagna noodles in a baking dish with chanterelle mix, béchamel sauce, and spinach. Top with the béchamel sauce and bake in the oven for 40 minutes.
6. Garnish with the chanterelles you set aside earlier and serve right away.

72. Atlantic Herring with Roasted Garlic and Lime

For this recipe, I roast the garlic. The roasting causes the stickiness of the onion to disappear and it becomes mild and sweet. My husband doesn't like raw garlic, so I'm always careful to roast them when he's not around.

4–6 SERVINGS
6 pickled herring fillets
10 garlic cloves
oil for sautéing
¾ cup (200 ml) mayonnaise (see page 109)
1¼ cups (300 ml) sour cream
½ cup (100 ml) finely chopped parsley
1 red onion, finely chopped
1 lime, zest and juice
salt, freshly ground white or black pepper

DIRECTIONS:
1. Peel the garlic cloves and roast in a little bit of oil until they turn soft and golden brown. Mash the garlic cloves.
2. Cut the herring diagonally into pieces and mix them together with garlic, mayonnaise, sour cream, parsley, red onion, and the lime zest and juice. Season with salt and pepper.
3. Let rest in the fridge for twenty-four hours before serving.

73. Spicy Ramlösa Atlantic Herring

I created this recipe while I was working at IKEA many years ago. I don't think I've ever gotten more requests for any other recipe before or since. I actually didn't have the recipe until now. . . . At IKEA we measured the herring in tons, and we didn't have a recipe for individual portions. I always make the Ramlösa herring for Christmas and bring the leftovers to our vacation home for New Year's Eve. It tastes even better then.

4–6 SERVINGS
8 pickled herring fillets
SPICE BRINE:
4 tsp fennel seed
4 tsp anise seed
3 star anises
1 tsp whole black peppercorns
1 silver onion, finely chopped
1 red onion, finely chopped
½ lemon, zest and juice
¾ cup (200 ml) of the brine from the pickled herring
3½ tbsp canola oil

DIRECTIONS:
1. Finely crush the fennel seed, anise seed, star anise, and black peppercorns in a mortar. Mix the spices, onion, lemon zest, lemon juice, brine from the herring, and canola oil.
2. Layer the spice mixture over the herring fillets and let rest overnight in the fridge—or better yet, for 2–3 days.

74. Mustard-pickled Herring

Yes, if you skip the herring part, you'll have a really tasty mustard sauce whenever you need one.

4–6 SERVINGS

10 Baltic herring fillets (approx. 14 oz [400 g])

BRINE:

2 cups (500 ml) water
⅔ cup (150 ml) white vinegar
1 tsp salt

MUSTARD SAUCE:

⅔ cup (150 ml) coarse-grain mustard
4 tbsp white wine vinegar
4 tbsp sugar
1¼ cups (300 ml) canola oil
½ tsp salt, freshly ground white or black pepper

DIRECTIONS:

1. Pull the skin off the herring fillets.
2. Mix the ingredients for the brine and let the herring fillets sit in the brine overnight in the fridge.
3. Drain the brine from the fish and lightly pat down the pieces with paper towels.
4. Mix all the ingredients for the mustard sauce and season to taste. Add the herring pieces and mix well. Let rest in the fridge for at least 24 hours before serving.

75. Pan-fried Pickled Herring

Breading the pickled herring with rye flour is my specialty, after having been in charge of the pan frying of herring at Ramlösa Tavern. Dad used to have a huge frying table that could probably fit a hundred herrings—so you had to move quickly!

4–6 SERVINGS

10 Baltic herring fillets (approx. 14 oz [400 g])
¾ cup (200 ml) coarse rye flour
salt, freshly ground white or black pepper
butter and oil for sautéing

BRINE:

1¼ cups (300 ml) water
¾ cup (200 ml) sugar
½ cup (100 ml) white vinegar
½ tbsp allspice
3 carrots
2 small yellow onions
2 bay leaves

DIRECTIONS:

1. Cut off the fins and rinse the herring. Salt and pepper the fillets and fold them in half.
2. Pour the flour onto a large plate and cover the fillets completely in the flour. Pan-fry them in butter and oil until they are golden brown.
3. Peel the onion and carrot. Thinly slice the onion and cut the carrot into coins. Mix the rest of the ingredients for the brine with a whisk until the sugar has dissolved. Add carrots, onion, and bay leaves.
4. Put the pan-fried herring into a bowl. Add the brine so it covers the fish completely. Let it rest in the fridge for at least two days before serving. The longer you allow the herring to rest in the brine, the better it will taste.

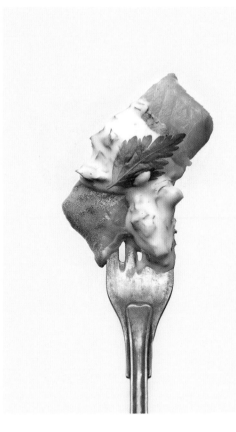

72. 73.

74. 75.

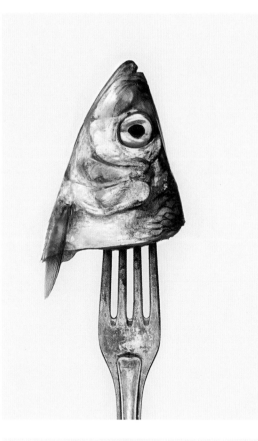

76.

77.

78.

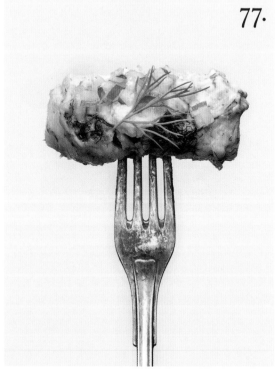

76. Warm Tomato and Sherry Herring

This recipe, as well as the following one, is great with mashed potatoes (see page 239).

4 SERVINGS

15 Baltic herring fillets
⅔ cup (150 ml) tomato paste
2 tbsp sugar
1 tbsp white vinegar
⅔ cup (150 ml) drained pearl onions
⅓ cup (75 ml) sherry
3½ tbsp water
½ cup (100 ml) coarsely chopped parsley
salt, freshly ground white or black pepper

DIRECTIONS:

1. Preheat the oven to 350°F (180°C). Pull the skin off the herring fillets. Season with salt and pepper. Roll them up with the skin side out and place the rolls onto an oiled baking dish.
2. Mix tomato paste, sugar, vinegar, and parsley. Season with salt and pepper. Pour the mixture onto the herring rolls and bake in the oven for 20–30 minutes.

77. Kerstin's Caviar Herring

A recipe from Ramlösa Tavern.

4 SERVINGS

15 Baltic herring fillets (approx. 1⅓ lbs [600 g])
salt
¾ cup (200 ml) mayonnaise + ½ cup (100 ml) milk
2 tbsp caviar
½ red onion, finely chopped
½ cup (100 ml) finely chopped dill

DIRECTIONS:

1. Preheat the oven to 350°F (180°C).
2. Grease a baking dish. Cut or pull off the back fins on the herrings. Season with salt, roll up the fillets with the skin side out, and place them in the dish.
3. Stir the mayonnaise with the milk and caviar. Add the onion and half of the dill. Pour the mixture over the herring fillets. Sprinkle the rest of the dill on top and bake in the oven for 20–30 minutes. Serve with mashed potatoes.

78. Pickled Herring
Boquerones

Boquerones are often served as tapas in Spain, but instead of herring they use sardines. Keep in mind that it takes some time to prepare the herring.

4 SERVINGS

15 Baltic herring fillets (1⅓ lbs [600 g])
1 cup (250 ml) freshly squeezed lemon juice
1½ tbsp salt
rind strips from 2 lemons
1¼ cups (300 ml) olive oil (for preserving)
freshly ground black pepper
3 garlic cloves, crushed
1 bunch of fresh herbs, for example, thyme and parsley

DIRECTIONS:

1. Remove the skin from the herring fillets. Marinate the fillets in lemon juice and salt until the meat has turned white (6–8 hours in the fridge).
2. Drain the lemon juice. Layer the herring with all other ingredients in a glass jar—the oil should cover the fish. Let it rest in the fridge for 24 hours before serving.

Barbecue

Grilled Watermelon with Peanut Sauce
Lobster with Dill and Lemon Butter
Grilled Oysters with Lemon and Green Tabasco
Grilled Whole Salmon with Green Pea Guacamole
Texas Burger with Blue Cheese Cream
Feta Cheese Salad with Mint and Maple Syrup
Cinnamon-glazed Pork Belly
Bulgogi with Sides
Kimchi—Fermented Cabbage
Sesame Sprouts
Pickled Chili Cucumber
Grilled Lamb Shoulder, Apple Vinaigrette, and Tomato
Salad with Breadcrumbs
Ketchup with Horseradish, Ginger, and Lime
Barbecue Sauce
Chimichurri

I USUALLY DREAD THE FIRST BARBECUE OF THE SEASON, which is almost always a spur of the moment thing. What will we find stuck on the grill grate this year? Last year's pork loin? Or perhaps a bit of leftover corn-fed chicken? And the bowl that I've been looking for all winter can always be found under the grill, filled with a bunch of frozen insects that got trapped when the cold came. Here I've included some silly tips and ideas for the grilling season, as I take you over a few grilling basics. *Lump charcoal or briquettes*? Lump charcoal comes from wood and doesn't make too much dust, which makes for easy cleaning. It also lends your food a nice flavor. Lump charcoal can reach high temperatures quickly, which is good for certain kinds of grilling. Briquettes consist of compressed wood by-products and hold temperatures both longer and more evenly than coal does. The downside is that they're messy and made with chemicals. My way is to not choose sides, but rather to use both coal and briquettes. I use the briquettes for the even heat and the coal for the high heat and taste. To *marinate or not to marinate*? Many people marinate . . . and marinate . . . and marinate . . . and as the summer draws to an end, they've become marinated as well.

Truth be told, the marinade doesn't make that much of a difference. If you do marinate, you should make sure the meat is fatty, and it should be left to marinate for a few days; this allows the fibers to break down, and the meat tenderizes. If you do want a marinade, it's better to apply it while the meat is on the grill, meaning that you glaze the meat several times during the grilling process or afterward. Glazing meat with chimichurri right before serving is something I love to do! You can also *rub* the meat with a spice mix right before you grill it.

Direct grilling. This is the way I usually do it—right over the heat/live coals. It's hot enough and the cooking time is short.

Indirect grilling. This is a little like using the oven. You don't place the food to be grilled right on top of the heat but rather around it. The grill lid should be closed to let the heat come from both below and above.

Asado grilling. This is when you grill over an open fire. This originally comes from the South American kitchen. Sometimes, the burning coal is just thrown in a big pit.

79. Grilled Watermelon with Peanut Sauce

When I grilled watermelon at Torekov's camping grounds one summer, many people frowned at me. But watermelon really does taste delicious when grilled. You can also grill it ahead of time. Just add the peanut sauce and serve it at a big buffet dinner.

6–8 SERVINGS

1 small watermelon (approx. 4½ lbs [2 kg])
olive oil for glazing

PEANUT SAUCE:

¾ cup (200 ml) roasted and salted peanuts
2 tbsp water
½ lemon, juice
2 tbsp olive oil
possibly ½ tsp salt

DIRECTIONS:

1. Mix the peanuts and about ½ tablespoon water into a smooth mixture. Add the rest of the water and all the other ingredients for the sauce and mix some more. If needed, season with some salt.
2. Cut the melon into wedges or whole slices as in the picture on the previous page. Glaze them with olive oil and grill for 2 minutes on each side. Let them get a charred grill pattern.

80. Lobster with Dill and Lemon Butter

With all due respect to the lobster, in this dish the butter steals the show. It's super tasty with any kind of seafood. Or spread some of the butter on a piece of toast. Lobster is expensive, so make sure you treat it well and don't burn it or make it tough.

2–4 SERVINGS

1 live lobster (approx. 12 oz [350 g])

DILL AND LEMON BUTTER:

2 sticks (200 g) butter, room temperature
1 small red onion, finely chopped
½ cup (100 ml) coarsely chopped dill
1 lemon, zest + 2 tbsp juice
½ tsp salt, freshly ground white or black pepper

DIRECTIONS:

1. Mix all the ingredients for the butter. Let it rest in the fridge. The butter is pictured on page 161.
2. Split the live lobster down the middle with a sharp knife (start by cutting the head with the tip of the knife and work your way down the body). If you do this quickly and decisively, the lobster will die right away.
3. Put the lobster halves meat-side-up in aluminum foil and spread the butter on top of each piece. Wrap them up and place them on the grill grate. Grill the lobster halves until their shells turns red. Cook them on the edges of the grill for another 10 minutes so the meat springs back after you touch it.
4. Plate the lobster and drizzle the delicious butter from the pan on top. Serve with a dollop of green pea guacamole (see page 252). Enjoy!

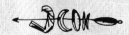

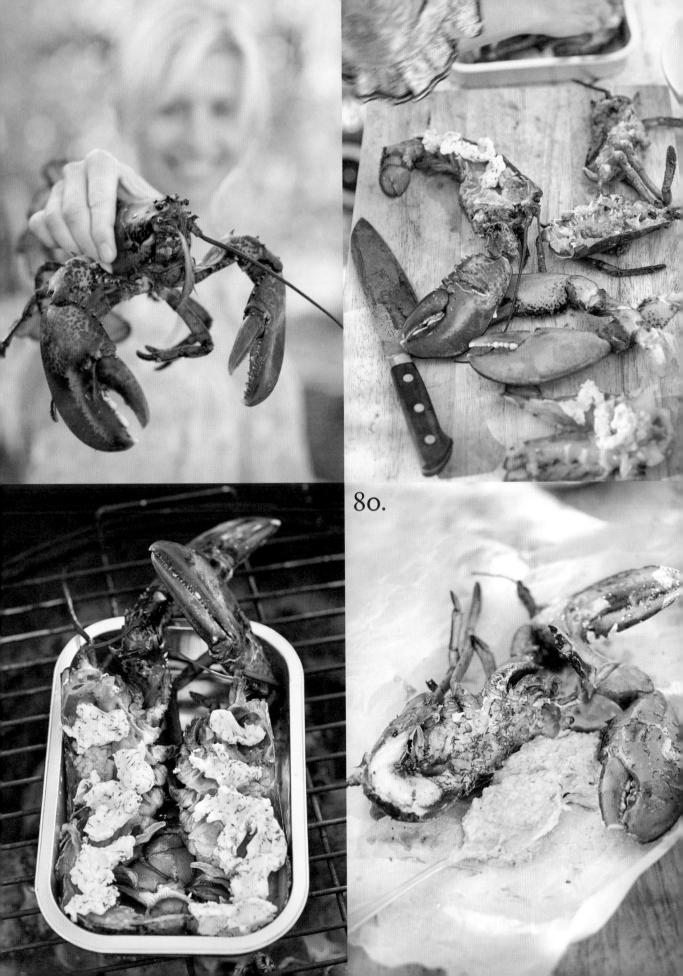

80.

81. Grilled Oysters with Lemon and Green Tabasco

Eight oysters are enough for four, unless you're oyster crazy and end up eating them all on your own! Watch your tongue, though, when you slurp the hot oysters, since I actually burned mine the first time I ate one. Blow, blow, and then blow some more. And yes, the oysters are definitely alive when you eat them raw and don't die until they're in your stomach. That's just the way it is! The ones that are already dead should be thrown away. Also, green Tabasco is milder than the red version.

4 SERVINGS
8 oysters
1 lemon
a few dashes of green Tabasco

DIRECTIONS:
1. Open the oysters by sticking in a knife through the hinge between the two valves and twisting until you hear a popping sound. Continue to open the oyster by following the edge with your knife.
2. Put the oysters right on top of the burning coals. Grill them for 2–3 minutes, until they're hot and the liquid starts to bubble.
3. Place the oysters on a serving platter, squeeze some lemon juice on top, and season with Tabasco. Serve right away.

82. Grilled Whole Salmon with Green Pea Guacamole

This dish is really great if you have a nice piece of wood to place the salmon on—a piece of birch, for example. It's a nice way to serve the fish. I'll usually put the wood on a tray so guests can serve themselves. Serve this dish with the Caesar salad on page 28.

6–8 SERVINGS
1¾–2¼ lbs (800 g–1 kg)
TERIYAKI MARINADE:
½ cup (100 ml) Teriyaki sauce
2 tbsp green curry paste
¼ tsp turmeric
½ tsp salt
freshly ground white or black pepper
GREEN PEA GUACAMOLE:
See recipe on page 252

DIRECTIONS:
1. Begin by soaking a piece of wood in water for 24 hours—this is important—otherwise it'll catch on fire!
2. Mix all the ingredients for the marinade.
3. Cut the salmon to fit the piece of wood you're using as a platter. Put the salmon on the wood with the skin side down and glaze with plenty of marinade. Then place the wood on top of the glowing coals and cover it with the grill lid. Since the smoke will give the fish some of its flavor, it's important to be patient and not to lift the lid when it starts to smoke.
4. After 15 minutes, lift the lid. If the sides of the salmon are done (and if you prefer your salmon a little on the rare side), you can remove it. If you want it more well-done, just leave it in for another 5 minutes. The core temperature should be between 113°F (45°C) and 118°F (48°C).
5. Serve the salmon as is on top of the wood with some green pea guacamole and some boiled new potatoes.

82.

83. Texas Burger with Blue Cheese Cream

An awesome burger made with ground wild boar meat, but you can, of course, use whatever meat you like. The blue cheese cream and the roasted onion make this a burger with a capital B. The cheese cream is also delicious as a dip for carrots or to serve with pie.

4 SERVINGS

1¾ lbs (800 g) ground beef or wild boar
2 tbsp Dijon mustard
½ tbsp paprika powder
1 tsp ground nutmeg
¼ tsp cayenne pepper
2 tsp smoked Ancho chili powder
2 tsp salt

BLUE CHEESE CREAM:

¾ cup (200 ml) crème fraîche (or sour cream)
3½ oz (100 g) crumbled blue cheese
½ lemon, zest and juice
salt, freshly ground white or black pepper

FOR SERVING:

4 small yellow onions
1 garlic clove
4 hamburger buns
olive oil for drizzling over the bread
8 slices prosciutto
romaine lettuce

DIRECTIONS:

1. Wrap each onion in aluminum foil. Place the wrapped onions on top of the hot coals and turn them over every so often. Let them stay on the coals until the onions turn soft, about 20 minutes.
2. Mix all ingredients for the blue cheese cream and season with salt and pepper.
3. Mix the minced meat with mustard and spices. Shape into patties and place them on the grill. If you use beef, the meat can still be pink in the middle. If you do use wild boar, however, it needs to have a core temperature of 155°F (68°C) or be thoroughly cooked.
4. Split the garlic clove and rub it on top of the hamburger buns. Drizzle some olive oil on top and put them on the grill until they get a nice color.
5. Grill the prosciutto slices very quickly. They should turn a little crispy.
6. Remove the onions from the grill and squeeze out the middle part, which should now be soft and buttery.
7. Smear some blue cheese cream on the bottom of the buns with a leaf of lettuce, the burger, onion, and lastly the grilled prosciutto. Cover with the top of the bun and serve.

84. Feta Cheese Salad with Mint and Maple Syrup

For this salad, get a high-quality Greek feta cheese. This dish has just a hint of mint.

4 SERVINGS

1⅓ lbs (600 g) Greek feta cheese
½ lemon, juice
1 handful fresh mint leaves (approx. 1 oz [30 g])
2–3 tbsp maple syrup
freshly ground black pepper

DIRECTIONS:

1. Break the cheese into small pieces and spread it out on a plate. Squeeze the lemon juice over the cheese and shred the mint leaves on top. Season with some freshly ground black pepper and top with a drizzle of maple syrup. Serve with grilled meat or poultry.

83. 84.

85. Cinnamon-glazed Pork Belly

My inspiration for this recipe comes from the restaurant Heberleins in Förslöv. Sometimes I used to sneak in there before I went to work at Torekov to have a piece of pork and a slice of dark rye bread. It was absolute heaven! In this recipe, I'm preparing the pork in one whole piece, but sometimes I'll cut it up into cubes and leave out the apricots and thyme. The pork makes a great addition to a barbecue buffet, along with all the other grilled meats.

4 SERVINGS

1⅓ lbs (600 g) whole smoked pork belly
   with rind
½ cup (100 ml) dried apricots
2 tbsp maple syrup or honey
2 tbsp white wine vinegar
1 tsp cinnamon
1 bunch of fresh thyme
freshly ground white or black pepper

DIRECTIONS:

1. Score the pork rind deeply until it is "ribbed" throughout. Stuff the scores with apricots.
2. With a sharp knife, score across and grill the pork with the rind down.
3. Remove the pork from the grill and put it on a double-folded square of aluminum foil. Pour syrup and vinegar over it. Season with cinnamon and spread some thyme on top.
4. Put the pork back on the grill and let it cook for about 30 minutes until it has gotten really hot, and then turn it over so the marinade soaks in on both sides.
5. Cut the pork into slices and serve.

86. Bulgogi with Sides

Bulgogi is a Korean dish that is eaten with the side dishes seen on the next page: kimchi, sesame sprouts, and pickled chili cucumber. This is a recipe that requires some preparation and is the only dish I preach that you marinate.

4 SERVINGS

2 lbs (1 kg) whole entrecote
2 tbsp oil for sautéing

MARINADE:

½ cup (100 ml) Japanese soy sauce
½ cup (100 ml) sherry, sake, or red wine
½ tbsp sesame oil
⅓ leek, finely chopped
1 garlic clove, shredded
1 tsp freshly ground white or black pepper
1 tbsp sugar

FOR SERVING:

kimchi, sesame sprouts, and pickled chili
   cucumber (see page 160)

DIRECTIONS:

1. Cut the entrecote into slices ¼–½ inch (½–1 cm) thick.
2. Mix the ingredients for the marinade in a spacious bag. Put the meat in the bag and tie it up. Massage the marinade into the meat. Refrigerate for at least 24 hours.
3. Remove the meat and lightly dab it with a paper towel. Flash-grill it on both sides over live coals.
4. Serve right away with kimchi, sesame sprouts, and pickled chili cucumber.

AN EASIER WAY TO CUT THE MEAT
The entrecote will be easier to cut into thin slices if you put it in the freezer and let it cool down for about 30 minutes before cutting it.

87. Kimchi—Fermented Cabbage

Kimchi is the Asian answer to milk-fermented vegetables and is a very common, everyday dish. Milk-fermented is the same as fermented.

4–6 SERVINGS
1 head of Napa cabbage

BRINE:
2 quarts (2 liters) water
3½ tbsp salt

KIMCHI MIXTURE:
¾ cup (200 ml) shredded Napa cabbage
½ tbsp paprika powder
2 tbsp Sambal oelek
2 shredded garlic cloves
3 tbsp oyster sauce
2 tbsp finely chopped ginger
1 tbsp sugar

DIRECTIONS:
1. Mix the ingredients for the brine and let the Napa cabbage soak in it overnight.
2. Drain the brine and rinse the cabbage under cold water for about 10 minutes until most of the saltiness has disappeared.
3. Mix the ingredients for the kimchi mixture. Smear the mixture onto each leaf, and then put the cabbage in a plastic bag and seal it shut. Let the bag rest at room temperature for 24 hours and then place the bag in the fridge for at least five days—the longer it rests, the better it will taste.
4. Cut the cabbage into slices and serve with the bulgogi and other side dishes.

88. Sesame Sprouts

Sprouts and beans are cheap, and they make great side dishes to pretty much everything. Try flavoring the sprouts with some finely chopped dill and lemon juice instead of sesame seasoning.

4 SERVINGS
1⅔ cup (400 ml) mung bean sprouts
½ leek, finely sliced
3 tsp sesame oil + 1 tbsp canola oil
2 tbsp toasted sesame seeds
salt, freshly ground white or black pepper

DIRECTIONS:
Mix all ingredients and season with salt and pepper. Serve with the bulgogi, kimchi, and chili cucumber.

89. Pickled Chili Cucumber

A twist on traditional pickled cucumber.

4 SERVINGS
2 cucumbers
3 tbsp white vinegar
2 tbsp sugar
4 tsp Sambal Oelek
2 garlic cloves, shredded
½ cup (100 ml) roasted and peeled almonds

DIRECTIONS:
Wash the cucumbers and slice thinly lengthwise with a cheese grater. Leave out the core and the seeds. Mix all ingredients and let it rest for about 30 minutes or longer. Serve with the bulgogi, kimchi, and sesame sprouts.

86.

87.

88.

89.

90.

90. Grilled Lamb Shoulder, Apple Vinaigrette, and Tomato Salad with Breadcrumbs

Lamb shoulder is not usually found on a grill. It can be bought at a great price, but you'll have to go to a store with a meat counter. If you find it difficult to de-bone, just ask the staff at the counter to do it for you. The apple vinaigrette is the headliner in this recipe. Let it become one of your favorites. It's so incredibly delicious with the apple purée and the mustard. Great for a big barbecue or for Sunday dinner.

6–8 SERVINGS
approx. 4½ lbs (2 kg) de-boned lamb shoulder
1 head of garlic
1 bunch of fresh rosemary
1 tbsp salt
freshly ground black pepper
½ cup (100 ml) olive oil

TOMATO SALAD WITH BREAD CRUMBS:
2 lbs (1 kg) mixed tomatoes
cooking juices from the lamb
salt, freshly ground white or black pepper
7 oz (200 g) light sourdough bread
1–2 tbsp olive oil

APPLE VINAIGRETTE:
2 shallots, finely chopped
½ cup (100 ml) olive oil
2 tbsp raw dark brown sugar
1 lemon, juice
3 tbsp water
¾ cup (200 ml) applesauce
2 tbsp coarse Dijon mustard
salt, freshly ground white or black pepper

DIRECTIONS:

1. Begin by grilling the meat on all sides until the outside is browned. Put the lamb in a baking dish and rub the meat with garlic, rosemary, salt, black pepper, and half of the olive oil.

2. Push the live coals to the side of the grill and place the baking dish on top of the grill grate—this is indirect grilling. Close the lid and open the valve. After 10 minutes, begin glazing the lamb with the rest of the oil. Flip the meat over from time to time.

3. Grill the lamb until it reaches a core temperature of 136°F (58°C) (if you are using a digital thermometer) or for 20–30 minutes. Let the meat rest on a platter for about 10 minutes before you cut into it. Save the grilling juices for the tomato salad.

4. Put onion, oil, sugar, lemon juice, and water for the apple vinaigrette in a pot. Bring to a boil and let it simmer for about 5 minutes. Add applesauce and mustard. The vinaigrette should be runny but with a slight thickness to it. Season with salt and pepper.

5. Split the tomatoes in half. Place them in a bowl and mix with 3–4 tbsp of the lamb juices and the vinaigrette.

6. Cut the bread into thick slices and grill it until golden brown and crispy. Crumble the bread and mix it into the tomato salad.

7. Serve the lamb shoulder cut into slices with the tomato salad.

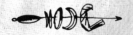

91. Ketchup with Horseradish, Ginger, and Lime

The easiest recipe in the world! It's quick to make and leaves a feeling of both finesse and accomplishment. I love, really *love* when only a few ingredients can create a symphony in my mouth. This tastes great with anything grilled.

APPPROX. 2½ CUPS (600 ML)
- ¾ cup (200 ml) shredded fresh horseradish
- 1 tbsp shredded fresh ginger
- ¾ cup (200 ml) ketchup
- ¾ cup (200 ml) chili sauce
- 1 lime, zest
- ¼ tsp salt

DIRECTIONS:
Mix horseradish and ginger with ketchup, chili sauce, and lime zest. Season with salt.

92. Barbecue Sauce

This homemade barbecue sauce works with any kind of grilled or pan-fried items: fish, poultry, beef, or vegetables.

APPROX. 2 CUPS (500 ML)
- 1 red onion
- 3 garlic cloves
- ½ red chili
- 1 tbsp fennel seeds
- 1 tbsp coriander seeds
- 1 tbsp paprika powder
- ½ tsp black peppercorns
- 3½ tbsp Japanese soy sauce
- 1 tbsp white wine vinegar
- 3½ tbsp raw sugar
- 1¼ cups (300 ml) ketchup

DIRECTIONS:
1. Peel and finely chop the red onion. Peel the garlic cloves and core the chili. Bruise the garlic, chili, and the spices in a mortar.
2. Put the onions and garlic mix in a pot along with the soy sauce, vinegar, and sugar. Bring to a boil and let simmer for a few minutes. Put to the side and let cool.
3. Add ketchup to the mix and then let the sauce get cold. Pour into clean bottles and refrigerate. The sauce will last for at least two weeks.

93. Chimichurri

An Argentinean sauce or marinade. I usually make a really big batch and keep it in the fridge for a salad dressing, sauce for boiled carrots, or glaze for grilled meats and fish. A universal sauce suitable for everything. It's not pictured.

APPROX. ⅔ CUP (150 ML)
- 2–3 tbsp olive oil
- 2 tsp cumin
- 3 tsp paprika powder
- 2 tsp smoked paprika powder
- 1 bunch of parsley, chopped
- 1 bunch of fresh oregano, chopped
- 1 lemon, zest and juice
- 1 garlic clove, shredded
- salt

DIRECTIONS:
Mix olive oil, spices, chopped parsley, and oregano. Add lemon zest and garlic. Squeeze the lemon juice over it and season with salt.

91.

92.

Meat & Poultry

Question:
What is the most important tool in the kitchen?

Answer:
The hand!

A Much-too-pricy
Beef Wellington!

FORGETTING THINGS IS PART of my nature. Like, for example, the charger for my computer that is often hidden somewhere in the house. I usually have to come racing back to the house after dropping the kids off, speeding up the driveway and rushing in to search before heading out again. Of course, I know you're not supposed to do that to the environment! But in my defense, I do make trips to the recycling center every weekend. It's not easy to live right all the time. . . .

When it comes to my own domain—food, and how and what we should buy—I can hear myself preaching about sustainability and the environment at the same time that I'm looking at the box of strawberries in my shopping cart . . . out of season. Why don't I practice what I preach?

One weekend when the kids and I had woken up with the rooster, and I finally had time to read the whole newspaper (even the classifieds), I had found an ad for a children's yard sale. All of a sudden, the hands-on mom in me snapped awake, and I tried to explain to my children the concept of second-hand as well as I could. But they only heard what they wanted to hear: "Buying new toys!"

But first we had to swing by the supermarket, since we were expecting some guests that evening and, in a moment of weakness, I had offered to make Beef Wellington baked in puff pastry. You know—that proper, old-fashioned dish. We were dressed and ready with our teeth brushed in two seconds flat. The kids and I chose a supermarket that we normally don't go to, and you could tell we caused a bit of a ruckus in there, which was fun.

"Food-Tina, food-Tina!" someone shouted from the cheese counter! "Would you like to try our cheeses?"

After having tried a thin slice of a really delicious cheese, I, of course, felt obligated to buy something. But I really had to control myself when I saw the price tag. Ten dollars for one tiny piece of cheese! I had just finished paying the last of the bills from our wedding the day before, and I was basically flat broke at that point.

Pushing the shopping cart with that small piece of cheese, the kids and I started searching for the beef. I had already decided to buy a cut that was imported from as far away as possible, because I simply couldn't afford anything local and organic that day. This is a bit embarrassing, but I tried to justify myself by remembering that trip to the recycling center the weekend before.

"Where can I find beef tenderloin?" I asked the guy at the meat counter. He recognized me of course right away as "Food-Tina" and said quickly, "Only the best for the best! I take it you want our best organic Swedish fillet. . . ."

What could I say? I talk about buying local, organic meat every day in both the newspapers and on TV. I couldn't exactly say, "Actually, between you and me, you wouldn't happen to have a cheap Danish piece, would you?" In short, I ended up walking away from the counter with a beef tenderloin that cost me nearly 100 dollars, and it was going to be served baked in puff pastry! All the children and I could do was head to the register and pay for the beautiful piece of meat.

But, of course, the meat ended up tasting amazing! I treated it with care and let it rest at room temperature for a long time, sautéed it nicely, and seasoned it with love. Just to make sure the meat stayed its best inside that puff pastry. When it finally ended up in our mouths, it melted like butter.

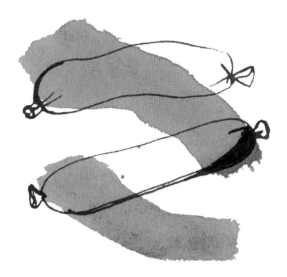

If we were all to practice what we preach and feel bad every time a cow passes gas, we would all have to become strict vegetarians—and self-sustaining ones at that. But I know that I'm not the only one who has difficulties merging ideals with lifestyle. I don't feel alive if

I don't have a chance to sink my teeth into a nicely aged sirloin or beef tenderloin once in a while.

However, it's not something I need to eat each and every day. Today, beef is a luxury item and should be treated as such. When you do eat it, be sure to enjoy it, so you can look a cow in the eye with a good conscience. When I was younger, I used to go with my dad to buy goose blood for black soup for St. Martin's Day. In those days, the meats were not wrapped in plastic. You either bought the animal whole or half. Over the years, after working at various restaurant kitchens, I've had to learn butchery from scratch. I remember the time my now husband came to fetch me from the restaurant Petri

Pumpa while I was arm-deep in dismembering half a cow. The fact is, I love butchering meat just as much as I love cooking an animal whole. An animal should never die in vain; therefore, the care and consideration of every little detail of the meat is important to me.

To cut up the various parts of the animal and use the meat for rolls, steaks, and minces is incredibly stimulating. Today's renewed interest in all this makes me happy. Stuffing sausage, making liver pâté, and preparing bone marrow are making a comeback, and it's wonderful that so much cooking knowledge is making its way back into the collective consciousness. So, if you're thinking of making Beef Wellington one of these days, perhaps you should actually buy organic, local meat after all. Only eat a small portion of the meat, and treat the sides and vegetables as the main dishes.

173

THINK LIKE TINA

HOW CAN I TELL IF MEAT IS TENDER?

Tender meat should retain its juices. So when you buy meat, always go for a package with as little blood in the wrapping as possible.

SEASON WITH SALT BEFORE OR AFTER COOKING?

What's the rule again? Season the meat with salt and pepper before or after you cook it? Yes, the salt will absorb the juices, but only if you have salted the meat the day before. You can definitely season with salt and pepper just before you cook it.

ROOM TEMPERATURE

Remove the meat from the refrigerator well before you intend to cook it, so it can reach room temperature. If you put a steak straight from the fridge onto a hot frying pan, it will cool the pan significantly, and rather than pan-frying the meat, you will boil it.

DON'T FLIP THE STEAK OVER TOO SOON

Let the meat get a nice color on the first side before turning it over to cook it on the other side so the meat becomes pan-fried instead of boiled.

THE MAILLARD EFFECT

The French professor and chemist Louis Camille Maillard realized that when you fry a piece of meat, chemical reactions will occur. The proteins inside the meat caramelize on the surface, and this is what makes the meat taste good. You can either get this effect by frying the meat in a pan on both sides or by cooking it in the oven on low heat and then finishing by broiling it.

SLOW COOKING MEAT

When you cook meat, it initially shrinks and gets tough and chewy, but if you slow cook it in the oven or in a slow cooker, it will tenderize at the same time. The fibers break down, and your meat becomes tender and delicious. The secret to a really delicious stew is patience. Put the meat in the pot and add enough water that the meat is only just covered and bring to a boil. Remove the foam that floats to the top. Add vegetables and spices after you have removed the foam and cook the stew for a long time.

THE MEAT DOES NOT HAVE TO BE HOT

If you're preparing a dinner with meat, you can actually cook the meat the day before. Remove the meat from the refrigerator well ahead of time the day of the dinner, and let it reach room temperature before slicing. Place the meat on warmed plates to serve (see next section for heating plates), and pour a hot sauce or gravy over the meat. The meat doesn't need to be hot because the gravy and plate already are.

SERVE ON WARMED PLATES

It feels luxurious to have your food served on warm plates. Place a stack of plates in the microwave and turn it on at full blast for a few minutes. Or heat them in the oven at 200°F (100°C).

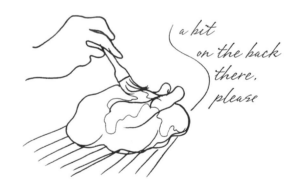

a bit on the back there, please

A DELICIOUS CHICKEN IDEA

Chicken is easy to season and it easily becomes a delicious dish. Cut a chicken breast or thigh into strips and mix with the miso marinade on page 102. Sauté in a hot frying pan or in the oven at 425°F (225°C). Serve with Thai cabbage and celery salad (see page 33). There are also a million and one ways to season the chicken. Rub spices on the skin or under it when cooking a whole chicken or individual pieces. Choose herbs, garlic, and a variety spices.

94. Beef Tenderloin with Baked Tomatoes and Béarnaise Sauce

Most everyone loves this dish. Treat the meat well and try not to rush. Beef tenderloin is too high quality a meat to allow for any rushing.

4 SERVINGS

1¾ lbs (800 g) beef tenderloin
butter and oil for sautéing
20 cherry tomatoes on the vine
1 garlic clove, crushed (outer skin and all)
½ tbsp brown sugar
salt, freshly ground white or black pepper

BÉARNAISE SAUCE:

1 shallot, finely chopped
2 tsp dried tarragon
1–2 tbsp butter for sautéing
4 tbsp white wine vinegar
3½ tbsp water
3 egg yolks
2 tbsp (200 g) melted butter
1 bunch tarragon, freshly chopped (approx. ¾ oz [20 g])
salt, freshly ground white or black pepper

DIRECTIONS:

1. Preheat the oven to 425°F (225°C).
2. Put the tomatoes and garlic clove in a baking dish and sprinkle sugar on top. Season with salt and pepper. Bake in the oven for 10–15 minutes. Remove the tomatoes and reduce the temperature to 225°F (110°C).
3. Season the meat with salt and pepper. Pan-fry the tenderloin in butter and oil for 3–5 minutes per side. Place it on an oven rack and stick a thermometer into it. Cook it in the oven until the core temperature is 130°F (54°C); this way, the inner meat will be nice and pink. Let the meat rest for a few minutes before serving.
4. Flash-fry the onion and dried tarragon in butter. Add water and vinegar and bring to a boil. Reduce to 2 tbsp. Remove the pot from the heat and whisk in the egg yolks. Whisk for a minute. Add the butter in a thin, steady stream while whisking constantly. Add the fresh tarragon. Season with salt and pepper.
5. Serve the sliced meat with baked tomatoes and béarnaise sauce.

95. Sliced White Pepper Beef Tenderloin with Sauce Morel

This dish is a remnant of the '80s and is both simple and rustic—and I like that. The beef tenderloin is really peppery.

4 SERVINGS

4 pieces of beef tenderloin (each approx. 6–7 oz [180–200 g])
plenty of coarsely ground white pepper
butter and oil for sautéing

SAUCE MOREL:

3½ oz (100 g) parboiled morels (canned)
1 tbsp butter
1 shallot, finely chopped
1 tsp crushed white pepper
2 tbsp sherry
1¼ cups (300 ml) heavy cream
½ tsp salt

DIRECTIONS:

1. Rinse the morels and sauté them in butter with onion and white pepper. Add the sherry and heavy cream. Bring to a boil and let simmer until the sauce thickens. Season with salt.
2. Press the tenderloins into the coarse white pepper so the whole surface of the tenderloins are covered. Pan-fry them for 3–5 minutes per side in butter and olive oil. Let the meat rest for a few minutes. Serve with morel sauce and a mixed green salad.

94.

95·

96. Beef Wellington with Mushroom Filling

A classic recipe from the '80s. I can thank my physical therapist for this, because she pretty much forced me to try it. The baking sheet must be super hot to start cooking the puff pastry immediately—if you ignore this part, the bottom pastry will end up unpleasantly chewy. The name Wellington comes from the Duke of Wellington, who defeated the mighty Napoleon at the Battle of Waterloo.

6–8 SERVINGS
2 lbs (1 kg) beef tenderloin, the middle part (i.e., cut off the ends so the length is all of equal size)
butter and oil for sautéing
½–¾ tsp salt, ½ tsp freshly ground white or black pepper
6 big slices of prosciutto (approx. 5 oz[150 g])
1–2 tbsp Dijon mustard
2 sheets of puff pastry + a little bit of flour
egg yolk for glazing

MUSHROOM FILLING:
10½ oz (300 g) mushrooms
3 chopped shallots
butter for sautéing
¾ cup (200 ml) heavy cream
¼ tsp salt, ¼ tsp freshly ground white or black pepper

MADEIRA SAUCE:
1⅔ cups (400 ml) Madeira wine
3½ tbsp (50 ml) balsamic vinegar
2 tsp light soy sauce
2 tsp brown sugar
2 shallots, thinly sliced
¼ tsp freshly ground white or black pepper
1 tbsp olive oil to thin the sauce

MUSHROOMS AND BRUSSELS SPROUTS:
10½ oz (300 g) mixed mushrooms
butter and oil for sautéing
7 oz Brussels sprouts, with outer leaves removed
1 bunch of coarsely chopped parsley
¼–½ tsp salt, ¼–½ tsp freshly ground white or black pepper

DIRECTIONS:

1. In a food processor, mix the mushrooms with the onion. Sauté the mushrooms in butter and let the mushrooms absorb the liquid. Add the heavy cream. Let simmer until the mixture is creamy. Season with salt and pepper and let it cool.

2. Reduce all ingredients for the Madeira sauce—except the olive oil—in a pan, until the mixture is reduced by half. Drizzle the olive oil on top when you serve; gently pour the oil over the top of a spoon so the sauce turns into beautiful pearls. This makes the sauce more of a warm vinaigrette than anything else. Season with salt and white or black pepper.

3. Season the tenderloin with salt and pepper. Flash-fry it in a frying pan in butter and oil. Let it cool.

4. Wrap a cutting board with plastic wrap and layer the prosciutto on the board. Spread out the mushroom mix, and place the tenderloin in the middle. Top the meat with some mustard. With the help of the plastic wrap, roll everything together so it's all held together firmly.

5. Preheat the oven to 450°F (230°C).

6. Layer the puff pastry and roll them out thoroughly with plenty of flour so they don't stick. Remove the meat from the plastic wrap and place it on top of the puff pastry. Roll the meat up into the puff pastry and pinch the edges together. "Glue" it together with whisked egg yolk. Score a few diagonal lines in the top of the dough; this will ensure that the steam can escape during cooking and will prevent the meat from boiling.

7. Put the puff pastry roll seam-side down on the hot oven plate and stick a thermometer into the meat. Place the oven pan in the middle of the oven. After 10 minutes, reduce the heat to 325°F (160°C). The meat should be done after 25–35 minutes, or once it has reached a core temperature of 130°F (54°C).

8. Sauté the mushrooms in butter for a few minutes. Add the Brussels sprouts and sauté them as well. Season with salt, pepper, and parsley.

9. Serve the sliced meat with the sides.

97. Venison Roast and Vinegar Pork with Potato and Apple Compote

The vinegar pork in this recipe is so delicious! And the compote of apple, lemon, and shallot is super fresh and easy to make. It doesn't matter if you choose venison or elk.

4 SERVINGS
 1⅔–2¼ lbs (800 g–1 kg) venison roast
 salt, freshly ground white or black pepper
 butter and oil for sautéing

VINEGAR PORK:
 10½ oz (300 g) pork belly
 ½ cup (100 ml) white wine vinegar
 ½ cup (100 ml) maple syrup or honey

POTATO AND APPLE COMPOTE:
 1⅔ lbs (800 g) firm potatoes
 2 apples, peeled
 1 lemon, zest + ½ lemon, juice
 1 shallot, finely chopped
 2 tbsp olive oil
 2 tbsp crème fraîche (or sour cream)
 3½ tbsp coarsely chopped parsley
 ½ tsp salt
 freshly ground white or black pepper

DIRECTIONS:

1. Preheat the oven to 225°F (110°C).
2. Season the venison roast with salt and pepper. In a frying pan, sear the meat on all sides in butter and oil. Put the roast in a baking dish. Cook in the oven until the core temperature is 135°F (57°C). Cook the meat just a little bit longer if you prefer a more well-done meat.
3. Cut the pork into big cubes, about 1" x 1" (2 x 2 cm). Put them in a pot and pour vinegar and syrup on top so they're almost completely covered. Let it simmer for about 30 minutes. The pork should have a reddish-brown color and will have a sweet and sour taste to it.
4. Peel the potatoes and boil in salted water. Drain the water and lightly mash the potatoes. Shred the apples into the potatoes and add the lemon zest and juice. Add onion, olive oil, crème fraîche (or sour cream), and parsley. Season with salt and pepper.
5. Serve the hot, thick slices of roast with the vinegar pork and the potato and apple compote.

HERBS MAKE EVERYTHING DELICIOUS

Try cooking meat with a delicious herbal paste. In a mortar, mash 3½ tbsp fresh or ½ tbsp dried rosemary, 3½ tbsp fresh or ½ tbsp dried sage, 1 garlic clove, zest from 1 lemon, and 1 tbsp olive oil into a smooth paste. Rub the paste onto the meat and cook it in the oven according to the recipe.

98. Cordon Bleu

A favorite at our house! Try to get a hold of Japanese panko breadcrumbs rather than using standard breadcrumbs, as the panko breadcrumbs make this dish so much tastier. You ought to be able to find them in a well-stocked supermarket, but if not, try an Asian grocery. A real wienerschnitzel is always made of veal. To make it cordon bleu, use Emmentaler cheese and ham.

4 SERVINGS

4 large flattened veal schnitzels (approx. 1⅓ lbs [600 g])
8 slices of Emmentaler cheese
4 slices of prosciutto
4 tbsp Dijon mustard
salt, freshly ground white or black pepper
butter and oil for sautéing

DOUBLE BREADING:

3 eggs
1 cup (200 ml) flour
salt, white or black pepper
1 cup (200 ml) panko breadcrumbs

DIRECTIONS:

1. Spread the veal schnitzels on a cutting board. Season with salt and pepper. Put two slices of cheese, one slice of ham, and a little bit of mustard onto one side of each veal schnitzel. Fold together.
2. Whisk the eggs. In another bowl, add the flour and season with salt and pepper. In a third bowl, add the breadcrumbs. Begin by dipping the schnitzels into flour, then into the egg mixture, and lastly into the bread-crumbs. Make sure the meat gets thoroughly coated at each step.
3. Pan-fry the schnitzels in butter and oil until they are golden brown in color—about 5–7 minutes on each side. Don't turn the burner to too high of a temperature; otherwise the meat will burn. While cooking, baste the meat with the butter and oil mixture.
4. Serve the cordon bleu with mashed potatoes (see page 239) and a salad.

99. Beef Strindberg with Fingerling Potatoes

This dish from my first cookbook. It's named after August Strindberg, even though nobody knows for sure if he ever actually ate this dish. The parsley potatoes pair well with many other dishes, especially during the summertime. You can actually use parsley on pretty much everything and anything—grilled vegetables, boiled ears of corn, salads. . . .

4 SERVINGS

4 sirloin steaks (each approx. 7 oz [200 g])
4 tbsp Dijon mustard
4 shallots, finely chopped
salt, freshly ground white or black pepper
flour for breading
butter and oil for sautéing

FINGERLING POTATOES:

8 fingerling potatoes
1 fennel
1 garlic clove
1 cup (200 ml) parsley
3½ tbsp olive oil
salt, freshly ground white or black pepper

DIRECTIONS:

1. Spread the steaks on top of a cutting board. Spread 1 tablespoon of mustard on one side of each steak, and distribute the onion on top. Season with salt and pepper. Carefully turn the steaks over in flour and sauté them in butter and oil with the onion side first.
2. Peel the potatoes and boil them. Mix the boiled potatoes with thin slices of fennel (which is easily done with help of a mandolin). Peel and shred the garlic. Mix the parsley, oil, and garlic into a smooth oil. Season with salt and pepper. Combine the potatoes and fennel with the parsley oil.
3. Serve the steaks with the potatoes.

98. 99.

100. 101.

100. Beef Rouladen with Potato Cake and Warm Cucumber

Ask the store to hammer out the beef to crush the fibers, which lets the meat cook faster. You can fill the rouladen with practically anything: celery, ajvar relish, parsnip, mushrooms, scorzonera. . . . Let the fridge decide! The cool warm cucumber is also great with gravlax, pan-fried fish, or atop whole-grain bread with a thick piece of smoked sausage.

4 SERVINGS

*1⅓ lbs (600 g) topside or minute steaks in
    thin slices*
Dijon mustard
5⅓ oz (150 g) spicy sausage, for example, chorizo
2 small carrots
¼ celeriac
½ leek
salt, freshly ground white or black pepper
butter and olive oil for sautéing

SAUCE:

1 yellow onion
1 tbsp tomato paste
1⅔ cups (400 ml) porter + 2 tbsp water
2 bay leaves
1 tbsp cornstarch + 2 tbsp water
salt, freshly ground white or black pepper
butter or oil for sautéing

POTATO CAKE:

2 lbs (1 kg) potatoes
2 tbsp butter, melted
*1 tsp salt, a pinch of freshly ground white or
    black pepper*
butter or oil for sautéing

WARM CUCUMBER:

½ cucumber
butter for sautéing + 1 tbsp water
salt, freshly ground white or black pepper
1 tbsp finely chopped shallot
3½ tbsp finely chopped parsley

DIRECTIONS:

1. Preheat the oven to 350°F (175°C).
2. Peel the carrots and celeriac. Rinse the leek. Cut carrots, celeriac, leek, and sausage into sticks.
3. Spread a little bit of mustard onto each piece of beef. Distribute the root vegetables, onion, and sausage onto the steak slices. Roll them up and insert a toothpick into each roulade to hold them together. Season with salt and pepper. Pan-fry the roulades in some butter and oil, and place them in a casserole dish.
4. Peel and slice the onion for the sauce and pan fry it in butter or oil until soft. Add tomato paste, porter, water, and bay leaves. Bring to a boil, reduce heat, and let simmer for 10 minutes. Pour the beef stock over the rouladen and cook them in the oven for about 1 hour. Test with a toothpick to make sure they're fully cooked. When cooked, remove the rouladen from the oven and take out the toothpicks holding them together.
5. Strain the juices from the casserole dish into a pot and bring to a boil. Thicken the sauce by adding cornstarch that has been mixed with water until it is a thick paste. Season the sauce with a few pinches of salt and a few turns of the peppermill.
6. Peel and shred the potato on the roughest side of the grater. Squeeze out the juices. Pour in the melted butter (the secret of achieving a delicious-looking cake is in the fat, so don't skimp!). Season with salt and pepper. Flatten the shredded potatoes into a cake shape and pan-fry some butter or oil for 5–10 minutes, until it has a lovely golden-brown color. Flip the cake over with the help of a lid or a plate. Cook the other side on low heat until both sides have a beautiful color and the cake is really soft. Poke it with a knife to make sure it's done.
7. Peel and core the cucumber. Cut it diagonally into pieces. In a saucepan, melt some butter and add the cucumber and some water. Season with salt and pepper. Heat the cucumber on low heat. Add the finely chopped onion and parsley just before serving.
8. Place the rouladen in the sauce to heat them up. Serve with the potato cake and the warm cucumber.

101. Topside Beef and Roasted Garlic Butter with Carrot and Jerusalem Artichoke Mash

For this recipe, I use tender cuts of beef from highland cattle; the meat is as tender as I feel after the first day of cross-country skiing in the wintertime. The butter highlights the sweetness of two sources: the roasted garlic and the mango chutney. Even if you're one of those people who frown at garlic, you'll certainly enjoy this garlic butter. When you roast the garlic, it turns mild and "un-sticky," and is a lot tastier. You may want to make a double batch of the butter and serve it on a baked potato the next day.

4 SERVINGS
> 4 topside beef cuts, preferably from highland cattle (each approx. 7 oz [200 g])
> 1 bunch of thyme
> salt, freshly ground white or black pepper
> 2 tbsp Dijon mustard
> freshly squeezed lemon juice

CARROT AND JERUSALEM ARTICHOKE MASH:
> 1 lb (500 g) carrots
> 1 lb (500 g) Jerusalem artichokes
> 3 shallots
> 1 tbsp butter
> 1 tbsp olive oil
> 1 tsp freshly squeezed lemon juice
> ¼ tsp salt
> ¼ tsp freshly ground white or black pepper

ROASTED GARLIC BUTTER:
> 5 garlic cloves
> olive oil for sautéing
> 1 stick + 2½ tbsp (150 g) butter at room temperature
> 2 tbsp mango chutney
> 1 lemon, zest
> ½ tsp salt
> freshly ground white or black pepper

DIRECTIONS:

1. Peel and pan-fry the garlic cloves in some olive oil until they turn soft and golden brown in color. Mash them with a fork; mix the garlic mash into the butter. Add the rest of the ingredients for the roasted garlic butter. Season with salt and pepper.

2. Peel carrots, Jerusalem artichokes, and onions. Cut these into pieces and boil in lightly salted water until soft. Drain the water and add butter, olive oil, and lemon juice. Mash the vegetables coarsely with a potato masher or a hand mixer and season with salt and pepper.

3. Rub the beef with thyme, salt, and pepper. Sear the meat in a grilling pan or frying pan for a few minutes on each side. Place the beef on a plate and let it rest for a while.

4. Glaze the top of the meat with some mustard. When serving, squeeze lemon juice on top to add freshness and great flavor. Serve the beef with the mash and the delicious butter.

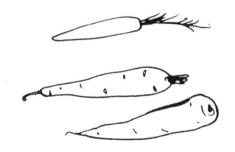

102. Beef Bourguignon

What would a hefty cookbook be without a recipe for Boeuf Bourguignon? Be bold enough to cut thick chunks of meat and let it cook for a long time. When it's done, it should literally fall apart. At first, when cooking meat, it shrinks and is tough and chewy, but when it's cooked slowly in the oven or in a slow cooker, it will become tender. The fibers of the meat break down and when it's ready, you'll have a tender and tasty meat. So dare to cook it for a very long time. You might even start cooking a day in advance, as that will only improve the taste and texture.

4 SERVINGS

3⅓ lbs (1½ kg) chuck roast
2 tbsp (30 g) butter
1½ tbsp flour
7–10½ oz (200–300 g) smoked pork belly
2 large carrots
1 yellow onion
3 garlic cloves
1 tbsp tomato paste
3 cups (700 ml) red wine
2 cups (500 ml) water
3 sprigs of thyme
3 bay leaves
18–20 pearl onions
14 oz (400 g) small button mushrooms
butter for sautéing
salt, freshly ground white or black pepper

DIRECTIONS:

1. Cut the beef into chunks roughly 1¼" x 1¼" (3 x 3 cm). Sear the beef chunks in butter. Sprinkle the flour on top and let the surface of the beef turn a lovely brown color. Put the chunks into a large pot. Pour ½ cup (100 ml) of water into the frying pan in which you seared the beef, and bring to a boil before pouring it over the beef chunks in the pot.
2. Peel carrots, yellow onion, and garlic. Cut the onion into eight wedges and crush the garlic. Cut the carrot into pieces.
3. Sauté the pork belly, carrots, yellow onion, and garlic with the tomato paste. Pour all of this into the pot, and pour in the red wine and water. Bring to a boil and add in the thyme and bay leaves. Let the stew simmer for 2–2½ hours.
4. Peel the pearl onions, and sauté in butter with the mushrooms. Ladle some of the stew into the frying pan and let the onions simmer until they turn soft. Pour the pearl onion and mushroom mixture into the stew and season with salt and pepper.
5. Serve the stew with boiled or mashed potatoes (see page 239).

MY BEEF STOCK

Instead of using store-bought beef stock, I prefer to use water and let the ingredients provide the flavor themselves. But if you have time and are up for it, there's nothing better than homemade beef stock you can pull from the freezer to use in stews and sauces. It definitely tastes better than store bought!

2 lbs (1 kg) chicken wings
1 lb (500 g) oxtail slices
2 carrots, in large pieces
1 parsnip, in large pieces
2 yellow onions, in pieces
1 head of garlic
water
3 bay leaves
10 white peppercorns
1 tsp dried thyme

DIRECTIONS:

Preheat the oven to 475°F (250°C). Roast the chicken wings, oxtail, root vegetables, and garlic in the oven for about 25 minutes until they turn golden brown. Put everything in a large pot and pour in enough water to cover all ingredients. Bring to a boil and skim off the fat and impurities. Add the spices and let simmer for 3–4 hours. If it looks cloudy, strain the stock, and let it cool to room temperature before refrigerating. It will last for 5–6 days in the fridge.

103. Maqluba

If you want it to be a true Maqluba, you have to prepare the "magical" spice mix! Go ahead and make a large supply, as it will last for a long time. Then, use it as seasoning—it makes a more flavorful rice, for one example. Fun fact: Maqluba means "turn upside-down" in Arabic, which is exactly what we're doing here.

4 SERVINGS

1¾ lbs (800 g) veal shoulder, bone-in
2 yellow onions
5 garlic cloves
butter for sautéing
1 tbsp "magical" spice mix (see page 213)
1 eggplant
1 tsp salt
1 tbsp butter + 2 tbsp olive oil
1 zucchini
1 cup (200 ml) roasted almonds (see page 28)
1¼ cup (300 ml) basmati rice
lemon slices for serving

DIRECTIONS:

1. Cut the meat as needed so it will fit into the pot. Peel and finely chop the onion. Peel and crush the garlic cloves.
2. Sear the meat in butter inside a large pot. Add the onion, garlic, and spices. Sauté for a few minutes. If there's not enough space left in the pot, just lift up the meat so the onion has room to finish frying. Add enough water to cover the meat completely and then some. Cover the pot with a lid and let it simmer for about 1 hour.
3. In the meantime, slice the eggplant and put it in a bowl. Sprinkle salt over the eggplant slices. Let it rest for 20 minutes. Then, soak up the liquid from the eggplant with some paper towels, and sauté the eggplant slices in butter and oil.
4. Slice the zucchini.
5. When the meat has cooked for an hour, pour its stock into a separate pot and set it aside. Keep the meat in the pot. Place the eggplant on top of the meat. Pour in the raw rice and the broth you set aside. If you don't have enough broth, you can add a little bit of water, but you'll need to add some salt as well. Add the zucchini and let simmer under a closed lid until the rice is cooked—about 20 minutes.
6. Turn the pot upside-down onto a plate. Top off the Maqluba with some roasted almonds and serve it with lemon sliced Russian style (see below).

THE RUSSIAN LEMON

When my colleague Benny and I were guests in Moscow, we were taught a new way to cut lemons. With a few simple slices, the lemon juice will drip right onto your plate rather than shooting into your neighbor's eye!

DIRECTIONS:

Stick the knife through the lemon as shown in the drawing. Make an incision lengthwise through the lemon, from one side to the other. Now turn the knife over so that the other side of the lemon comes up and make an incision equal to the first. Now you can split the lemon and remove the knife. Cut off the top and bottom of the lemon so that the halves lay steadily on the plate.

Russian Lemon

103

104. Indian Lamb Stew with Chorizo

Curry, cumin, and cinnamon are great spices to use when cooking lamb. Let the lamb cook for an extended period of time until the tomato sauce has turned a deep red in color. If you like, you can use my recipe as the "basic" recipe; simply omit all the spices I call for and choose your favorite spices instead. You might discover a brilliant new spice combination!

4 SERVINGS

1¾ lbs (800 g) lamb shoulder, deboned
2 carrots
2 parsnips
1 head of garlic
2 tbsp tomato paste
1 bunch of thyme
2 tsp salt
2 cups (500 ml) water
2 cans of whole tomatoes (each approx. 14 oz [400 g])
3 shallots
7 oz (200 g) smoked pork belly
5 small chorizo sausages
½ lemon, juice
freshly ground white or black pepper

SPICE MIX:

1 tbsp curry
½ tbsp cumin
½ tbsp cinnamon

DIRECTIONS:

1. Cut the meat into chunks of 2" x 2" (5 x 5 cm).
2. Peel the carrots and parsnips. Cut them into large pieces. Split the head of garlic into two.
3. In a large pot, sear the lamb chunks in oil, with the tomato paste, garlic, thyme, salt, and spice mix. Add the water and whole tomatoes with their juice and bring to a boil. Skim the fat off the surface.
4. Peel and slice the shallots. Add the root vegetables, pork belly, and shallots to the stew. Let the meat simmer for 1–1½ hours until it is soft and tender.
5. Cut the chorizo into large pieces and add to the stew. Bring to a boil and season with pepper and lemon juice.
6. Serve with tortillas (see page 243) and a dollop of Greek yogurt.

Pork with an International Twist

I will now present something completely new to you—so sit down and hold on! Yes, I created this "basic recipe" as an antidote to the boredom of routine, everyday food. I've heard that most of us rotate between fourteen or so dishes per year, that we just keep repeating over and over again. Now, imagine if these fourteen dishes could each taste fourteen different ways. The same recipes but with different flavors and shapes and colors and methods of cutting the ingredients. So stock up your spice rack. You can change so many elements of your meal by just changing up basic flavors. Here you go! The same pork is sometimes party pork and sometimes everyday pork. Same basic recipe, but all with different results.

105. Basic Pork

Sure, you can certainly stick to the ingredients of the basic recipe. And it will taste great. But the basic recipe is meant to be a foundation for all the other stews in this chapter. Dare to try your own flavor combinations as well.

4 SERVINGS

1⅓ lbs (600 g) pork
2 carrots, peeled
¼ celery root
1 onion, finely chopped
3 garlic cloves
butter and olive oil for sautéing
1 cup (200 ml) water
1¼ cup (300 ml) heavy cream
1 lemon, zest and juice
1 tsp salt
freshly ground white or black pepper

DIRECTIONS:

1. Cut the meat whatever way you want. Peel and cut the root vegetables and onion diagonally into strips or cubes. Sear the meat and vegetables in a frying pan in butter and oil.
2. Add water, heavy cream, lemon zest, and juice. Reduce until only half the liquid remains. Season with salt and pepper.
3. Serve with rice (see page 236).

106. Asia with Heat

Sometimes shredded coconut tastes better in the stew than coconut milk. The flavor is gentler, and you'll have the texture of the shredded coconut too. It's a great dish for everyone, except perhaps for those who don't like pulp in their orange juice.

4 SERVINGS

1 batch of basic pork recipe
1⅓ lbs (600 g) boneless pork loin, sliced
FLAVORING:
5 tbsp (75 ml) shredded coconut
1 lemongrass, coarsely crushed
½ red chili, seeded and in strips
fresh cilantro
1 lime

DIRECTIONS:

1. Cut the meat into strips. Peel the root vegetables and onion listed in the basic recipe and cut them diagonally into strips or cubes. Sear them with the meat and coconut in a frying pan with butter and olive oil.
2. Add water, heavy cream, lemon zest and juice, lemongrass, and chili. Reduce to half its volume and season with salt and pepper.
3. Serve with noodles and top with cilantro. Squeeze some lime juice on top before serving.

106.

107.

108.

107. European Tenderloin Delight

This dish is all about the traditional flavors from my side of the world, and with the horseradish for a finisher, you'll have a clean and fresh stew that everyone will enjoy.

4 SERVINGS

1 batch of basic pork (see page 195)
   that uses 1 pork tenderloin (approx. 1⅓ lbs [600 g])

FLAVORING:

4 sardine fillets
½ tbsp dried tarragon
1 tbsp spicy brown mustard
½ cup (100 ml) shredded fresh horseradish

DIRECTIONS:

1. Clean the tenderloin and cut it into medallions. Peel the root vegetables and onion listed in the basic recipe, and cut them diagonally into strips or cubes. Sear the tenderloin and vegetables in a frying pan with butter or oil.
2. Add water, heavy cream, sardines, tarragon, and mustard. Reduce to half its original volume. Season with salt and pepper.
3. Sprinkle the horseradish on top and serve with mashed potatoes (see page 239).

108. Africa in Sunshine

My kids absolutely love these flavors! Go ahead and try them. Your kids will be delighted!

4 SERVINGS

1 batch of basic pork (see page 195)
   that uses 2 pork chops bone-in (1⅓ lbs [600 g])

FLAVORING:

½ cup (100 ml) blanched and peeled almonds
3½ tbsp yellow sultana raisins
½ tsp ground cloves
1 tsp ground nutmeg
a pinch (½ g) saffron (1 packet)

DIRECTIONS:

1. Season the meat with salt and pepper. Sear it in a frying pan in butter and oil.
2. Peel the root vegetables and onions listed in the basic recipe and cut diagonally into strips or cubes.
3. Roast the almonds in a dry pan until they turn golden brown. Drizzle some oil on top and add vegetables, heavy cream, raisins, cloves, nutmeg, and saffron. Reduce until half its original volume. Season with salt and pepper.
4. Serve with rice (see page 236).

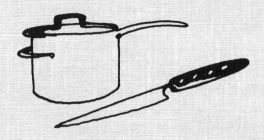

109. Pork Knuckle Ossobuco with Gremolata

This is a mock version of the Italian Ossobuco, which is supposed to be made using veal shank. I even fry the gremolata to make it less sticky from the garlic and lemon zest, and it does wonders. Perfect harmony!

4 SERVINGS

4½ lbs (2 kg) sliced pork knuckles (approx. 2 inches [5 cm] thick)
butter and oil for sautéing
¼ celery root
2 carrots
2 yellow onions
2 parsnips
a few sprigs of thyme
2 cans of crushed tomatoes (each approx. 14 oz [400 g])
1¼ cup (300 ml) white wine
2½ cups (600 ml) water
1½ tsp salt
freshly ground white or black pepper

GREMOLATA:

1¼ cup (300 ml) finely chopped parsley
2 garlic cloves, shredded
1 lemon, zest

DIRECTIONS:

1. Peel and cut the celery root, carrots, onion, and parsnip into small pieces.
2. Sear the pork knuckles in butter and oil inside a large pot (preferably cast iron).
3. Add the celeriac, carrots, onion, parsnips, and a few sprigs of thyme into the pot and let it simmer all together for a little while.
4. Add the crushed tomatoes, the wine, and water. Close the lid and let the stew simmer over medium heat for 1–1½ hours. The meat is ready when it falls off the bone.
5. Mix all the ingredients for the gremolata and flash-fry with olive oil in a pan.
6. Spread the gremolata over the Ossobuco and serve with tasty bread, for example, Manitoba baguettes (see page 268).

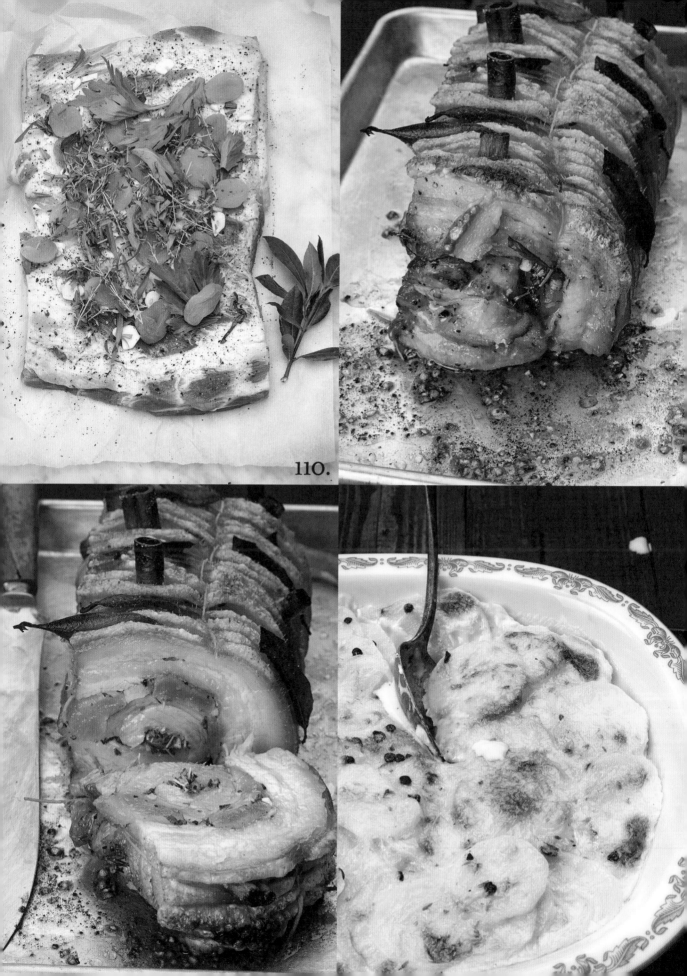

109

110.

110. Porchetta with Potato and Turnips Au Gratin

This recipe for porchetta (which means "little sow" in Italian) was a dish I prepared with Magnus Nilsson in Fäviken when I was there filming a TV program. To make it, he gave me a cut from his Christmas pig, which was one of the fattest and nicest looking pigs I've ever seen. And the porchetta turned out so incredibly delicious because of it! Pork belly is unsliced bacon, and I cut it without actually slicing it all the way through. Then I spread it open, fill it up, and roll it together.

4–6 SERVINGS

3⅓ lbs (1½ kg) pork belly
1 tsp salt
freshly ground white or black pepper
1 cup (200 ml) dried apricots (approx. 3 oz [150 g])
5 garlic cloves
a handful of fresh herbs, for example, oregano, parsley, thyme, rosemary
cooking string
2 tbsp olive oil
2 tsp salt
4 cinnamon sticks
1¼ cup (300 ml) apple juice

POTATO AND TURNIPS AU GRATIN:

1⅓ lbs (600 g) potatoes
5 turnips
½ yellow onion
½ tbsp ground allspice
butter and oil for sautéing
salt, freshly ground white or black pepper
1⅔ cup (400 ml) milk
1¼ cup (300 ml) whipping cream
3½ oz (100 g) spiced cheese, shredded

DIRECTIONS:

1. Preheat the oven to 475°F (250°C).
2. Split the pork belly lengthwise without cutting it all the way through. Spread it wide open. Season heavily with salt and pepper.
3. Cut the apricots into strips. Peel and crush the garlic cloves with a knife.
4. Spread the apricots, garlic, and herbs onto the pork belly. Roll it up tightly and bind it with cooking string. Rub the rolled-up meat with olive oil and salt. Score the rind of the pork belly and insert the cinnamon sticks into the scored meat. Place the porchetta onto a baking pan and put it in the oven. After about 20 minutes, flip the meat over so it will get a nice, even color before reducing the temperature to 300°F (150°C). Pour the apple juice on top and cook the porchetta for about 1½ hours, until it is tender. Baste the porchetta every 30 minutes.
5. Thinly slice the potatoes and turnips, preferably in a food processor or with a mandolin. Peel and thinly slice the onion. Sauté the onion with the allspice in some oil and butter. Add the milk and the heavy cream and bring to a boil. Add the sliced potatoes and turnips and season heavily with salt and pepper (the potatoes will absorb a lot of salt). Cook the potatoes and turnips until they are soft and their consistency is creamy, for about 3–5 minutes. Be sure to stir consistently—do not walk away from the stove. Pour the creamy root vegetables into a casserole dish and sprinkle the cheese on top. Put all this delightfulness into the oven beside the porchetta. Bake for 30–40 minutes. Poke it with a fork to check if it's done.
6. Remove the porchetta when it's done and increase the oven temperature back to 475°F (250°C) or set it to broil. Keep the potato and turnips au gratin in the heat to get some color.
7. Serve the sliced porchetta with the potato and turnips au gratin.

111. Polynesian Spare Ribs with Red Cabbage and Apple

Polynesian spare ribs are famous worldwide. The marinade can be used for many different things—as a glaze for pork, for example. Or you can mix strips of pork loin in a bag with the marinade and fry it all up later. It's great with salad.

4 SERVINGS

3⅓–4½ lbs (1½–2 kg) thick spare ribs

MARINADE:

3½ tbsp chili sauce

4 garlic cloves, shredded

3½ tbsp sweet soy sauce (preferably Indonesian sweet soy sauce)

½ tbsp red wine vinegar

2 tbsp Dijon mustard

2 dashes of red Tabasco

1 tbsp Worcestershire sauce

SWEET AND SOUR RED CABBAGE WITH APPLE:

Approx. 14 oz (400 g) red cabbage

1 yellow onion

5⅓ oz (150 g) smoked pork belly, cubed

oil for sautéing

3½ tbsp red wine vinegar

½ cup (100 ml) water

2 tbsp brown sugar

1 sour apple cut into cubes

1 lemon, juice

½ tsp salt

freshly ground white or black pepper

BAKED APPLES:

4 apples

4 garlic cloves

4 bay leaves

butter

DIRECTIONS:

1. Preheat the oven to 300°F (150°C).
2. Mix all the ingredients for the marinade together and rub it onto the ribs. Let the ribs marinate overnight for a more robust flavor. Put the ribs bone-side down on a baking rack (with a baking sheet under it to catch the drippings) and roast in the oven until the ribs are thoroughly cooked. This will take about 1½ hours.
3. In the meantime, cut the cabbage into wedges and remove the stem on each wedge. Slice the cabbage into thin strips. Peel the onion and cut into thin slices. Sauté the onion, pork, and cabbage in a wide pan with a little bit of oil. Add the red wine vinegar, water, and brown sugar and let simmer under a closed lid for about 30 minutes. Finally, mix the cubed apple into the pan and season with lemon juice, salt, and pepper.
4. Put the four apples on a baking sheet lined with parchment paper. Score the apples and insert a garlic clove and bay leaf into each. Smear some butter on top of each apple and bake in the oven with the ribs until they are soft, for 20–25 minutes.
5. Feel free to put the ribs back in the oven and broil just before serving to give them a really nice surface. Serve the spare ribs hot with the red cabbage and the baked apples.

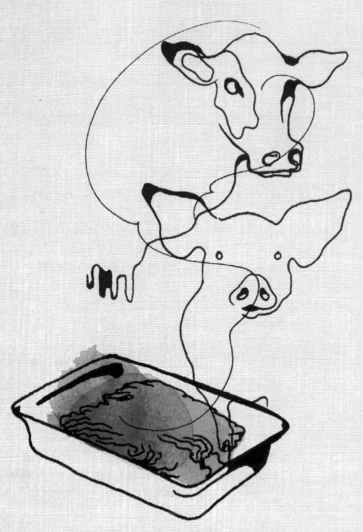

One Kind of Ground Meat, Three Different Kitchens

You can dress up ground meat for any nationality: one day it might be in a German dirndl, and the next it might be rocking modern studs and leather. You can season, roll, or shape ground meat in any way you like. It can also be fun to grind your own meat: so if you want your meal to have a mild lamb flavor, combine equal amounts of ground lamb with ground pork. The pork is necessary because of its fat content; you'll need lots of fat when sautéing smaller pieces of ground meat, because they dry up easily. Don't be afraid of fat, but do use common sense!

I use white bread instead of bread crumbs, because the taste and texture are better when you choose bread. It makes the ground meat lighter and less dense, and on top of that, the meat you have will go further and will feed more people. Remove anything called soda water from the meatball-making process. Yes, the meat does expand when you add soda water but trust me, the water and carbonation will both evaporate in the pan, and the meatballs will be really dry.

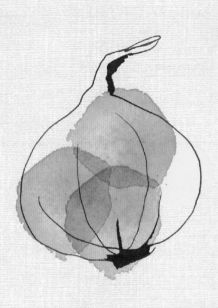

113.

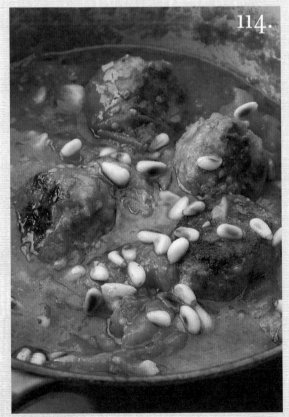

114.

115.

112. Basic Meatball Recipe

Another great basic recipe to memorize. Works just as well with lean as with fatty meats.

4 SERVINGS
> 1 egg
> ⅔ cup (150 ml) milk
> 1 slice fresh white bread without crust
> 1 tsp salt, freshly ground white or black pepper
> 1 lb (500 g) ground meat of choice, for example, veal, beef, lamb, pork, or wild game

DIRECTIONS:
1. Mix egg and milk in a bowl. Add the bread and let it soak up the liquid until it turns soft, about 10 minutes.
2. Add the ground meat and mix to a paste. Season with salt and pepper.

113. Tina's Meatballs with White Cabbage

In this recipe, I use ground pork with sardines and spicy brown mustard, which results in a delicious balance of salty and sweet that I absolutely adore.

4 SERVINGS
> 1 batch of basic minced meat made with 1 lb (500 g) ground pork (see above)

FLAVORING:
> 1 tbsp chopped sardines with liquid from the can
> ⅔ cup (150 ml) finely chopped leek
> 2 tbsp spicy brown mustard

STEWED WHITE CABBAGE:
> ½ white cabbage, cut into pieces
> butter and oil
> 1 tbsp flour + 1¼ cup (300 ml) milk
> salt, freshly ground white or black pepper
> 1 shallot, finely chopped
> ½ cup (100 ml) coarsely chopped parsley

DIRECTIONS:
1. Follow the directions for the basic meatball recipe and stir in the flavoring. Let rest for 10 minutes.
2. Sauté the cabbage in a pot with oil and butter. Sprinkle some flour on top and add the milk. Let the mixture cook for about 10 minutes until the cabbage has turned soft. Season with salt and pepper and add the shallot and parsley.
3. Wet your hands and shape the meat into meatballs. Pan-fry them in butter and oil for about 10 minutes.
4. Serve the meatballs with the stewed cabbage.

114. Italian Meatballs with Tomato Sauce

Forget the pasta! Serve this delicious concoction on its own with just some bread to soak up the extra sauce.

4 SERVINGS
> 1 batch of basic meatballs made with 1 lb (500 g) ground veal

FLAVORING:
> ½ cup (100 ml) freshly shredded Parmesan
> 2 tsp dried tarragon
> 1 lemon, zest
> ½ onion, finely chopped
> 1 garlic clove, shredded

ORIGINAL TOMATO SAUCE:
> 1 shallot
> 3 garlic cloves
> 1 box of cherry tomatoes
> ⅓ cup (75 ml) high-quality olive oil
> ½ cup (100 ml) water
> 1 can of crushed tomatoes (approx. 14 oz [400 g])
> 1 tbsp white wine vinegar
> ½ tsp salt, freshly ground white or black pepper
> a pinch of sugar
> 3½ tbsp roasted pine nuts

DIRECTIONS:

1. Follow the basic meatball recipe and stir in the flavoring. Let rest for 10 minutes.
2. Prepare the sauce: Peel and cut the shallot into smaller pieces and crush the garlic cloves. Sauté the onion, garlic, and fresh tomatoes in olive oil. Add water and the crushed tomatoes and let simmer until it becomes a sauce-like consistency. Season with vinegar, salt, pepper, and a little bit of sugar.
3. Wet your hands and shape the meat into meatballs. Pan-fry them in butter and oil for about 10 minutes.
4. Drop the pan-fried meatballs into the tomato sauce and let simmer over low heat for 10 minutes.
5. Sprinkle some pine nuts on top and serve with some delicious bread.

115. Greek Lamb Balls with Vegetables

Delicious lamb meatballs like these are enough to make you feel like you're in Greece.

4 SERVINGS
1 batch of basic meatballs with 1 lb (500 g)
   ground lamb

FLAVORING:
   ½ yellow onion, finely chopped
   ½ cup (100 ml) chopped Kalamata olives
   1 tbsp dried oregano

VEGETABLES:
   ½ eggplant
   ½ zucchini
   1 yellow onion
   2 garlic cloves
   1 red pepper
   3½ tbsp oil
   ½ cup (100 ml) water or white wine
   ⅔ cup (200 ml) cooked large white beans
   ¾ tsp salt
   freshly ground white or black pepper
   fresh basil

FOR SERVING:
   Greek yogurt
   feta cheese cubes

DIRECTIONS:

1. Follow the basic meatball recipe and stir in the flavoring. Let it rest for 10 minutes.
2. Peel the eggplant, onion, and garlic. Cut the eggplant, onion, zucchini, and red pepper into large pieces. Flash-fry the vegetables and onion in a pot with the olive oil. Add the water or wine and the beans. Let simmer under a closed lid until the eggplant is soft. Season with salt and pepper.
3. Wet your hands and shape the meat into large meatballs. Pan-fry the meatballs in butter and oil for about 10 minutes.
4. Serve the meatballs and the vegetables sprinkled with fresh basil and a bowl of yogurt on the side. Top it all off with some feta.

116. Wallenberg Burger with Clarified Butter, Peas, and Potato Purée

This Swedish classic was named after Marcus Wallenberg, whose father-in-law, Charles Emil Hagdahl, happened to be the author of cookbooks. In case you can't get ground veal, you can make a "Broström burger" from lean ground pork instead. The fresh bread crumbs, which hold together the loose ground meat, are really important here, and they offer a crispier surface. Keep in mind that the ground meat contains a lot of fat, so be sure to keep all ingredients cold. It's easiest to mix the ground meat in a food processor.

4 SERVINGS

1 lb (500 g) ground veal
4 egg yolks
1⅔ cups (400 ml) heavy cream
salt, freshly ground white or black pepper
5 slices of white bread
butter and oil for sautéing

PEAS:

1¼ cup (300 ml) frozen peas
salt, freshly ground white or black pepper
a pinch of sugar

POTATO PURÉE:

2 lbs (1 kg) potatoes
3½ tbsp (50 g) butter
⅔ cup (200 ml) milk
½–¾ tsp salt
freshly ground white or black pepper

CLARIFIED BUTTER:

1 stick + 2½ tbsp (150 g) butter

FOR SERVING:

cognac lingonberries (see page 110)

DIRECTIONS:

1. Peel and boil the potatoes.
2. Make sure that the ingredients for the burger patty are really cold, otherwise the patty may fall apart. In a food processor, mix the meat with salt and pepper for a few seconds. Mix in the egg yolks and ¾ cup to 1 cup (200 ml) of the heavy cream, a little bit at a time.
3. Whisk ¾ cup (200 ml) heavy cream lightly. Pour onto the meat mixture and fold in the lightly whisked cream. Let the meat rest in the fridge for a little while, so the burgers will be easier to shape.
4. In the meantime, cut the crusts off the bread and crumble into bread crumbs. Pour them onto a plate.
5. With wet hands, shape four burgers and turn them around in the crumbled bread.
6. Pan-fry the burgers slowly in butter and oil, for about 6–7 minutes on each side, until they are golden brown.
7. Drain the water from the potatoes and dump the hot potatoes into a bowl. Add the milk and butter. Whisk until you have reached a smooth purée consistency. Season with salt, pepper, and a little bit of sugar.
8. To "clarify" means to melt the butter and skim the top off. Serve right away with the Wallenberg burgers, potato purée, peas, and cognac lingonberries.

116. 117.
118. 119.

117. Stuffed Cabbage Rolls À La Nada

My lovely neighbor Nada is a pro at making these stuffed cabbages (and according to her husband, mine are not as delicious as hers . . .). Whole cabbage leaves can be found in the supermarkets. Buy several of them and stick them in the freezer. The human stomach just loves to get to work with such acidic vegetables as these.

4 SERVINGS
1⅓ lbs (600 g) ground pork salt, freshly ground white or black pepper
⅔ cup (200 ml) cooked rice
1 head of white cabbage, with the stem removed
butter and oil for sautéing
SPICE BOUILLON:
1 large yellow onion, chopped
2 sausages, sliced
1½ tsp ground coriander
1½ tsp cumin
1½ tsp dried oregano
1 tbsp paprika powder
½ tbsp ground cardamom
1 tbsp butter
2 tbsp tomato paste
2 cups (500 ml) water

DIRECTIONS:
1. Preheat the oven to 350°F (175°C). Pan-fry the onion, sausage, and the spices for the bouillon in butter. Add the tomato paste and let it all simmer for a few minutes. Add the water and simmer for another 15 minutes.
2. Pan-fry the ground pork lightly without letting it cook thoroughly. Season with salt and pepper. Mix the meat with rice.
3. Separate the cabbage leaves. Put some of the meat and rice mix in the middle of each cabbage leaf and roll them up. Place the stuffed cabbage leaves onto a greased baking pan. Pour the bouillon over the cabbage leaves and bake in the oven for about 40 minutes.
4. Serve with some delicious bread and sour cream.

118. Beef À La Lindström on Toast

It's said that this recipe was named after Henrik Lindström, who was born and raised in St. Petersburg. When he visited Hotel Witt in Kalmar, Sweden, with some friends, he wanted to treat them to some authentic Russian cuisine and ordered all the ingredients for making Beef à la Lindström.

4 SERVINGS
1 lb (500 g) ground beef
½ red onion, chopped
½ cup (100 ml) chopped pickled red beets
½ cup (100 ml) chopped pickled cucumber
1–2 tbsp capers
½ tsp salt
¼ tsp freshly ground white or black pepper
butter and oil for sautéing
4 slices of white bread
4 egg yolks
BROTH:
2 tbsp Worcestershire sauce
1 tbsp soy sauce
2 tbsp red wine
1 pat of butter

DIRECTIONS:
1. Mix the ground beef with the onion, red beets, cucumber, and capers. Season with salt and pepper. Shape into beef patties and pan-fry in butter and oil for about 5 minutes per side. It's alright if they're still a little bit pink inside.
2. Put the patties to the side, and add the ingredients for the sauce to the pan. Bring them to a boil.
3. Pan-fry the bread in butter and arrange the beef patties on top. Spoon some broth over the patties and garnish with some extra chopped red beets, cucumber, and capers. Top with the egg yolk. Sprinkle with a few turns of the pepper mill.

119. Meatloaf with Apricots, Prunes, and Cream-stewed Parsley Potatoes

An everyday dish that can be easily made festive with just a bit more work and a few added ingredients. Just as in many other recipes, you can use this as a base. Omit the apricots and prunes or the lemon zest. Use any spices you like, and add some pearl onions, leeks, or strips of smoked sausage. If there's any meatloaf left over, it will make a great sandwich on some bread or will be a delicious dinner with a fried egg and a salad.

4–6 SERVINGS

7 oz (200 g) dried apricots and prunes
1 yellow onion
3 garlic cloves
1 egg
⅔ cup (150 ml) milk
2 slices of white bread
2 lemons, zest
2 lbs (1 kg) mixed ground meat (pork and beef)
salt, freshly ground white or black pepper
10 oz (140 g) bacon strips, uncooked

CREAM-STEWED PARSLEY POTATOES:

14 oz (400 g) boiled and peeled potatoes
2 tbsp butter
½ yellow onion, finely chopped
3 tbsp flour
½ cup (100 ml) milk
1 cup (200 ml) heavy cream
salt, freshly ground white or black pepper
chopped parsley

DIRECTIONS:

1. Preheat the oven to 350°F (175°C).
2. Cut the dried fruit into pieces. Peel and finely chop onion and garlic.
3. In a bowl, mix the egg and milk for the meatloaf. Cut off the crusts of the bread and throw them away. Put the bread slices in the bowl and let them soak up the liquid. This will take about 10 minutes.
4. Mix the ground meat with the bread, onion, garlic, lemon zest, and dried fruit. Season with salt and pepper. Shape the meat into a "loaf" on a greased baking dish, loaf pan, or baking sheet. Lay the bacon strips diagonally across the meatloaf and tuck in the edges to keep it all together. Cook in the oven for about 50 minutes. The meatloaf is ready when the liquid runs clear.
5. In a new pot, melt the butter for the cream-stewed potatoes and sauté the chopped onion. Sprinkle the flour on top and add the milk and cream while stirring to create a smooth and creamy sauce. If the stew becomes too thick, add some more cream and milk. Let the stew simmer for a few minutes. Season with salt and pepper and with plenty of parsley. Chop the boiled potatoes into smaller pieces and mix them into the creamy stew.
6. Slice the meatloaf and serve with the cream-stewed parsley potatoes.

120. Lebanese Beef Croquettes with Roasted Peppers

This isn't my own recipe, but rather one that I made together with my good friend Amal. Once again, the "magical" spice mix comes in handy, just as with the Maqluba (see page 188). You don't need any potatoes, pasta, or rice, just some amazing bread and aged cheese.

4 SERVINGS

1 yellow onion
1 lb (500 g) ground beef
½ tsp salt
1 tbsp "magical" spice mix (see below)
2 tbsp olive oil
parsley for garnish

ROASTED PEPPERS:

5 peppers of various colors
2 tsp olive oil
sea salt, freshly ground white or black pepper

"MAGICAL" SPICE MIX:

½ tsp ground white pepper
1 tsp ground nutmeg
2½ tsp ground cloves
2½ tsp ground cardamom
2½ tsp cinnamon
3 tsp cumin
3 tsp ground ginger

DIRECTIONS:

1. Start with combining all the spices for the "magical" spice mix. Keep the spice mix in a tightly sealed jar.
2. Preheat the oven to 450°F (230°C).
3. Peel and finely chop the onion. Mix the ground beef with the magical spice mix, onion, and salt. Work the meat mixture well and let it rest for about 10 minutes.
4. Set the whole peppers on a baking tray. Drizzle with some olive oil and season with salt and pepper. Roast them in the oven for about 10 minutes, until the peppers are a golden brown but are not too soft. They should have some resistance left in them!
5. In the meantime, shape the ground beef into croquettes and pan-fry the beef in oil. Flatten them slightly while cooking to shorten the cooking time—thus ensuring that everything will be done cooking at the same time. When they're finished, arrange the beef croquettes and peppers on a big platter. Garnish with some parsley and serve with a few drops of chimichurri (see page 164), if you so desire.

121. Ragù Bolognese

Let's sit down and read this recipe carefully. Spaghetti and meat sauce is something many people can cook with their eyes closed, but we're about to make this everyday classic by following every rule in the book. In a real ragù Bolognese, you're supposed to use white wine and chicken liver—everything else is pretty straight forward. Think of it as a dish for festive occasions and prepare it as a treat for your friends. It's a great food for making an impression! Just be sure to know the recipe by heart—just in case someone should ask. It will give your self-confidence a definite boost.

4–6 SERVINGS

1½ lbs (700 g) beef chuck, in small cubes
5⅓ oz (150 g) chicken liver, in large chunks
7 oz (200 g) pancetta or smoked bacon, in cubes
3 tbsp olive oil
3 tomatoes on the vine, in wedges
1 carrot
1 red onion
4 garlic cloves, crushed
3 celery stalks
3 bay leaves
2 sprigs of thyme, chopped
1 bunch of basil, chopped
½ can tomato paste
1¼ cup (300 ml) white wine
1⅔ cup (400 ml) water
2 tbsp heavy cream
1 tsp salt
freshly ground white or black pepper

FOR SERVING:

14 oz (400 g) uncooked pasta
Approx. 3–4 tbsp shredded parmesan cheese
chopped parsley for garnish

DIRECTIONS:

1. Peel the carrot, red onion, and garlic. Cut the carrot and red onion into large cubes. Crush the garlic cloves. Cut the celery into slices.
2. Sear the beef chuck, chicken liver, and pancetta in a large pot with olive oil. Add all the other ingredients except the heavy cream. Simmer over low heat for about 45–60 minutes until the meat is tender.
3. Add cream at the end and season with salt and pepper.
4. Boil the pasta in salted water. Drain the pasta. At the time of serving, mix the pasta with the ragù. Top it with shredded parmesan and chopped parsley.

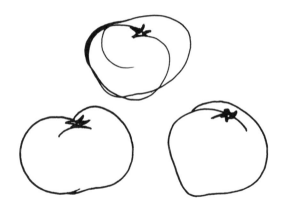

121

122. Chanterelle and Ground Beef Pie

This pie is simple to make and you don't have to make the pie dough in advance. And once you've made this pie a few times, you can start varying the ingredients. Keep the same amount of ground beef, the pie cover, and the pie dough, but try leaving out the chanterelles and season with cumin, paprika, and oregano (see page 243 for the taco spice mix recipe). And there you have it: taco pie!

4 SERVINGS
PIE DOUGH:

3½ tbsp (50 g) butter, room temperature
1⅔ cups (400 ml) flour
⅔ cup (150 ml) milk
2 tsp baking powder
½ tsp salt

FILLING:

2 yellow onions or 2 large shallots
2 garlic cloves
1 lb (500 g) chanterelle mushrooms
oil for sautéing
1¾ lbs (800 g) ground beef
salt, freshly ground white or black pepper

PIE COVER:

2 cups (500 ml) crème fraîche (or sour cream)
4 tbsp mayonnaise (see page 109)
1⅔ cups (400 ml) grated cheddar

DIRECTIONS:

1. Preheat the oven to 400°F (200°C).
2. Knead all the ingredients together for the pie dough. Roll out the dough and put it in a pie dish.
3. Peel and thinly slice the onion. Peel the garlic cloves and crush them with a kitchen knife. Clean the chanterelles.
4. Pour some oil into a frying pan and sauté the onions, garlic, and chanterelles until they each have gotten some color. Push the mixture to the edges of the frying pan and sear the ground beef in the middle. Mix the beef with the chanterelles and season with salt and pepper. Pour the mixture onto the pie crust.
5. In a bowl, mix the crème fraîche (or sour cream) and mayonnaise. Spread the mixture over the beef and chanterelle filling and cover it with cheese. Bake the pie in the oven for 20–30 minutes.
6. Serve with a fresh salad.

124

123. Chanterelle-topped Veal Patties

You have to make this dish! Both your eyes and mouth will be beaming with joy.

4 SERVINGS

1 lb (500 g) ground veal
1 egg
⅔ cup (150 ml) milk
1 slice of white bread with the crust removed
1 yellow onion, finely chopped
1 tsp sea salt
¼ tsp freshly ground white or black pepper
butter and canola oil for sautéing

CHANTERELLE TOPPING:

4 cups (1 liter) chanterelles (approx. 12 oz [350 g])
1 shallot, finely chopped
2 garlic cloves, peeled and sliced
butter for sautéing
2 tbsp crème fraîche (or sour cream)
1 egg yolk
1 cup (200 ml) shredded parmesan cheese

DIRECTIONS:

1. Preheat the oven to 425°F (225°C) and broil.
2. In a bowl, whisk together the egg and milk and add the bread. Let it soak for about 10 minutes.
3. Mix the onion and the minced meat with the bread. Season with salt and pepper. Shape the meat mixture into four patties. Sear them in butter and oil for about 4 minutes per side.
4. Sauté the chanterelles, shallot, and garlic in butter. Let the liquid in the chanterelles evaporate, and then sear them over high heat. Season with salt and pepper. Pour the chanterelles into a bowl. Add crème fraîche (or sour cream), egg yolk, and parmesan. Distribute the mixture onto the veal patties and bake in the oven for a couple of minutes.
5. Serve right away; it makes a great accompaniment to cream-marinated red currant salad (see page 33).

124. Goulash Soup with Ground Beef

This is a quick version using ground beef. I really love the spices in goulash! Just be sure to follow the recipe so the measurements are right, and this soup will turn out wonderfully!

4 SERVINGS

1 yellow onion
2 garlic cloves
3 potatoes
¼ celery root
2 red peppers
14 oz (400 g) ground beef
butter and oil for sautéing
2 tsp paprika
1 tsp dried marjoram or oregano
1 tsp ground cumin
¼ tsp cayenne pepper
1½ tbsp tomato paste
1 can crushed tomatoes (approx. 14 oz [400 g])
4 cups (1 liter) water
2 tsp salt, freshly ground white or black pepper

FOR SERVING:

Greek yogurt

DIRECTIONS:

1. Peel and finely chop the onion and garlic. Peel the potatoes and celery root and cut into cubes. Core the peppers and cube them.
2. Sear the ground beef in a pot with plenty of butter and oil. Add onion, garlic, potatoes, celeriac, and peppers. Season with paprika, marjoram, cumin, and cayenne pepper. Add the tomato paste and stir. Add the crushed tomatoes and the water. Season with salt and pepper. Simmer for about 20 minutes.
3. Serve with some rustic-style bread and a dollop of Greek yogurt.

125. Pork Sausage with Butternut Squash and Sweet Potato Mash

The two lead players in this dish are the sausage and the syrup marinade. The mash is, of course, also delicious but can be replaced by traditional mashed potatoes if need be (see page 239).

4 SERVINGS

2 rings of fresh pork sausage (each approx. 9 oz [250 g])
2 bay leaves
5 whole allspice corns

BUTTERNUT SQUASH AND SWEET POTATO MASH:

2 sweet potatoes (each approx. 9–11 oz [250–300 g])
½ butternut squash
2 bay leaves
8 whole allspice corns
1½ tsp salt
2 tbsp butter
½ shallot, peeled and sliced

MOLASSES MARINADE:

½ cup (100 ml) light molasses
1½ tsp white vinegar
½ shallot, finely chopped
1 tsp coarsely crushed allspice

DIRECTIONS:

1. Peel the sweet potatoes and the squash. Cut them into large even-sized pieces. Put the pieces in a pot and pour in water until the pieces are just barely covered. Add bay leaves, allspice corns, and salt. Gently simmer while covered. Drain the water. Add the butter and onion, and mash it all coarsely with a fork.
2. In a large bowl, mix the ingredients for the syrup marinade.
3. Poach the sausage in salted water with 2 bay leaves and 5 allspice corns for about 10 minutes.
4. Distribute the mash onto plates. Top with the sausage and drizzle with molasses marinade.

126. Flatbread Wrap with Chorizo, Sauerkraut, and Ajvar Relish

I made this for a band of hunters once. I admit, I don't consider myself a hunter, but I will happily cook for them. Butchering and cooking is more my style! This Swedish flatbread is made from the same recipe as the one for taco bread in the "Tacos" chapter. It's perfect for both purposes. If you don't want to or don't have the time to make your own bread, you can just use store-bought pita or tortilla wraps.

4 SERVINGS

1⅔ cups (400 ml) sauerkraut
4 chorizo sausages
approx. ½ cup (100 ml) Ajvar relish
Dijon mustard

FLATBREAD:

1 cup (250 ml) water, room temperature
½ oz (12 g) active dry yeast
½ tsp salt
2½ cups (600 ml) wheat flour

DIRECTIONS:

1. Begin making the flatbread dough by mixing the water and yeast. Stir in a little bit of salt and flour at a time. Knead until it has turned into smooth dough. Let it rise for 30 minutes.
2. Divide the dough into smaller pieces and roll them out into thin, round cakes. Bake in a hot frying pan for 2 minutes on each side.
3. Score the sausages and then pan-fry or grill them.
4. Distribute the sauerkraut onto the flatbreads. Spread each flatbread with approximately 1 tbsp Ajvar relish and a little bit of mustard. Place the sausage in the middle and fold it all together. Wrap it in a napkin and serve right away.

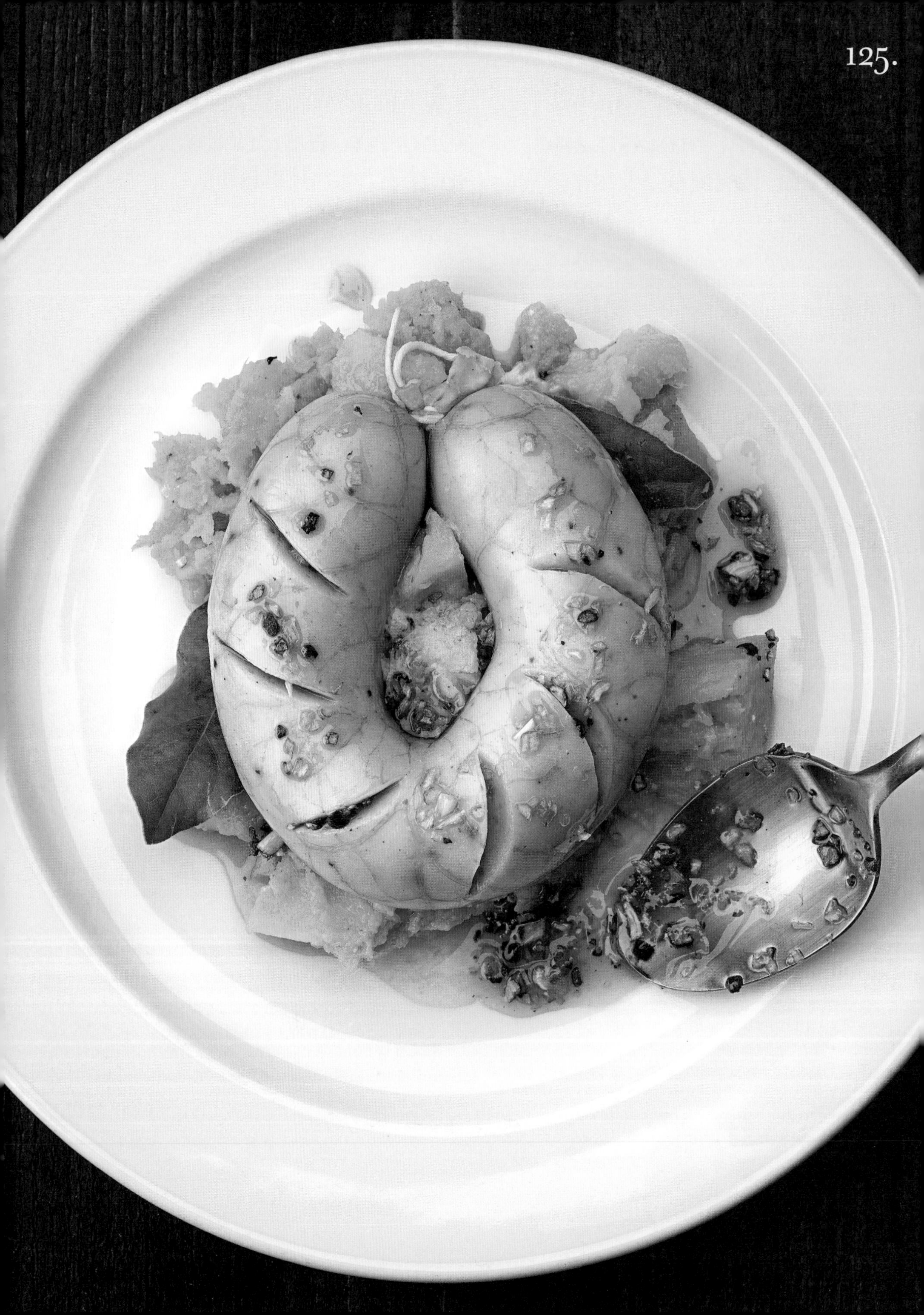

127. French Chicken Stew with Polenta-fried Potatoes

This is a recipe that everyone loves, and once you've tried it you'll be hooked! It has a bit of restaurant flair to it. No one spice demands center stage but rather they harmonize as one. At least once, you should substitute the chicken for pork loin or fresh salmon. Again, do as you please as long as you stick to the basics.

4 SERVINGS

1 lb (500 g) de-boned chicken thighs, in pieces
7 oz (200 g) pearl onions
butter and oil for sautéing
¼ tsp dried thyme
½ tsp dried tarragon
¼ tsp ground nutmeg
2 tbsp Dijon mustard
1 cup (200 ml) beer
1¼ cups (300 ml) heavy cream
salt, freshly ground white or black pepper
2–3 sprigs fresh tarragon for garnish

POLENTA-FRIED POTATOES:

2 lbs (1 kg) fingerling potatoes
½ cup (100 ml) coarse polenta
3 tbsp olive oil
2–3 pinches sea salt
freshly ground white or black pepper

DIRECTIONS:

1. Season the chicken with salt and pepper. Sear it with the onion in a deep frying pan with some butter and oil. Add spices and mustard. Pour the beer on top of the chicken and bring to a boil. Mix in the heavy cream and let it all simmer for about 15 minutes, until the sauce has reduced and is creamy.
2. Preheat the oven to 425°F (220°C).
3. Boil the potatoes in lightly salted water for about 15 minutes. Drain the water and let the potatoes release the steam. Pour them into a casserole dish and add the polenta and olive oil. Shake the dish around a bit so the potatoes get fully covered with polenta. Season with salt and pepper. Bake in the oven for 25–30 minutes until they are crispy and golden brown.
4. Serve the chicken stew garnished with some fresh tarragon and with the polenta potatoes on the side.

127

128. Roasted Whole Chicken with Parsnips and Cold Bean Sauce with Lemon

Roasting a whole chicken . . . you know you can do it! The bean sauce is done in 5 minutes and is great for so many things—vegetable dip or for the fresh summer potatoes. Or why not serve at your shrimp party instead of mayonnaise?

4 SERVINGS
1 whole chicken
8–10 parsnips
1 lemon
7 tbsp (100 g) butter
salt, freshly ground white or black pepper
1 bunch of fresh rosemary, chopped

COLD BEAN SAUCE WITH LEMON:
1 can white beans (approx. 14 oz [400 g])
3 tbsp olive oil
1 lemon, juice
3½ tbsp juices from the cooked chicken (optional)
salt, freshly ground white or black pepper

DIRECTIONS:
1. Preheat the oven to 425°F (220°C).
2. Peel the parsnips and cut them into long strips. Wash and slice the nonzested lemon.
3. Remove the backbone from the chicken. To do so, lay it on its back and use a knife or poultry shears. Spread (butterfly) the chicken out.
4. Put the parsnips and lemon slices in an oven pan and put the butterflied chicken on top. Dollop some butter onto both the parsnips and the chicken and sprinkle some rosemary all over. Roast in the oven for about 45 minutes.
5. Mix all the ingredients for the sauce with a hand mixer. Season with salt and pepper. Optionally, stir the juices from the chicken into the sauce.
6. Serve the chicken hot with the cold bean sauce.

129. Corn-fed Chicken with Juniper-glazed Sauerkraut

Fast food at its finest! A delicious, whole corn-fed chicken, juniper berries, and a can of sauerkraut. Don't omit the juniper berries, because they make all the difference. Your taste buds will smile at the pairing of the juniper berries' flowery flair with the cream and the acidity from the cabbage. Juniper-glazed sauerkraut is also perfect with smoked sausage or any other type of sausage.

4 SERVINGS
4 corn-fed chicken breasts with skin
salt, freshly ground white or black pepper
butter and oil for sautéing

JUNIPER-GLAZED SAUERKRAUT:
1 silver onion
1 high-quality spicy sausage
butter and oil for sautéing
1 tbsp crushed juniper berries
25 oz (700 g) canned sauerkraut
1 cup (200 ml) heavy cream
salt, freshly ground white or black pepper

DIRECTIONS:
1. Season the chicken breasts with salt and pepper. Sear them skin-side down in a frying pan with butter and oil. Flip them over and fry the other side until the chicken is thoroughly cooked. Set aside and let them rest.
2. Peel and slice the onion. Cut the sausage into thin slices. Sauté the onion and sausage in a little bit of butter and olive oil. Add the juniper berries and the heavy cream, and let it simmer for a few minutes. Drain the sauerkraut and add it to the cream reduction.
3. Cut the chicken breasts into smaller portions. Plate the sauerkraut and chicken.
4. Serve right away, preferably with a tasty white bread such as a Manitoba baguette (see page 268).

129.

130. Green Chicken Tenders with Paprika Dip

For this recipe, we're making chicken tenders from scratch. Fresh bread crumbs make them extra crispy. The sauce it a little bit like Mojo Rojo but is somewhat easier to make.

4 SERVINGS
 2–3 chicken fillets without skin
 salt, freshly ground white or black pepper
 oil for sautéing
 4 slices of white bread
 1 bunch of parsley (1–1¾ oz [30-50 g])
 1 garlic clove

PAPRIKA DIP:
 2 tsp paprika powder
 5 ⅓ oz (150 g) canned grilled peppers, in strips
 2 garlic cloves
 2 egg yolks
 2 slices of white bread
 ½ lemon, zest and juice
 1 cup (200 ml) olive oil
 1 tsp salt

DIRECTIONS:
1. Remove the crusts from the bread. Mix the bread, parsley, and garlic until the combination has turned an intense green and bursts with parsley flavor.
2. Cut each chicken fillet lengthwise into four slices. Dip the slices into the green breading.
3. Pan-fry the chicken pieces in hot oil until they are well done and crispy. Season with salt and pepper.
4. Mix all the ingredients for the paprika dip (except the oil) with a hand mixer. Pour in a little bit of oil at a time while stirring until the sauce thickens. Season with salt.
5. Serve the chicken tenders and paprika dip with a fresh greens salad.

131. Tom Kha Gai

There are as many recipes for this soup as I have shoes in the closet—which means there are a LOT. For some of the ingredients you might need to stop in at an Asian grocery. Other than that, this soup is very easy to make. Just remember that the flavors need a little time to develop. And in the future, use this stock as a base recipe; it's great with vegetables or with fish.

4 SERVINGS
 1 silver onion
 2 garlic cloves
 1 red chili
 6 kaffir lime leaves
 1 stalk lemongrass, crushed and split in half
 oil for sautéing
 2 cans of coconut milk (each approx. 14 oz [400 g])
  + 1 can water
 2 limes, juice
 1½ tsp salt
 3 tbsp fish sauce
 2 chicken breast fillets
 1 tbsp fresh cilantro, chopped

DIRECTIONS:
1. Peel the onion and garlic and cut into thin slices. Core the red chili and cut it into strips.
2. Sear the onion, garlic, chili, lime leaves, and lemongrass in some oil until the onion softens, about 2 minutes.
3. Add coconut milk, water, lime juice, salt, and fish sauce. Let it all simmer for 15 minutes. Remove the soup from the heat and let it rest for another 15 minutes.
4. Cut the chicken into strips. Heat up the soup again and add the chicken. Let it simmer for about 10 minutes. Check to see if the chicken is fully cooked by cutting one of the pieces in half.
5. Sprinkle chopped cilantro on top and serve the soup right away.

131.

132. Creamy Chicken Soup with Dill

This recipe is incredibly easy to make but it does take some time. I made it for an episode of a TV show with Barbro "Lill-Babs" Svensson in her garden. It turned out that she had never touched a raw chicken before! Well, there are first times for everything!

4–6 SERVINGS

CHICKEN STOCK:

2 chicken thighs

2 sprigs fresh thyme

1 sprig fresh rosemary

3–5 stalks of dill

1 bay leaf

2 tsp dill seed

2–3 tsp salt

6 white peppercorns

approx. 6 cups (1½ liters) water (enough to cover the chicken)

SOUP:

3 cups (700 ml) chicken stock from above recipe

½ cauliflower head

1 bunch of carrots

2 parsley roots

1 small leek

2 tsp flour

1⅔ cups (400 ml) milk

⅔ cup (200 ml) heavy cream

salt, freshly ground white or black pepper

⅔ cup (200 ml) frozen green peas

½ lemon, juice

FOR SERVING:

coarsely chopped dill

DIRECTIONS:

1. Put the chicken thighs and spices for the chicken stock into a large pot. Add water and bring to a boil. Skim the white residue off the top. Let simmer until the chicken meat is falling off the bone, for about 20 minutes. Set aside for the time being.

2. Strain about 3 cups of the chicken stock and pour it into a new, large pot. Save the rest of the stock for later.

3. Separate the cauliflower into small florets. Peel and slice the carrots and parsley roots. Slice the leek thinly on the diagonal. Put the carrots and parsley roots into the pot with the stock and let it all simmer for about 2–3 minutes. Then add the cauliflower and leek. Let it simmer for a minute more. Remove the vegetables with a perforated ladle and set to the side.

4. Create a thickening agent by stirring flour into ½ cup (100 ml) of the milk. Add it into the stock while stirring. Pour in the rest of the milk and cream, and let it all simmer for 3–5 minutes. Season with salt and freshly ground pepper.

5. Add the vegetables and the peas, and bring the soup to a boil once more. Finish it off by adding some lemon juice. Add the vegetables

6. Heat the chicken thighs in the chicken stock you set aside earlier. Serve the chicken on the side or pick the meat from the bones and heat it in the soup.

7. Sprinkle the dill over the soup and season with freshly squeezed lemon juice. Serve hot with an open bread and cheese sandwich.

Four Ways to Make Rice

I like the kitchen staples—the foods you can switch up without having to think too much. By staples I mean those dishes we make out of habit but that can easily be adapted into something new. Rice is a perfect example. We tend to take it for granted and rarely allow it to take center stage. Rice, potatoes, and pasta can all be seasoned to become something more than just a side dish. They make great leftovers or to serve plain with a salad. By changing up the rice you serve, you'll have the opportunity to teach your kids new flavors, but you have to be patient: it takes time for children's palates to become accustomed to new things. Generally you'll have to serve a new dish five times for the child to recognize its flavor and learn to like it.

Here are four delicious and completely different flavors from something as simple as rice.

Basic Rice Recipe

4 SERVINGS
1⅓ cups (300 ml) basmati rice
1 tsp canola oil
1½ tsp salt
2½ cups (600 ml) water

DIRECTIONS:

1. Rinse the rice under cold water as needed. Flash-fry the rice in a pot with oil, salt, and any other seasoning from the following recipes that you like.
2. When the rice has turned translucent, pour in the water and let it all simmer for about 20 minutes.

133. Moroccan Rice

My favorite rice! This is a perfect accompaniment to lamb. Add some roasted almonds (see page 28) and raisins!

1 batch of basic rice recipe (see left)
1 tsp turmeric
1 tsp cumin
1 tsp ground coriander
¼ tsp ground cardamom
6 cloves, lightly crushed

134. Nordic Rice

A sweet and sour rice that tastes delicious with meat or fish. Don't hold back on the horseradish!

1 batch of basic rice recipe (see left)
1 tbsp dill seeds, lightly crushed
5–6 thin slices of fresh horseradish, approx ⅒ inch (3 mm)
3 tbsp white vinegar
2 tbsp sugar

135. Thai Rice

The kaffir lime leaves give the rice a distinct character. It's delicious boiled for dinner and fried the next day for a snack.

1 batch of basic rice recipe (see left)
5 kaffir lime leaves
2 tbsp ground ginger
1 tbsp dried mint

136. Italian Rice

A beautifully colored rice that's delicious with smoked meats and chicken.

1 batch of basic rice recipe (see left)
4 garlic cloves, crushed
1 tbsp dried rosemary
2 tbsp tomato paste + 1 tomato cut into small pieces

133.

134.

135.

136.

137.

138.

139.

140.

Four Ways to Make Mashed Potatoes

This is along the same vein as the rice recipes on page 236—simple mashed potatoes made up in several unique styles. Let these dishes play the lead role. Suddenly you can pick side dishes to go with the mashed potatoes instead of the other way around!

Basic Mashed Potatoes Recipe

4 SERVINGS
1 lb (500 g) potatoes
water + salt
⅔ cup (150 ml) milk
7 tbsp (100 g) butter
1 tsp salt, freshly ground white or black pepper

DIRECTIONS:
Boil the potatoes in salted water. Drain the potatoes and mash them. Add milk and butter. Season with salt and pepper.

137. Garlic Mashed Potatoes

Great with meatballs.

1 batch of basic mashed potatoes recipe (see above)
6 garlic cloves, peeled and roasted in 1 tbsp
  of olive oil
2 tbsp capers + 1 tbsp capers juice

DIRECTIONS:
Mash the roasted garlic cloves and mix them with the capers and the juice from the capers. Combine the mixture with the mashed potatoes. Season with salt and pepper.

138. Olive Mashed Potatoes

This kind of mashed potatoes is perfect for parties. It tastes amazing with red meat of all shapes and sizes, but it's also quite tasty with fish.

1 batch of basic mashed potatoes recipe (see left)
1 bunch of tarragon, chopped
½ cup (100 ml) cored and chopped Calamata olives

DIRECTIONS:
Sauté the butter listed in the basic recipe before mixing it into the mashed potatoes. Add tarragon and olives. Season with salt and pepper.

139. Tomato Mashed Potatoes

These taste heavenly with ground meat dishes: croquettes, patties, or loaves. Or try the potatoes with strips of smoked meat or sausage.

1 batch of basic mashed potatoes recipe (see left)
2 tomatoes, cut into small pieces
1 bunch of chives, chopped
1 garlic clove, peeled and shredded

DIRECTIONS:
Fold tomatoes, chives, and garlic into the mashed potatoes.

140. Mashed Potatoes with Lemon

Tasty with baked fish or grilled pork tenderloin.

1 batch of basic mashed potatoes recipe (see left)
1 lemon, zest + ½ lemon, juice
1 bunch of dill, chopped (approx. 1 oz [30 g])

DIRECTIONS:
Stir the lemon zest, lemon juice, and dill into the mashed potatoes. Season with salt and pepper.

Tacos

Tortillas
Salsa
Taco Spice Mix
Ground Beef, Feta, and Capers with Russian Walnut Dip
Pulled Pork with Hoisin Sauce and Chili-roasted Corn
Chicken Thighs with Herbed Chickpeas and Green Pea Guacamole
Roasted Duck and Radish with Hoisin Sauce on Chinese Pancakes
Tempura-style Flounder with Salted Cucumber and Sour Cream
White Bean Tacos with Salsa Verde and Vegetable Strips
Russian Walnut Dip
Hoisin Sauce
Chili-roasted Corn with Hazelnuts
Green Pea Guacamole
Salted Cucumber
Salsa Verde

TEX-MEX IS WHAT WE CALL American food that draws inspiration from Texas and Mexico. Typically this includes tortillas, fajitas, nachos, tacos, salsa, guacamole, and beans. Funnily enough, Norwegians and my native Swedes eat the most Tex-Mex of all Europeans. How did that happen?

One reason might be that one of Sweden's biggest supermarkets decided to emphasize their exotic product lines, and after about six years of heavy marketing, us Swedes were hooked. Now we appreciate the many flavors and diverse uses of corn, as well as the admirable relationship between avocado, ground beef, cumin, oregano, and peppers. Tacos are the Mexican equivalent to the Swedish smörgåsbord. Swedes love to handpick their own food for their plates, buffet-style, and we revel in the many different flavors we can choose from. But one big difference between tacos and the smörgåsbord is that up until now most people have enjoyed their tacos while wearing their sweatpants! Now it's time to take our cherished taco dinners to a whole new level, so ditch those sweatpants and try something a bit more daring!

Here is a whole plethora of updated tacos to choose from. Different meats—chicken, duck, fish, and even vegetarian— along with all kinds of sauces and toppings. Everything in this chapter is easy to make, though some of the recipes have a lengthy prep time.

141. Tortillas

This might seem a little ambitious, but it's a lot of fun to bake your own tortillas when you have some spare time. And it makes a huge difference! The tortillas are fluffy and not as compact as the ones you buy in the store, and I like the little burnt bits here and there. Try to bake it in a panini press.

8 PIECES OF BREAD
½ oz (12 g) active dry yeast
1 cup (250 ml) water, room temperature
½ tsp salt
2½ cups (600 ml) flour
corn oil for sautéing

DIRECTIONS:
1. In a bowl, dissolve the yeast in a little bit of the water. Gradually add the rest of the water with the flour and salt. Mix until the dough is smooth, and let it rise under a kitchen towel for 30 minutes.
2. Divide the dough into 8 small pieces and roll them into balls. Flatten them with a rolling pin until they are ¼ inch (½ cm) thick.
3. Pan-fry the bread in some corn oil for a few minutes per side.

142. Salsa

Not much to mention here—salsa is a must for any classic taco! Make sure you get the seasoning right so you get the desired flavor. If you want it more spicy, just add some more cayenne pepper. Make a large batch of salsa to snack on later; it keeps in the fridge for 10–14 days and tastes better after it's been allowed to sit for a time.

APPROX. 2 CUPS (500 ML)
1 shallot, thinly sliced
3 garlic cloves, crushed
⅓ cup (75 ml) olive oil
3 tbsp dried oregano
1½ tbsp paprika powder
2 tbsp ground cumin
¼ tsp cayenne pepper
1½ tsp salt
1 box cherry tomatoes (approx. 9 oz [250 g])
1 can crushed tomatoes (14 oz/400 g)
½ cup (100 ml) white wine vinegar

DIRECTIONS:
1. Pan-fry the onion, garlic, and spices in half of the olive oil. Add all other ingredients and let simmer over low heat for 10–15 minutes.
2. Mash the salsa coarsely with a fork or mortar and pestle. If possible, let the sauce rest in the fridge for 24 hours before serving.

143. Taco Spice Mix

Use the taco spice mix for classic tacos made of ground beef, salsa, tortillas, and sour cream. Use 2 tbsp taco spice mix per ¾–1 pound (400–500 g) of ground beef.

APPROX. 1/2 (200 ML) CUP
3 tbsp cumin
2 tbsp Ancho chili powder
1 tsp paprika
1 tsp chili flakes
2 tsp garlic powder
3 tsp dried oregano
3 tsp dried coriander
½ tsp cayenne pepper
2 tsp salt
1 tsp sugar

DIRECTIONS:
Grind the spices in a mortar and pestle. Store the spice mix in a jar with a tightly closed lid.

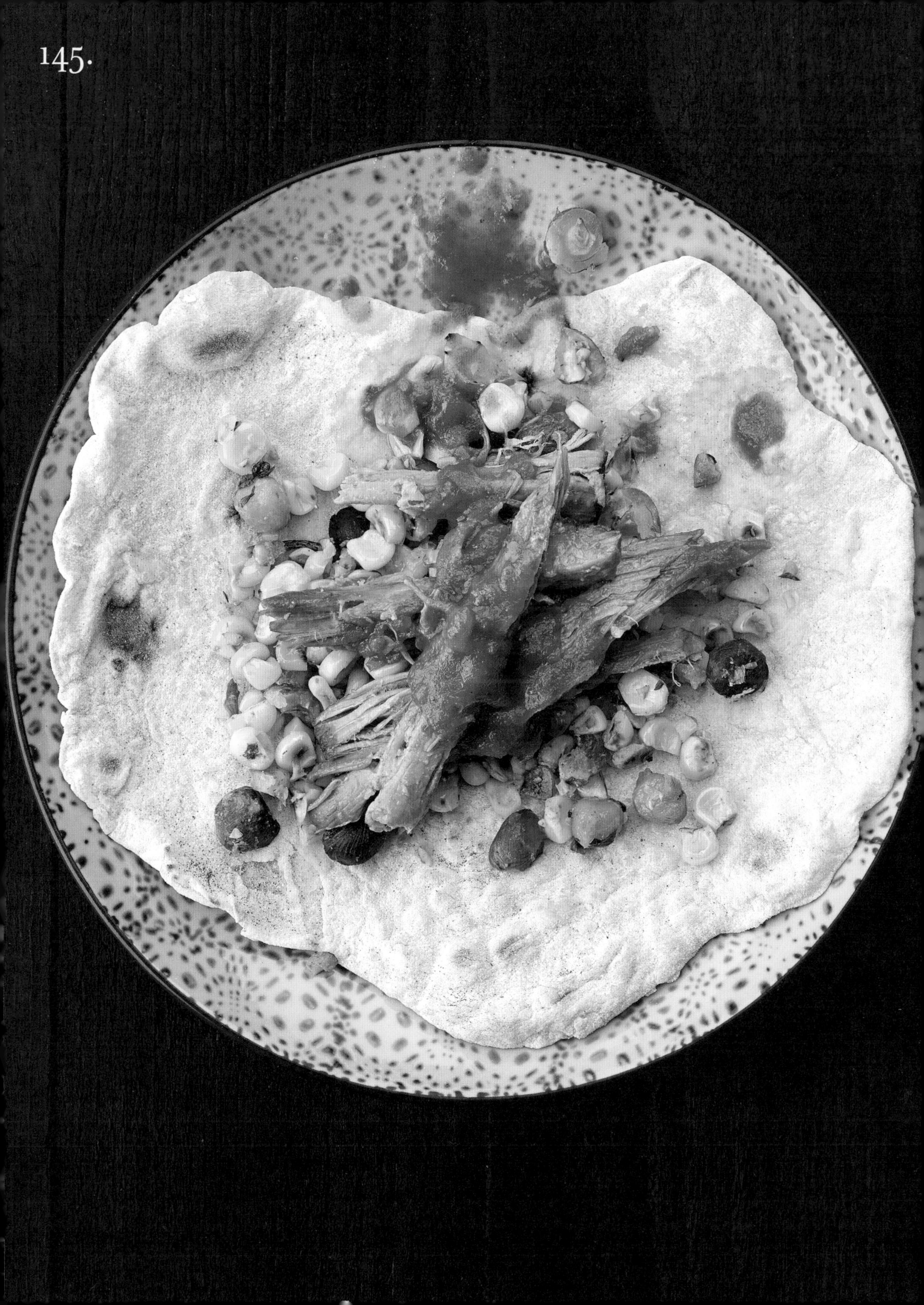

144. Ground Beef, Feta, and Capers with Russian Walnut Dip

This recipe was actually concocted by mistake. While we were sautéing the ground beef, we put the cheese to the side of the pan to make sure it wouldn't melt—which is exactly what happened. And the dish turned out better than we could ever have imagined! Serve any extras from this dish with some leftover Moroccan rice (see page 236), and you'll have a whole new meal.

4–6 SERVINGS

14 oz (400 g) ground beef
1½ tbsp capers
3½ oz (100 g) feta cheese
⅔ cup (150 ml) walnuts
olive oil for sautéing
1½ tbsp Dijon mustard
½ tsp salt
freshly ground white or black pepper

FOR SERVING:

tortillas (see page 243)
Russian walnut dip (see page 251)
shredded carrot
leek, thinly sliced

DIRECTIONS:

1. Coarsely chop the capers. Crumble the feta cheese. Finely chop the walnuts and sauté them in a frying pan with olive oil. Add ground beef, capers, feta cheese, and mustard. Season with salt and freshly ground white or black pepper. Serve the meat on tortilla bread with the shredded carrot and leeks. Top with the Russian walnut dip.

145. Pulled Pork with Hoisin Sauce and Chili-roasted Corn

This is easiest dish in the world to make! I simply put the pot in the oven, brush my teeth, and go off to bed. By the time I'm sipping my morning coffee, the pulled pork is done. It's a perfect dish to prepare the day before you're expecting company. You can just heat it up right before serving. And it's super-delicious for a lazy Friday night at home.

4–6 SERVINGS

3⅓ lbs (1½ kg) whole pork shoulder, de-boned
salt, freshly ground white or black pepper (as needed)

MARINADE:

1 cup (200 ml) barbecue sauce
2 tbsp white wine vinegar
1 tbsp paprika
½ tsp cayenne pepper

FOR SERVING:

tortillas (see page 243)
Hoisin sauce (see page 251)
chili-roasted corn with hazelnuts (see page 251)

DIRECTIONS:

1. Preheat the oven to 250°F (120°C).
2. Place the meat in a large, lidded pot that can handle being in the oven. Mix the ingredients for the marinade and pour it over the meat. Place the pot in the oven and cover it with the lid. Let it cook for 8–9 hours.
3. Pull the pork apart with a fork and season with salt and pepper as needed. Serve on tortillas with Hoisin sauce and chili-roasted corn with hazelnuts.

146. Chicken Thighs with Herbed Chickpeas and Green Pea Guacamole

Another of my favorites! I love when food looks a little disorganized but has the flavor to knock your socks off. Everything in one pot, nutritious and low-maintenance to boost.

4–6 SERVINGS
   4 chicken thighs, with skin
   3 tbsp olive oil
   3 shallots, thinly sliced
   5 garlic cloves, peeled and crushed
   1 bunch of fresh herbs (e.g., sage, rosemary, parsley, tarragon)
   1¼ cups (300 ml) soaked, uncooked chickpeas + water from the chickpeas
   2 bay leaves
   6 white peppercorns
   6 cloves
   salt, freshly ground white or black pepper
FOR SERVING:
   tortillas (see page 243)
   green pea guacamole (see page 252)

DIRECTIONS:
1. Season the chicken thighs with salt and sear them with the onion, garlic, and herbs in a thick-bottomed pot with olive oil herbs.
2. Add chickpeas and spices along with the water from the chickpeas so that everything is almost covered. Bring to a boil and let simmer over low heat for about 2 hours. (The bouillon should have almost completely evaporated).
3. Remove the chicken and pull the meat off the bones. Fold the meat into the chickpea mix and season with salt and pepper.
4. Serve on tortillas with green pea guacamole.

147. Roasted Duck and Radish with Hoisin Sauce on Chinese Pancakes

Can you really serve something as fancy as duck on a pancake? You bet! Everyone will love it so much that they'll be cartwheeling around you!

4 SERVINGS
   2 duck breasts
   salt, freshly ground white or black pepper
CHINESE PANCAKES:
   2 cups (500 ml) milk
   1⅔ cups (400 ml) flour
   4 eggs
   1 tsp salt
   1 lemon, zest + ½ lemon, juice
   2 garlic cloves, shredded
FOR SERVING:
   finely shredded radish
   Hoisin sauce (see page 251)

DIRECTIONS:
1. Preheat the oven to 300°F (150°C).
2. Wipe the skin of the duck breasts and score the breasts through the skin a few times.
3. Put the duck breasts skin-side down in a hot frying pan. Season with salt and pepper. Reduce the heat and fry the duck breasts for a couple of minutes until the skin turns crispy. Flip them over and lightly sear the other side. Place the duck breasts on a baking rack with a baking sheet underneath to catch the drippings and bake in the oven until the duck breasts have a core temperature of 129°F (54°C). Let them rest for a few minutes and then cut into slices before serving.
4. Mix the pancake batter and fry the pancakes in butter over low heat. They're supposed to be pale in color and very thin.
5. Serve the duck on the Chinese pancakes. Top with shredded black radish and a dash of Hoisin sauce.

148. Tempura-style Flounder with Salted Cucumber and Sour Cream

I made this flounder once at the Torekov camp grounds for several hundred campers. The tortillas were made over an open flame. The flounder should be served straight from the fryer. Feel free to drizzle some vinegar on top when serving; it will neutralize the fatty oil.

4 SERVINGS

4 flounder fillets (approx. 4½ oz [125 g] per person)
canola oil for frying
salt, freshly ground white or black pepper

TEMPURA BATTER:

2 eggs
½ cup (100 ml) cornstarch

FOR SERVING:

salted cucumber (see page 252)
sour cream

DIRECTIONS:

1. Whisk the egg and cornstarch until it becomes a smooth, runny batter. Dip the fish fillets in the batter.
2. Fry the fish until they are golden brown, for about 2–3 minutes. Season with salt and pepper. Serve on tortillas with pickled cucumber and sour cream.

HOW TO DEEP FRY

Pour the sunflower oil into a deep saucepan and heat it until it reaches a temperature of 350°F (180°C). Measure the temperature with a kitchen thermometer or gently place a piece of bread in the oil. If the bread turns brown within one minute, you've reached the right temperature. Make sure to keep a lid handy just in case the oil catches fire. NEVER try put out an oil fire with water! And don't fry too much at a time because this will reduce the temperature of the oil. Place the fried strips on paper towels afterward to soak up any excess oil.

149. White Bean Tacos with Salsa Verde and Vegetable Strips

Beans and cumin *are* tacos. Children love these tacos.

4–6 SERVINGS

3 shallots, thinly sliced
butter and oil for sautéing
2–4 garlic cloves, peeled
½ tbsp ground cumin
½ cup (100 ml) chopped parsley
1 can white beans (approx. 14 oz [400 g])
½ cup (100 ml) tahini
½ tsp salt, freshly ground white or black pepper
1 whisked egg
panko bread crumbs for breading
canola oil for frying

FOR SERVING:

salsa verde (see page 252)
scallion cut into fine strips
shredded carrot

DIRECTIONS:

1. Flash-fry the onion in a frying pan with butter and oil until the onion softens but hasn't gotten any color. Add garlic and seasonings.
2. Drain the beans and pour the beans into the pan along with the tahini. Season with salt and pepper. Mash everything with a fork to make the mixture easy to shape. Or put everything in a bowl and mix with a hand mixer. Shape the mixture into small balls and roll them first in the whisked egg and then in the panko bread crumbs. Fry the balls in oil until they turn golden brown, for about 2–3 minutes.
3. Serve your tacos on tortillas with scallion strips and shredded carrots. Top with a scoop of salsa verde.

146. 147.
148. 149.

150.

141.

152.

153.

142.

154.

155.

150. Russian Walnut Dip

I was inspired to make this dip after a trip to Moscow with my colleague, Benny. It's a completely new kind of sauce to me, loaded with walnuts and a distinct cumin flavor. It's a match made in heaven with the ground beef, feta, and capers (see page 246). It's also amazing with the green chicken tenders (see page 232) and even makes a tasty dip for bread.

APPROX. 2 CUPS (500 ml)
2 shallots
2 garlic cloves
⅔ cup (200 ml) walnuts
½ tbsp olive oil
1 tsp ground cumin
1 tsp ground coriander
1 tbsp paprika
½ tsp cayenne pepper
⅔ cup (200 ml) crème fraîche (or sour cream)
¼ tsp salt

DIRECTIONS:
1. Peel the shallots and garlic cloves. Chop the walnuts, shallots, and garlic extremely fine. Put these in a pot and add the oil and spices. Sauté for about 2 minutes.
2. Add the crème fraîche (or sour cream). Stir and bring to a boil. Season with salt and pepper. Let it cool.
3. Serve the walnut dip chilled.

151. Hoisin Sauce

This is my homemade version of the East Asian sauce. It's flavorful and a little syrupy, with notes of coffee, tahini, and vinegar. It's perfect for pulled pork. This red sauce is pictured on page 240, poured into a bottle.

APPROX. 1 CUP (200 ml)
1½ tbsp Kikkoman soy sauce
½ cup (100 ml) tahini (sesame paste)
2 tsp sesame oil
1 tsp Sambal oelek
1½ tbsp coffee
2 tbsp white wine vinegar
3½ tbsp honey

DIRECTIONS:
Mix all ingredients in a bowl.

152. Chili-roasted Corn with Hazelnuts

Corn is a fun taco side dish, especially mixed with cucumber and chopped tomatoes. This tastes best when the nuts are chopped coarsely, so you can really get their full flavor with each bite. Absolutely delectable with pulled pork (see page 246).

APPROX. 1⅔ CUPS (400 ml)
2 fresh or frozen ears of corn
1 cup (200 ml) coarsely chopped hazelnuts
1 tbsp olive oil
½ red chili, cored and finely chopped
1 lime, zest and juice
½ tsp salt

DIRECTIONS:
1. Peel the ears of corn, if needed. Place one end of the cob against a cutting board. With a sharp knife, slice the corn kernels off the cob.
2. Lightly fry the hazelnuts in a frying pan with oil. After a little while, add the chili. Add the corn and roast it all together in the pan until the hazelnuts are golden brown in color. Season with the lime zest and juice, along with some salt.

153. Green Pea Guacamole

A favorite dip of mine. It's also great with grilled salmon (see page 154). The green peas give the guacamole a sweetness and freshness. It's also a great topping on spicy sausage pizza.

APPROX. 2 CUPS (500 ml)
2 avocados
2 cups (500 ml) green peas
1 tbsp sour cream
2 tbsp olive oil
1–2 garlic cloves
½ tsp (or less) salt
5 dashes of green Tabasco

DIRECTIONS:
Halve the avocados. Remove the pits and scrape the avocado flesh from the skins. Coarsely mash together the peas, avocado, sour cream, and olive oil. Shred the garlic into the mixture and stir. Season with salt and Tabasco.

154. Salted Cucumber

Quick and easy to make. The salt makes the cucumber crunchy and with the skin peeled away it looks even prettier. Salted cucumber is also delicious in salads.

4 SERVINGS
1 cucumber
½ tsp salt

DIRECTIONS:
Peel and core the cucumber. Slice it diagonally and put the slices into a plastic bag. Pour the salt into the bag and shake. Let it rest for 10–15 minutes before serving. You can also put the cucumber slices in a bowl and combine it that way, but this will take longer.

WARM CUCUMBER WITH DILL
Heat the cucumber with a pat of butter and some dill and mix with steamed vegetables. Amazing what you can do with a simple cucumber!

155. Salsa Verde

Salsa verde is an Italian and Spanish sauce that's easy to overlook, but it's great with almost anything. And that's why you can find this recipe next to the pickled char on page 117. It's also great with bean tacos (see page 248) and with smoked salmon and new potatoes, or as a salad dressing.

APPROX. 1⅔ CUPS (400 ml)
1 bunch parsley
1 bunch cilantro
1 bunch mint
1¾ oz (50 g) fresh spinach
2 tbsp capers
2 garlic cloves, peeled
2 tbsp Dijon mustard
2 tbsp water
½ cup (100 ml) olive oil
a pinch of salt
freshly ground white or black pepper

DIRECTIONS:
Mix herbs, spinach, capers, garlic, mustard, and water with a hand mixer until it becomes a smooth green sauce. Pour in the olive oil in drops until the sauce thickens. Season with salt and pepper and let it rest in the fridge for 30 minutes before serving.

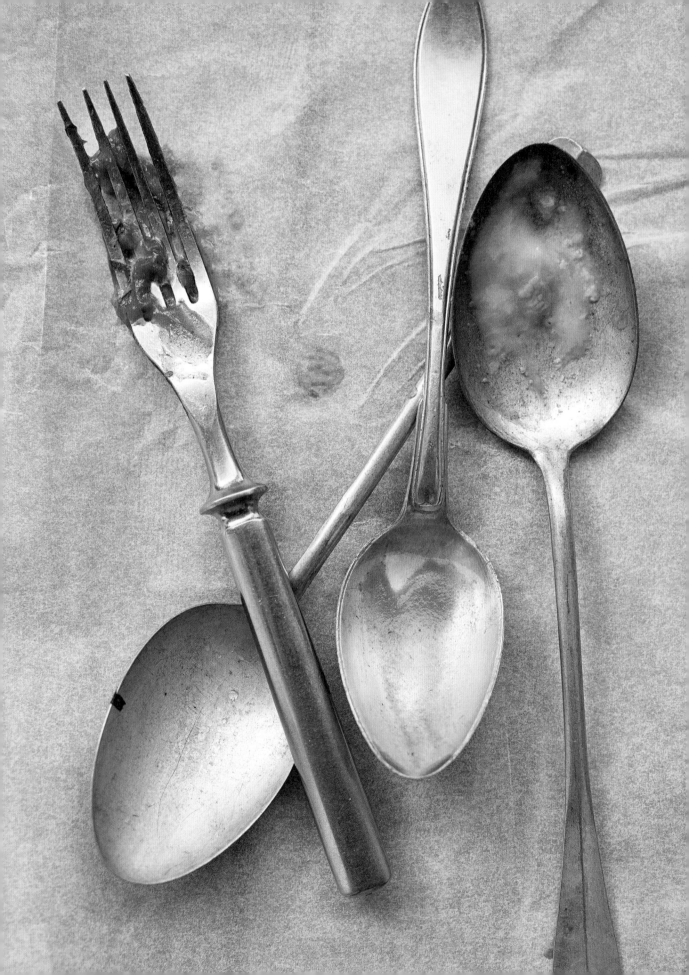

Bread & Pizza

Instead of an apron

The Dough in the Drawer!

NOT MANY WOULD HAVE thought I would end up a chef. When it came to baking and cooking at home, our kitchen was always ruled by my big brother, Peter. No, I always wanted to be a priest! Imagine a priest finishes each sermon by offering the congregation a new recipe for a Sunday roast with gravy, jellies, and homemade cucumber. Perhaps it still wouldn't be such a stupid idea to combine cookery and the clergy. I never did become a priest, but I did work as a sexton for few years. I would stand in the doorway and greet all the parishioners before the sermon, and I made sure they rose up when they were supposed to and sat down when they were told to during the service. I was also in charge of the collection. It was a side gig that included some responsibility and I liked that. The fact that the congregation complained about my skirts being too short was something I ignored completely. I just wanted to look nice! For the most part, cooking was notable in my life largely for its absence. Well . . . except for a few valiant attempts to excel in this area. I remember one time I had decided to surprise my mom, dad, and my brother by baking some fresh bread. Off I went to the local supermarket and bought all of the ingredients I needed for the baking. But when I put the dough in a bowl to rise I realized something awful: damn it, I had forgotten the salt! Back in those days I had no idea that it was perfectly okay to add the salt afterward. Everything just went blank.

Down the dough went into a plastic bag, and I dumped it all into a drawer filled with pajamas, t-shirts, and socks before rushing off to the store again to buy some more yeast and flour. I still had enough time to finish the bread before my mom and dad came home. And sure enough, before they walked in the door, the kitchen was clean and the coffee maker was bubbling with a fresh brew. Everything played out just as I had envisioned! I went to bed happy that night, Mom came in to say goodnight . . . that's when I realized the dough was still in the drawer! I laughingly told her about the

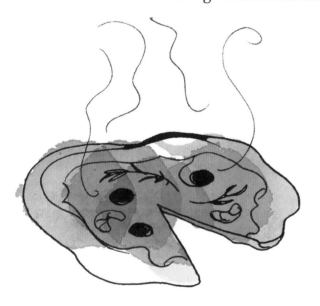

dough that had no salt, and until she opened that drawer up, all was quiet. But then, she yanked it open and out exploded a doughy mountain of pajamas, t-shirts, and socks—the entire mess spilling out over the side of the drawers and dripping onto the floor. Of course it did—it was leavening in a plastic bag all evening. Dough was everywhere! All Mom could do was laugh and laugh. It's a hilarious memory we'll be chuckling over for the rest of our lives.

These days, we'll always bake if we have the time and want to treat ourselves to something special. And of course we make the time to bake for Christmas and for parties. It all comes down to whether or not we feel like it and if we're not too busy. I do, however, believe that the warm, cozy feeling of baking bread will soon disappear. If we bake in the future, it will probably be for other reasons than making the house feel like a home. These reasons may include saving money and

choosing to make healthier, more nutritious bread so we can know exactly what is in it.

These days, there's no reason for us to eat anything but delicious bread. In most supermarkets there are shelves of bread made from many varieties of high-quality flour to choose from. Not to mention sourdough, which is slowly gaining popularity among today's consumers. If you have a sourdough starter in your fridge, you'll just need to be sure to leave it with the neighbors whenever you're going away for a few days so it won't starve. I've never managed to keep a sourdough starter alive at home—I always forget to feed it. But with a few basic bread recipes, you'll do just fine. And luckily for me and everyone else who's too forgetful to make our own sourdough, you can buy incredible sourdough at most bakeries. Bottom line: the future looks great for bread baking. Here are some of my favorite bread and pizza recipes!

THINK LIKE TINA

COLD OR WARM WET INGREDIENTS ?

When you want speedy baking, use wet ingredients that are warm. If you have more time on your hands and want better results, you should use cold wet ingredients. Then let it rise slowly no matter what it says in the recipe.

READ THE RECIPE CAREFULLY

If there's ever a time to follow a recipe to the letter, it's when it comes to baking. For example, it's essential that you measure the correct amounts for the recipe. If you make a mistake with the measurements, it can completely ruin everything. For the ease of American bakers, some of the US measurements included with the recipes have been rounded slightly. For more precise baking, you may wish to follow the metric measurements.

CHOOSE THE RIGHT KIND OF FLOUR

When you make bread—where you want gluten strands—you want to choose flour with a high level of protein in it, such as Manitoba flour. This will give you elastic and tasty bread. If you're making a pie crust, you do not want gluten strands, which will make the crust sink into the pan. This is why you should use flour with a low protein level, such as regular wheat flour, when you make pie. You should do the same for short-crust pastry and pancakes. High protein levels would be ¼ oz (12 g) per 3½ oz (100 g) flour.

WHAT SHOULD DOUGH BE LIKE FOR IT TO BECOME A GREAT LOAF OF BREAD?

The dough should be stringy and rubbery and not too firm. You'll achieve the best results by working the dough without salt for about 10–15 minutes. Then add the salt and work the dough quickly, but only for a few more minutes.

HEAT THE OVEN A LITTLE BIT HIGHER

Heat the oven about 50°F (10°C) hotter than the recipe calls for. When you open the oven door to put in the bread, you actually let out quite a lot of heat. After 10 minutes you can reduce the heat to its suggested temperature.

USE A THERMOMETER WHEN YOU BAKE

Insert a thermometer into the bread, and when it shows 208°F (98°C), it is done.

SEASON THE BREAD

Substitute the water for the dough liquid with crushed tomatoes or white wine (half water and half wine). You can also add sour milk, yogurt, ricotta cheese, or milk. Or perhaps try some colorful juices, like carrot, red beet, or tomato juice. Beer is always tasty in dark bread. Some classic bread spices are fennel, cumin, anise, and ginger. Use ½ tsp dried spice per every 2 cups (500 ml) of dough liquid.

LOVELY CRUSTS

It's really delicious to glaze the top of fresh baked bread with coffee or syrup. The crust will absorb the flavor and will become doubly delicious. Store bread standing up, with the cut edge toward the cutting board to maintain the crispy crust, or keep it in a paper bag. Never store bread in plastic bags.

BAKE WITH FRUIT

Make sure to soak any dried fruit, such as raisins, figs, or any other fruits that can absorb the moisture of the bread before baking. You can soak them in rum, sugar water, or apple juice. In doing so, you prevent the fruit from drying out the bread during the baking. The same rule applies for baking pastries.

156. Spiced Bread with Butternut Squash Purée

This bread has a little bit of sweetness to it, and it tastes great with aged cheese. Easy as 1-2-3 to bake; you just stir the dough, place it in a loaf pan, and drop the delicious concoction into the oven. It does take some time to bake, but it's worth the wait. Go ahead and experiment with different spices. The bread is also delicious with herbs such as rosemary, thyme, or marjoram.

2 LOAVES

1⅓ cups (300 ml) honey
½ cup (150 ml) raw sugar
1⅔ cups (400 ml) milk
2 tbsp ground anise
3½ tbsp cinnamon
1 heaping tbsp of ground or freshly shredded ginger
½ tbsp orange zest
1 tsp salt
2½ cups (600 ml) wheat flour
½ cup (100 ml) rye flour
1½ tbsp baking soda

BUTTERNUT SQUASH PURÉE:

½ butternut squash, peeled and in pieces (approx. 14 oz [400 g])
2 garlic cloves
1 tbsp olive oil
3½ tbsp blanched and peeled almonds
salt, freshly ground white or black pepper

DIRECTIONS:

1. Preheat the oven to 350°F (175°C).
2. Bring to a boil honey, raw sugar, milk, anise, cinnamon, ginger, orange zest, and salt. Let the mixture cool (you can let it sit overnight in the fridge if you want).
3. Add wheat flour, rye flour, and baking soda to the cold spice mixture. Stir until the dough is smooth in texture.
4. Grease two large loaf pans and divide the dough into the pans. Place in the oven and reduce the heat to 300°F (150°C). Bake for 45 minutes to an hour.
5. Remove the pans from the oven and let them cool for a little while before turning them over to release the loaves. Place onto a cooling rack.
6. Increase the oven temperature to 400°F (200°C). Peel the butternut squash and garlic cloves. Cut the butternut squash into chunks. Put the squash and the garlic cloves in a casserole dish and drizzle with some olive oil. Bake in the oven for about 20 minutes.
7. Mix the butternut squash, garlic, and almonds in a food processor or with a hand mixer. Season with salt and pepper. Let it cool.

Super Tasty

SPICED FRENCH TOAST

The spiced bread is incredibly delicious for making French toast (see page 347). Dip the bread in whisked egg and pan-fry it in butter. Top it off with powdered sugar sprinkled on top.

157. Stuffed Lemon Bread

This incredibly fresh-tasting bread is made from a simple bread dough with lemon mixed in. Great for picnics and an absolute must for buffets and any other large gathering. It's great for everything!

2 LOAVES

½ oz (12 g) active dry yeast

2½ cups (600 ml) cold water

3 lemons, zest

6 cups (1.4 liters) wheat flour

1 tbsp salt

1–2 tbsp polenta

FILLING 1: HAM, CHEESE, AND PEPPERS:

15 slices aged cheddar

5 slices ham of any variety (optional)

3 whole pickled peppers, cut into pieces

½ cup (100 ml) chopped fresh tarragon and rosemary

2 tbsp olive oil

FILLING 2: BLUE CHEESE, NUTS, AND RAISINS:

5⅓ oz (150 g) blue cheese

⅔ cup (150 ml) coarsely chopped mixed nuts (e.g., walnuts or almonds)

½ cup (100 ml) raisins

DIRECTIONS:

1. Preheat the oven to 450°F (230°C).

2. Dissolve the yeast in a little bit of the cold water. Pour in the rest of the water and stir in the lemon zest and flour. Work the dough in a food processor or by hand for about 10–15 minutes. Add the salt and work the dough for another couple of minutes. Let the dough rise covered for 2 hours (or in the fridge overnight).

3. Split the dough into halves and knead each half into a ball. Let them rest for 5 minutes.

4. Roll each dough ball out into a flat cake. Lay the aged cheese slices on top of one of the dough "cakes." Layer the ham, peppers, and herbs on top of and drizzle with some olive oil. On top of the second "cake," crumble the blue cheese and spread out the nuts and raisins on top.

5. Roll them both up and pinch in the edges to prevent the cheese from leaking out during the baking. Place the rolls on a baking sheet lined with parchment paper. Sprinkle some flour or polenta on top of each and let them rise for another 1 hour under a moist baking towel or plastic wrap.

6. Put the baking sheet in the center of the oven and reduce the heat to 400°F (200°C). To make the crust extra crispy, throw 3–4 tbsp (50 ml) water onto the bottom of the oven and then close the oven door quickly. The steam from the water will make the bread crispy and delicious. Bake for about 35 minutes and let it rest and cool before serving.

158. Manitoba Baguettes

In baker's terminology, this dough is considered "weak" and should not be kneaded. The high protein level of the Manitoba flour makes the baguettes springy and fluffy.

4 LARGE BAGUETTES

1 oz (25 g) active dry yeast
4 cups (1 liter) cold water
2 lbs (1 kg) Manitoba flour
⅔ cup (150 ml) sourdough starter from flour (1 jar)
1½ tbsp salt
½ lemon, zest
2 tbsp olive oil

DIRECTIONS:

1. Dissolve the yeast in some of the cold water. Pour in the rest of the water, and add the flour and sourdough starter. Mix the dough in a food processor on normal speed for 10 minutes.
2. Add salt and lemon zest, and mix on the highest speed for 5–8 minutes or until the dough releases from the bowl on its own. Pour into a greased bowl and let rise covered for about 2 hours.
3. Preheat the oven to 475°F (250°C).
4. Pour the dough out onto a floured surface. Divide the dough into four long, thin pieces with a spatula. Sprinkle flour on your hands and shape each piece of dough into baguettes. Place the baguettes on a baking sheet sprinkled with flour. Let the dough rest for 10–15 minutes on the baking sheet.
5. Bake the baguettes for about 15 minutes until they are golden brown and crispy on top. Let them cool down under a baking towel.

159. Focaccia

Do not for any reason add any extra flour to this recipe "just to be on the safe side." The dough is meant to be runny, and the bread will turn out nice and firm nevertheless. I used some lovely cherry tomatoes here, but go ahead and try some pearl onions, roasted garlic, capers, or fresh rosemary. Beautiful focaccia makes a wonderful hostess gift, so skip the bottle of wine next time you're invited to dinner.

1 LOAF

1 oz (25 g) active dry yeast
2¾ cups (650 ml) cold water
6 cups (1.4 liters) wheat flour
¾ cup + 4⅓ tsp (200 ml) graham flour
1 tbsp salt
3½ tbsp olive oil
7 oz (200 g) mixed tomatoes, in halves
approx. 3½ tbsp cored olives of your choice
1 tbsp dried herbs (e.g., rosemary or thyme)
a few sprigs of fresh herbs
1 tbsp coarse sea salt

DIRECTIONS:

1. Dissolve the yeast in some of the cold water. Pour in the rest of the water and add the flour. Work the dough with a food processor or by hand for 15 minutes. Add salt and work the dough for another couple of minutes. Cover and let rise for 45 minutes.
2. Line a baking sheet with parchment paper and grease it with olive oil. Grease your fingers, and press out the dough onto the pan. Press tomatoes, olives, and dried herbs into the dough. Let rise for about 45 minutes.
3. Preheat the oven to 475°F (250°C).
4. Drizzle olive oil onto the focaccia and top with fresh herbs and sea salt. Place the bread in the oven and reduce the heat to 425°F (225°C). Bake for about 20 minutes. Let cool.
5. Cut the bread into pieces and serve, preferably with some quality cold cuts. Perfect for a buffet meal!

160. Grissini

You can buy grissini ready-made in any grocery store. But I think the store-bought options are just too perfect. I think homemade grissini ought to be a little crooked in shape.

APPROX. 24 GRISSINI

1 oz (25 g) active dry yeast
1 cup (250 ml) water, room temperature
2½–3 cups (600–700 ml) wheat flour
2 tsp salt
5 tbsp canola oil
sea salt
poppy seeds

DIRECTIONS:

1. Dissolve the yeast in the water. Stir in half of the flour, salt, and oil. Stir in the rest of the flour and mix the loose dough. Let the dough rise covered for about 20 minutes until doubled in size.
2. Preheat the oven to 400°F (200°C).
3. Divide the dough into two halves and roll them out to ¼–½ inch (½–1 cm) thickness. Use plenty of flour when rolling them, so the dough doesn't stick. Glaze the dough with water and top with a sprinkling of salt and poppy seeds.
4. Cut the dough into ½ inch (1 cm) wide strips. Twist them and place them on a baking sheet lined with parchment paper. Let them rise covered for about 10–15 minutes.
5. Bake the grissini for about 20 minutes, until they are golden brown in color. If they're not crispy enough, you can dry them out in the oven. Just turn off the heat and open the oven door, and they will dry quickly. Store in a cool, dry place.

A SIMPLE AND TASTY SNACK FOR COCKTAIL HOUR

Buy a jar of whipped horseradish and some slices of smoked ham. Spread the whip onto the ham slices and wrap them around the Grissini. It's perfect for a cocktail hour. Or chop a bunch of herbs and roll the grissini in them before baking them in the oven.

161. Swedish Crisp Bread with Cumin

I think it's easier to bake crisp bread in a frying pan. It's quite traditional and delicious with gravlax and some lemon mayonnaise (see page 92). Or try some green pea guacamole (see page 252). You can even break the crisp bread into a bowl of tomato soup.

30–35 CRISP BREADS

3 cups (700 ml) wheat flour
1¼ cups (300 ml) rye flour
1¼ cups (300 ml) yogurt
½ cup (100 ml) olive oil
2 tsp baking powder
1 tbsp salt
6 tbsp ground cumin
2 tbsp ground anise seeds

DIRECTIONS:

1. Mix all ingredients into a smooth dough.
2. Roll the dough out into flat pieces and bake them for about 4–5 minutes per side in either a cast iron frying pan without any grease or oil, or in the oven at 425°F (225°C) on a baking sheet lined with parchment paper.
3. Store the crisp bread in a metal box in a dry location.

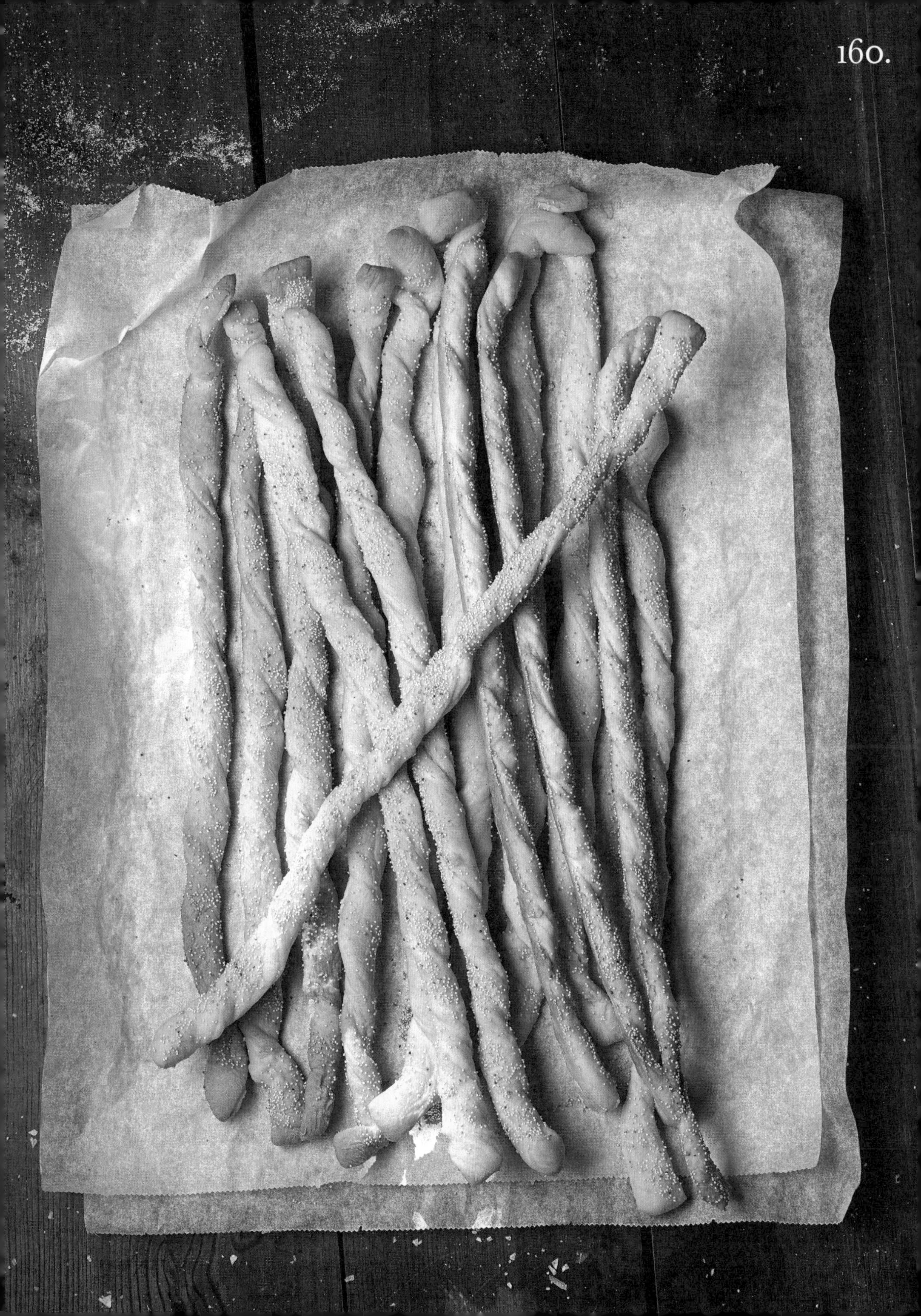

162. Oatmeal and Cardamom Scones

These scones should be served with lemon curd and clotted cream. Of course, if you're in a hurry you can cheat and buy store-bought lemon curd and substitute mascarpone cheese for clotted cream. Try using lemon curd as a filling for cute little pie crusts or in between almond crisps, and you'll have a quick, perfect little dessert for your coffee.

24 SCONES
- 7 tbsp (100 g) butter, room temperature
- 3⅓ cups (800 ml) wheat flour
- ½ cup (100 ml) oats
- 5 tsp baking powder
- 1 tsp salt
- 1⅔ cups (400 ml) milk or plain yogurt
- 1 tbsp sugar
- ½–1 tbsp ground cardamom

CLOTTED CREAM:
- 1⅔ cups (400 ml) heavy cream
- 1 tbsp crème fraîche (or sour cream)

LEMON CURD:
- ⅔ cup (150 ml) freshly squeezed lemon juice
- 3 lemons, zest
- ⅔ cup (150 ml) sugar
- 6 egg yolks
- 5 tbsp + 1 tsp (75 g) butter, room temperature

DIRECTIONS:

1. Bring the heavy cream to a boil and let simmer slowly until reduced by half. Stir occasionally. When there's about ¾ cup (200 ml) left in the pot, remove the pot from the stove. Stir in the crème fraîche (or sour cream). Pour the clotted cream into a bowl and let it cool in the fridge.

2. Whisk the freshly squeezed lemon juice, lemon zest, sugar, and egg yolks together in a pot and bring to a boil while stirring constantly. Let simmer gently for a few minutes until the mixture has thickened. Remove the pot from the burner. Fold the butter into the mixture until the lemon curd is smooth and silky. Cool the lemon curd in the fridge.

3. Preheat the oven to 425°F (225°C).

4. Mix all the ingredients for the scones, preferably in a food processor. Dollop six pieces of dough onto a baking sheet lined with parchment paper and flatten the pieces with your flour-covered hands. With a sharp knife, score an x in each scone. Bake the scones for about 15 minutes, until they turn golden brown.

5. Serve your freshly baked scones with lemon curd and clotted cream.

Super Tasty

TOAST YOUR LEFTOVER SCONES

Break your leftover scones into pieces and roast them in a hot frying pan with a dollop of butter and some olive oil. Top with some lemon zest just before they're finished. Serve as a topping on a green salad.

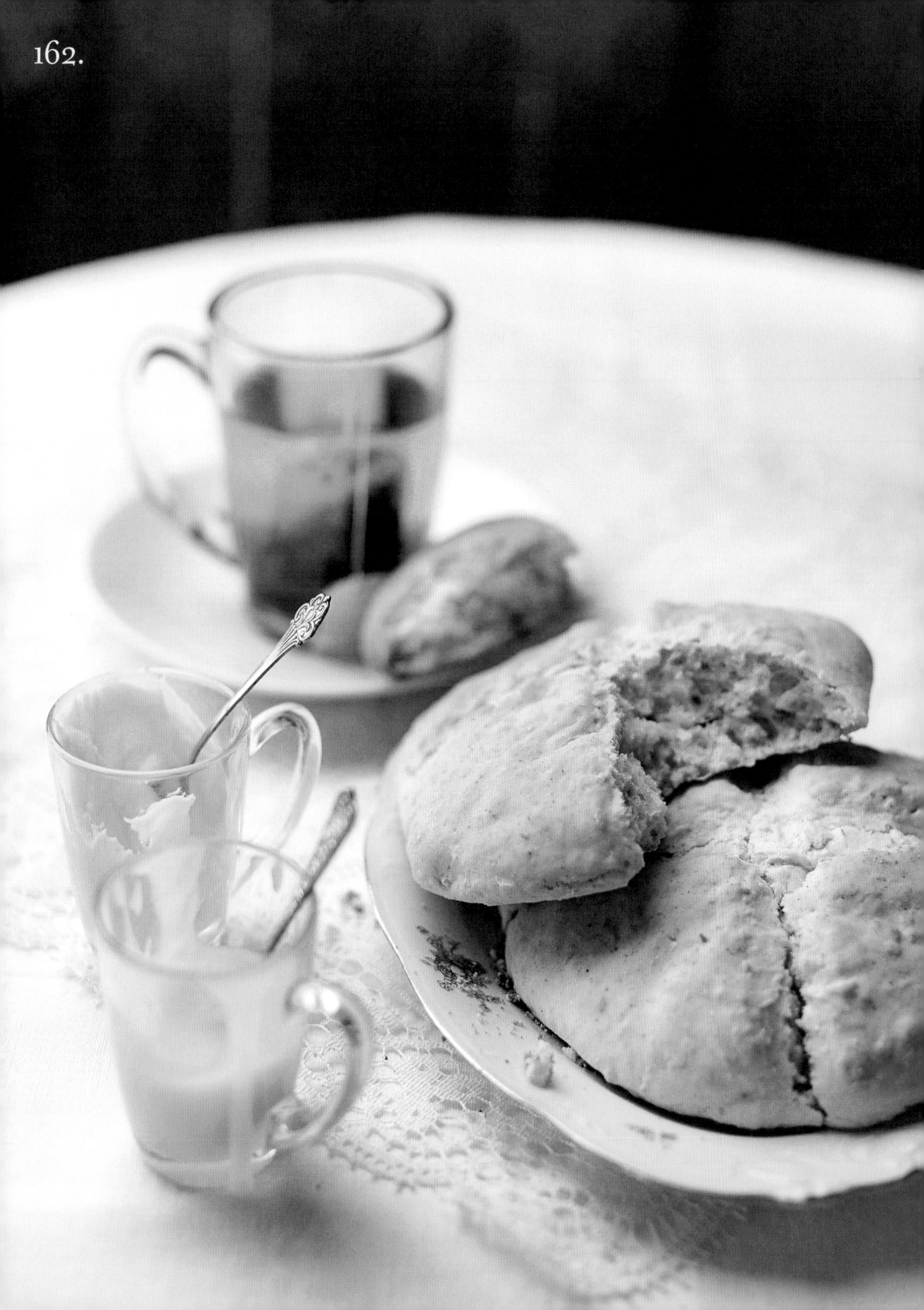

Pizza

I like thin-crust pizzas—not the thick ones that are similar to focaccia. If you want to make a really delicious pizza, great quality ingredients are a must. Another must is to preheat the baking sheet in the oven; this way, the heat rises from the bottom as well. Three flavors are more than enough for a pizza! All of these toppings work just as well on focaccia bread or stuffed in lemon bread.

4 SERVINGS
PIZZA DOUGH:

> *approx. ½ oz [12 g] active dry yeast*
> *1 cup (250 ml) water, room temperature*
> *½ tsp salt*
> *2½ cups (600 ml) wheat flour*

DIRECTIONS:
Dissolve the yeast in some of the water. Pour in the rest of the water and add salt and flour. Mix until the dough is smooth and let rise covered for about 30 minutes.

163. Pizza with Red Onion, Bacon, Emmentaler Cheese and Sour Cream

This recipe is inspired by the Alsace region, where they call their pizza *tarte flambé.*

4 SERVINGS
> *1 batch pizza dough (see above)*
> *4 red onions*
> *10 oz (280 g) bacon*
> *5⅓ oz (150 g) shredded Emmentaler cheese*
> *2 tsp white wine vinegar*
> *1 tsp salt*
> *1¼ cups (300 ml) sour cream for serving*
> *freshly ground white or black pepper*

DIRECTIONS:
1. Preheat the oven to 475°F (240°C). Place a baking sheet in the oven.
2. Peel and slice the onion thinly. Fry the bacon until the fat is released and the bacon turns golden brown. Add the onion and vinegar and sauté everything until the onion turns soft.
3. Roll the pizza dough out until it is thin and place it on parchment paper. Top with the cheese, bacon, and onion mixture. Remove the hot baking sheet from the oven and carefully slide the parchment paper with the pizza onto it. Bake for about 15 minutes.
4. Remove the pizza from the oven. Drizzle or dollop some sour cream on top and garnish with some freshly ground pepper. Serve right away.

164. Pizza with Shrimp, Artichoke Heart Cream, and Garlic

This artichoke cream is also perfect as a dip for vegetables or as a spread on fresh baked bread.

4 SERVINGS
> *1 batch pizza dough (see left)*
> *1 jar artichoke hearts (approx. 14 oz [400 g])*
> *1 cup (200 ml) shredded cheese*
> *10½ oz (300 g) peeled shrimp*
> *sprigs of dill for garnish*

ARTICHOKE HEART CREAM:

> *1 jar of artichoke hearts (14 oz [400 g])*
> *3 garlic cloves, peeled*
> *1 tbsp olive oil*
> *½ lemon, juice*

DIRECTIONS:
1. Preheat the oven to 475°F (240°C). Place a baking sheet in the oven.
2. For the artichoke heart cream, mix the artichoke hearts, garlic, oil, and freshly squeezed lemon juice into a cream.

274

3. Halve all artichoke hearts.
4. Roll the pizza dough out until it is thin and place it onto parchment paper. Distribute the cream across the pizza dough and spread out the remaining artichoke hearts. Sprinkle cheese on top. Remove the hot baking sheet from the oven and carefully slide the parchment paper with the pizza onto it. Bake in the oven for about 15 minutes.
5. Remove the pizza from the oven and top with the shrimp. Garnish with the dill and serve right away.

165. Chanterelle Pizza with Dill and Cumin Cheese

The chanterelles can be substituted for any other kind of mushroom if needed.

4 SERVINGS
1 batch pizza dough (see page 274)
14–17 oz (400–500 g) chanterelles
1 yellow onion
2 tbsp butter
1 bunch dill, finely chopped (approx. 1 oz [30 g])
¾ tsp salt, freshly ground white or black pepper
5⅓ oz (150 g) cumin cheese, coarsely shredded

DIRECTIONS:
1. Preheat the oven to 475°F (240°C). Place a baking sheet in the oven.
2. Clean the chanterelles. Peel and finely chop the onion. Sauté the chanterelles and onion in butter. Add dill and season with salt and pepper.
3. Roll the pizza dough out thinly and place it onto parchment paper. Distribute the chanterelles and cheese on the pizza. Remove the hot baking sheet from the oven and carefully slide the parchment paper with the pizza onto the baking sheet. Bake in the oven for about 15 minutes. Serve right away.

166. Broccoli Pesto Pizza with Prosciutto

This Swedish broccoli pesto is so tasty that it's a serious threat to the original Italian. Go Sweden!

4 SERVINGS
1 batch pizza dough (see page 274)
8 slices prosciutto for serving
freshly ground white or black pepper
BROCCOLI PESTO:
1 broccoli, cut into small pieces
½ cup (100 ml) hazelnuts
3 tbsp olive oil
½ cup (100 ml) shredded Parmesan
1 garlic clove
½ tsp salt

DIRECTIONS:
1. Preheat the oven to 475°F (240°C). Place a baking sheet in the oven.
2. Mix broccoli, nuts, oil, parmesan, garlic, and salt for the pesto.
3. Roll out the pizza dough thinly and place it on parchment paper. Distribute the pesto onto the pizza. Remove the hot baking sheet from the oven and carefully slide the parchment paper with the pizza onto it. Bake in the oven for about 15 minutes.
4. Remove the pizza from the oven and top with the prosciutto. Sprinkle with some freshly ground pepper and drizzle with some olive oil. Serve right away.

CHEESE FOR THE PIZZA
Use a combination of cream cheese and mozzarella to get the perfect, creamy consistency. When serving, garnish with some tasty Parmesan or Pecorino.

163.

164.

166.

165.

Tapas

Smoked Salmon in Puff Pastry
Catalan Breakfast—*Pa Amb Tomàquet*
Marinated Peppers with Goat Cheese and Sultan Raisins
Roast Beef with Julienned Vegetables and Horseradish Dip
Large White Beans with Chorizo
Potato Pancakes with Cheese, Bresaola, and Caramelized Lemon
Khachapuri
Toast Pelle Janzon
Roasted Eggplant with Sesame Seeds and Balsamic Vinegar
Black Beans with Mango and Cumin
Saganaki with Capers and Lemon Salsa
Chicken Salad with Truffle Mayo
Stuffed Phyllo Dough with Lemon-marinated Parsnips
Quail Eggs with Marinated Salmon Roe
Coppa-baked Ground Meat with Dates
Olive-baked Cabbage with Cress
Pan-fried Calamari
Carpaccio with Chanterelles and Artichoke Cream
Savory Oven Pancakes with Toppings

TAPAS, PINCHOS, CANAPÉS, APPETIZERS—call it what you will, these are small dishes that challenge the taste buds and tease the palate into wanting more. Ideally, these should be seasoned with something more than just salt and pepper. In Sweden, our tapas can be too polished, and I'm not just referring to the flavors, but rather how we eat them and how they look on the plate. Often in an environment that's a little too stylish, and with a murmur in the background that's a little too perfect, with wardrobes that are just a little too fashionable. But that's the way Swedes are, and I'm probably just the same. Maybe in other countries, their tapas and tapas experiences are less overly refined.

When serving your guests tapas, equip them with one simple fork, and plate the food a little haphazardly. This way, their focus will be on the flavors in the dish, and they won't be distracted. Put the plates on the table and serve with a glass of Cava. Dare to be spontaneous, even if you're in complete control. Don't play too perfect music and don't bother combing and bobby-pinning back your children's hair until they look impeccable but stiff. Just avoid being too polished. That's how I like it!

The pictures on pages 282, 286, and 291 show three different kinds of tapas menus, in which the dishes complement each other perfectly. But, of course, you can also combine all sorts of tapas dishes and serve it up as a buffet or as appetizers. Or you can choose your five favorite tapas, and make them your whole dinner!

167. Smoked Salmon in Puff Pastry

Puff pastry is folded dough that flakes when baked and becomes really crispy. Puff pastry should be cold when you work with it. One tip is to throw the rolling pin in the freezer to prevent the dough from sticking to it. You can buy great ready-made puff pastry dough, both refrigerated and frozen varieties. And if you bake puff pastry whole in the oven, you'll always achieve fantastic results.

4 SERVINGS

2 sheets of frozen puff pastry
4 silver onions
3½ tbsp (50 g) butter
10½ oz (300 g) smoked salmon
1 cup (200 ml) sour cream
salt, freshly ground white or black pepper

DIRECTIONS:

1. Preheat the oven to 475°F (250°C).
2. Roll out each puff pastry until it has doubled in length and width. Tear the sheets more or less in half and place them on a baking sheet lined with parchment paper.
3. Peel the onions and slice them thinly, preferably with a mandolin. Melt the butter in a frying pan and toss the onions. Let them absorb the fat and soften without getting any color. Divide the onion across the middles of the four pastry sheets, leaving a wide margin all around.
4. Bake the puff pastry in the oven for about 15 minutes until it puffs up and turns golden.
5. Put the smoked salmon pieces onto the puff pastry. Drizzle some sour cream on top and season with salt and pepper. Serve right away.

168. Catalan Breakfast— *Pa Amb Tomàquet*

A Catalan breakfast at its finest! To breakfast in a Catalonian household is something truly special. They serve freshly crushed tomatoes, their best olive oil, some white bread, and a cup of coffee so delicious it blows your mind. It's a far cry from the daily typical milk and cereal breakfast. This Catalan breakfast can be eaten in large quantities and at any time, even as an appetizer or a snack.

4 SERVINGS

4 thick slices of sourdough bread
3 garlic cloves
3 tomatoes
2–3 tbsp peppery olive oil
½ tsp sea salt
freshly ground white or black pepper

DIRECTIONS:

1. Bring a pot of water to a boil. Blanch the tomatoes by first scoring an "x" at the top of each tomato and then putting them in the boiling water for about 30 seconds. Remove them from the water and let them cool down in ice water.
2. Peel the tomatoes and cut them into pieces—remember to remove the stems. Place the tomatoes in a bowl and crush them haphazardly with a fork. Stir in 1 tbsp of olive oil.
3. Peel and crush the garlic cloves. Toast the bread and the garlic cloves in a frying pan with some olive oil until the bread is golden brown.
4. Serve the bread with a heaping helping of crushed tomatoes on top. Drizzle with some olive oil and season with sea salt and freshly ground pepper.

169. Marinated Peppers with Goat Cheese and Sultan Raisins

I've been "dragging" this dish around with me for a long time, and I've served it more times than I can remember for just about every kind of occasion. Mix it into a salad or eat it as is with some fresh bread.

4 SERVINGS
2 bell peppers (1 yellow and 1 red)
7 oz (200 g) goat cheese
fresh basil for garnish

MARINADE:
1 shallot, finely chopped
3½ tbsp olive oil
1 tbsp white wine vinegar
1 tbsp honey
salt, freshly ground white or black pepper
3½ tbsp roasted almond slices
3½ tbsp sultana raisins

DIRECTIONS:
1. Set the oven to broil.
2. Glaze the peppers with some oil and lay them in a baking pan. Place the pan in the oven and char the pepper skins. This will take about 10 minutes. Remove the peppers and put them in a plastic bag that you can close with a knot; it's easier to peel the peppers after they have steamed in the bag.
3. Mix all the ingredients for the marinade.
4. Remove the peppers from the bag. Peel them and cut them into thick slivers. Break the cheese into pieces. Arrange the cheese and peppers in a serving bowl, and pour the sweet and sour marinade over them. Top it all off with some almond slices and this dish is ready to be served!

170. Roast Beef with Julienned Vegetables and Horseradish Dip

One sunny day in Sandhamn, we were recording a TV program and made these roast beef roll-ups. Buy presliced roast beef to make them in a jiffy!

4 SERVINGS
8–10 slices of roast beef (cold cuts)
1 carrot
2 celery stalks
1–2 inches (a few cm) fresh horseradish

MARINADE:
3 tbsp olive oil
2 tbsp mirin
1 tbsp Japanese soy sauce
1 tbsp white wine vinegar

DIRECTIONS:
1. Julienne the celery and carrot (i.e., cut into thin strips). Shred the horseradish.
2. Roll up the roast beef, wrapped around the julienned vegetables.
3. Mix all the ingredients for the marinade in a bowl.
4. Place the roast beef rolls on a platter with some of the marinade and sprinkle the shredded horseradish on top. Guests can dip the rolls in the rest of the marinade.

167.

168.

169.

170.

171.

172.

171. Large White Beans with Chorizo

This is a favorite of mine. It only contains a few ingredients but still packs a punch. The acid from the vinegar is important, so feel free to apply it liberally. My colleague, Benny, and I made this simple farmer's dish in Barcelona. The beans were scooped onto rustic, chipped plates and didn't exactly look like fine dining. But to our palates, it was like arriving in heaven. I love this kind of food—where the focus is on *flavor*! You can also serve this dish as the main course.

4 SERVINGS

2 fresh chorizo sausages
1 can large white beans (save 3½ tbsp of the bean juice)
2 tbsp butter
½ tbsp white wine vinegar
1 garlic clove
salt, freshly ground white or black pepper

DIRECTIONS:

1. In a frying pan, sauté the sausages over medium heat until they are golden brown. Place them on a cutting board.
2. Pour the beans and the stock into the frying pan and mix in the butter and vinegar. Shred the garlic into the pan and mix. The beans should get hot.
3. Cut the sausages roughly on the diagonal—they shouldn't look pretty!—and serve with the beans. Season with salt and pepper. It's so simple and is delicious beyond belief!

172. Potato Pancakes with Cheese, Bresaola, and Caramelized Lemon

I once made these potato pancakes with Robert Aschberg at Högmarsö, just outside of Stockholm. Fat, juicy, and hearty. A substantial lunch dish. Rough and a little unpolished.

4 SERVINGS

4 potatoes
1 small piece of leek (approx. 2 inches [5 cm])
salt, freshly ground white or black pepper
9–11 oz (250–300 g) fresh cheese, with a white crust (e.g., Chaource or aged brie)
olive oil for sautéing
2 lemons
6–8 slices of bresaola or dry cured ham

DIRECTIONS:

1. Preheat the oven to 350°F (180°C).
2. Peel and coarsely shred the potatoes. Slice the leek finely. Combine the potatoes and leeks, and season with salt and pepper. Shape the potatoes into pancakes and pan-fry them in olive oil until they are crispy. Keep them hot.
3. Heat up another frying pan. Drizzle some olive oil into the pan and sprinkle in some salt. Flash-fry the cheese at high heat until it caramelizes (is nicely browned) and then stick it in the oven for a few minutes until it feels soft.
4. Caramelize the lemons in the frying pan by cutting them in half and frying the cut surface.
5. Plate the cheese and potato pancakes on a large platter and garnish with the bresaola. Squeeze fresh lemon juice on top of each potato pancake.

173. Khachapuri

Khachapuri is a traditional Georgian cheese bread and is served at parties in that country. A delicious little dish that complements other tapas dishes. My version includes some shortcuts.

4 SERVINGS

1 Sara Lee thick pizza dough
9 oz (250 g) mozzarella or other fatty cheese
½ red chili
1 bunch of sage (or thyme or rosemary)

DIRECTIONS:

1. Preheat the oven to 475°F (250°C).
2. Shred the cheese. Core and thinly slice the chili.
3. Place the pizza dough on a lightly floured surface. Sprinkle cheese, chili, and sage on half the dough. Fold the other half over it and pinch the edges together with your fingers, like you're making a calzone.
4. Bake the cheese bread in the oven for about 15 minutes. It should then be really tall and will have a crispy crust—the surface can even be a little charred. Remove the bread from the oven and let it rest for a minute before you cut it up and sink your teeth into it.

EASILY CORE A CHILI

Roll the whole chili between your fingers and then cut off the root. I promise all the seeds will fall out through the hole once you turn the chili upside down.

174. Toast Pelle Janzon

We all love to put tasty toppings on bread. Toast Pelle Janzon got its name from the Swedish opera singer Per Janzon. It's a less famous cousin of the classic Toast Skagen, but it's a success every time!

4 SERVINGS

9 oz (250 g) beef tenderloin
1 red onion, finely chopped
small, delicate lettuce leaves, such as radicchio
4 slices of white bread
2 tbsp (30 g) butter
4 tbsp fish roe
4 egg yolks
1 bunch of chives, finely chopped
sea salt, freshly ground white or black pepper

DIRECTIONS:

1. Clean the beef tenderloin of any tendons. Slice the meat into four thin slices and put them between two sheets of plastic wrap. Pound them with a meat tenderizer until they are thin. Since the beef tenderloin is so tender, you have to be careful not to break it when pounding it. Use a meat tenderizer.
2. Mix the red onion and lettuce in a bowl.
3. Pan-fry the bread in butter. Layer the raw meat, a dollop of fish roe, and egg yolk on top of the bread just as in the picture on page 286. Top it off with the onion and lettuce mixture, some chives, sea salt, and some freshly ground pepper.

PREPARE THE TOAST

Toast Pelle Janzon is perfect to serve at big gatherings. Pound out the meat, wrap it carefully, and then stick it in the freezer. When you take it out of the freezer, you can just put it on a plate and it will thaw in minutes!

173.

174.

175.

176.

177.

178.

175. Roasted Eggplant with Sesame Seeds and Balsamic Vinegar

It really can be this simple! A tasty roasted eggplant with roasted sesame seeds and the fine acidity of the balsamic vinegar. You can mix it all together with a hand mixer if you so desire. Add a little bit of olive oil, and you'll have yourself a delicious eggplant dip.

4 SERVINGS

2 eggplants
1 garlic clove
2 tbsp olive oil
salt, freshly ground white or black pepper
2 tsp freshly squeezed lemon juice
2 tbsp roasted sesame seeds
1 tbsp balsamic vinegar

DIRECTIONS:

1. Preheat the oven to 425°F (225°C).
2. Halve the eggplant lengthwise. Split the garlic and rub it into the eggplant halves. Add some olive oil. Place the eggplants with their open-side down on a baking sheet lined with parchment paper. Bake in the oven for about 30 minutes until they are lightly roasted and soft. Turn them over and sprinkle some sesame seeds on top.
3. Plate the eggplants and drizzle with balsamic vinegar. When serving, let your guests scoop the eggplant flesh directly onto their own plates.

176. Black Beans with Mango and Cumin

Perhaps not the prettiest dish but it's certainly tasty! Mango, cumin, and black beans make a heavenly combination. The cilantro and lemon are the cherry on top.

4 SERVINGS

1 large mango or a package of frozen mango chunks
1 cup (200 ml) canned black beans
¼ tsp sesame oil
½ tsp ground cumin
¼ tsp salt
1 lime
fresh cilantro for serving

DIRECTIONS:

1. Peel the mango and cut it into pretty pieces—big or small is up to you. A little hint from your coach: the taste is the same no matter what size you choose!
2. Drain the beans. Stir them together with the mango, sesame oil, cumin, and salt.
3. Squeeze the lime juice over the mixture and garnish with some fresh cilantro.

177. Saganaki with Capers and Lemon Salsa

The capers and lemon salsa is the key to this dish. Previously I used halloumi cheese, but then I discovered its Greek cousin saganaki, named for the frying pan it's made in. Freshly chopped lemon is really great for everyday salad, since you can forget about oil and vinegar.

4 SERVINGS

> 9 oz (250 g) saganaki cheese (or halloumi)
> ½ tsp olive oil

CAPERS AND LEMON SALSA:

> ½ cucumber
> 1 lemon
> 2 tbsp capers
> 1 bunch basil, chopped
> 3 tbsp olive oil
> freshly ground white or black pepper

DIRECTIONS:

1. Peel and core the cucumber and cut it into thin slices. Wash the lemon and zest it. Mix the cucumber, capers, and lemon zest in a bowl. Cut the pulp of lemon coarsely—just remember to remove the seeds first. Mix the red onion, basil, and olive oil into the bowl with cucumber, capers, and lemon zest. Season with pepper.
2. Heat up a frying pan on the stove. Pour in a small amount of oil, about ½ tsp, and then add the cheese. Let it sauté until it turns golden brown. Try to be patient and only lift the cheese after it has been in the pan for at least 30 seconds. Then flip it over and repeat the procedure.
3. Tear the cheese into large chunks. Pour the salsa on top and serve right away.

178. Chicken Salad with Truffle Mayo

Great with any tapas dish, as a stand-alone, or as part of a buffet. Be careful with the truffle oil as it can easily become overpowering. The mayo is also great with the carpaccio on page 292.

4 SERVINGS

> 10½ oz (300 g) chicken meat, pan-fried or from a
> store-bought roasted chicken
> 1 lb (500 g) wax beans, haricot verts, green
> beans, or fresh fava beans
> 2 shallots, finely chopped

TRUFFLE MAYO:

> 2 egg yolks
> ½ tsp Dijon mustard
> ⅔ cup (150 ml) neutral oil
> 1 tbsp heavy cream
> 2–3 drops truffle oil for flavoring
> ½ lemon, juice
> 2 small heads of lettuce
> salt, freshly ground white or black pepper

DIRECTIONS:

1. Bring a pot of water to a boil. Add all the beans, do a 10-second dance, and drain the beans. Rinse them in cold water. Let them dry on paper towels.
2. Mix the egg yolks and Dijon mustard in a bowl. Drip the oil into the mixture while whisking until the mayo has thickened. Add the heavy cream and season with truffle oil and freshly squeezed lemon juice.
3. Combine the chicken, beans, and onion in a bowl. Mix in the truffle mayo to make the salad "stick together." The chicken isn't supposed to be drowning in mayonnaise.
4. Plate the salad and season with salt and a hearty dose of freshly ground pepper.

179. Stuffed Phyllo Dough with Lemon-marinated Parsnips

My colleague, Benny, and I made this dish during a guest appearance in Moscow. Even though it has very few ingredients, it's quite a long "to do" list. It's not difficult, but it does take some time to prepare.

4 SERVINGS
2 parsnips
phyllo dough
3½ tbsp (50 g) butter, melted
sea salt flakes
LEMON MARINADE:
½ lemon
3½ oz (100 g) powdered sugar

DIRECTIONS:
1. Peel the parsnips and put them in water, preferably with some lemon juice so they don't change color. In the meantime, bring a saucepan of water to a boil and sprinkle in some salt. Add the parsnips and boil until soft.
2. Cut the lemon half into pieces and remove the seeds. Mix zest and pulp with powdered sugar until it turns into a thick sauce.
3. Add the parsnips and lemon marinade. Let them rest for as long as possible, preferably overnight but certainly no less than an hour.
4. Preheat the oven to 500°F (250°C).
5. Place two sheets of phyllo dough on a baking sheet lined with parchment paper. Glaze one-half of each sheet with butter and fold the sheets in half. You should end up with two sheets of double phyllo dough.
6. Place a cooked parsnip on each sheet of phyllo dough and add a little bit of marinade. Roll up the dough tight. Glaze the roll-ups with some butter and sprinkle some of the salt on top. Bake in the oven for 7–10 minutes. They should be golden brown and crispy when they are ready. Slice the rolls and serve them hot.

180. Quail Eggs with Marinated Salmon Roe

You might think it's difficult to get a hold of quail eggs, but that's not really the case. Go to a Polish supermarket to find them fresh and cheap. You'll have to buy the salmon roe at a fish counter though. The main thing about the salmon roe is that they need to be big to soak up as much of the marinade as possible.

4 SERVINGS
12 quail eggs
9 oz (250 g) salmon roe
MARINADE:
½ lime
3 tsp mirin
2 tsp rice wine vinegar
1 tsp finely shredded ginger

DIRECTIONS:
1. Boil the quail eggs for 3 minutes. Rinse them quickly in cold water. Peel the eggs (see below) and put them aside.
2. Mix all the ingredients for the marinade. Add the salmon roe and let it marinate for at least 30 minutes. The longer the better, since the roe will absorb the marinade and be really tasty.
3. Serve the salmon roe with the quail eggs as tapas or as an appetizer—preferably with some cream-marinated red currant salad (see page 33).

HOW TO PEEL QUAIL EGGS
Pour equal parts of white wine vinegar and water into a bowl. Put the quail eggs into the water-vinegar mix, and soon the quail shells will start to crackle and dissolve.

181. Coppa-baked Ground Meat with Dates

I got bored of making our traditional "jumping devils." It's like taking a sleeping pill—it's so mundane. I decided to update this dish and make these little devils. Give them a try—see if they're to your liking!

4 SERVINGS

- 14 oz (400 g) ground meat of your choice
- 3½ oz (100 g) cream cheese
- ½ tbsp green curry paste
- 1 tbsp chopped, pickled coriander (can be found in the Asian food section in the supermarket)
- 1 tsp salt
- ½ cup (100 ml) chopped and cored dates
- 15 slices coppa (air-dried pork shoulder)

DIRECTIONS:

1. Preheat the oven to 400°F (200°C).
2. Mix the ground meat with cream cheese, curry paste, coriander, salt, and dates.
3. Roll the meat mixture into little balls and cover them with the coppa (see picture opposite). Keep in mind to wrap the balls delicately so they're smooth on the surface.
4. Place the coppa balls on a baking sheet and bake them in the oven for 10–15 minutes. Serve the little devils hot.

182. Olive-baked Cabbage with Cress

Both my husband and I love cabbage, preferably roasted cabbage. When the cabbage comes out of the oven something magical happens, and the whole kitchen is filled with a sweet, nutty scent that is hard to beat. The pointy cabbage is great served cold for buffets and is a feast for the eyes.

4 SERVINGS

- 1 pointy cabbage
- olive oil
- salt, freshly ground white or black pepper
- tapenade (olive paste, which can be bought ready-made)
- watercress, arugula, or parsley for garnish

DIRECTIONS:

1. Preheat the oven to 400°F (200°C). Cut the cabbage into 8 wedges. Place them on a baking sheet. Drizzle some olive oil on top and season with salt and pepper. Bake in the oven until the cabbage has turned almost black, for about 15 minutes.
2. Dollop the tapenade in between the leaves. Then, remove the stem and roll up the cabbage into a ball. Garnish with watercress, arugula, or parsley.

183. Pan-fried Calamari

Calamari can be found frozen in most fish markets.

4 SERVINGS

- 9 oz (250 g) small, whole calamari (preferably frozen)
- 1 shallot + 1 garlic clove
- 2 tbsp olive oil
- 1 slice light bread, preferably Manitoba baguette
- salt, freshly ground white or black pepper
- lemon for serving

DIRECTIONS:

1. Toast the bread in a hot frying pan with some olive oil. Break the bread into pieces and put aside.
2. Peel and finely chop the onion and garlic. Sauté them in oil until they turn soft. Turn the heat up and add the calamari. Continue to sauté over high heat for another 2–3 minutes until the calamari appears springy and rolls up on itself. Season with salt and pepper. Add the bread pieces and squeeze the lemon on top. Serve straight from the pan.

180.

179.

181.

182.

183.

184.

184. Carpaccio with Chanterelles and Artichoke Cream

The last time I made carpaccio, I used elk tenderloin, but that can be a challenge to find, so using beef is perfectly fine. The artichoke cream is also perfect to dip vegetables or bread in.

4 SERVINGS
  9 oz (250 g) elk or beef tenderloin
CHANTERELLE MIX:
  2 cups (500 ml) chanterelles
  1 garlic clove
  butter for sautéing
  ½ cup (100 ml) fresh or frozen & thawed
    lingonberries (or cranberries)
  3½ oz (50 g) aged cheese
  olive oil
ARTICHOKE CREAM:
  1 jar artichoke hearts (approx. 14 oz [400 g])
  1 tbsp olive oil
  ½ lemon, juice
  salt

DIRECTIONS:
1. Clean the meat of any tendons or membranes. Cut it into thin slices and pound it flat between sheets of plastic wrap. Don't pound too hard on the tenderloin; you have to be gentle to prevent it from tearing. The bottom of a pot works well.
2. Mix the artichoke hearts (without the juice they come in) with olive oil and freshly squeezed lemon juice. Mix into a smooth cream. Season with salt.
3. Peel the garlic and crush it with the side of a knife blade. Pan-fry the chanterelles in butter with the garlic until they are crispy.
4. Spread out the meat onto individual plates or on a large platter. Dollop the cream on top of each piece and spread the chanterelle mixture on top. Sprinkle lingonberries and cheese over it. Drizzle with olive oil and enjoy it outside/inside/standing/sitting down.

HOW TO SAUTÉ MUSHROOMS

Sautéing mushrooms can be complicated because they contain so much water. If you don't have enough heat when sautéing them, the mushrooms have a tendency to boil rather than sauté. If that happens, just let the water evaporate! When all the water is gone you can just sauté the mushrooms until they're really crispy. Don't be afraid to burn them!

185. Savory Oven Pancakes with Toppings

Savory oven pancakes become glamorous when topped with something tasty. A Swedish tapas!

8–10 SERVINGS
  1 cup (250 ml) flour
  3 cups (700 ml) milk
  5 eggs
  ½ tsp salt
  2 tbsp (30 g) butter
TOPPINGS:
  bacon with lingonberries (or cranberries)
  smoked salmon with sour cream, dill, and
    horseradish
  boiled red beets with capers and lemon
  prosciutto with cream-sautéed mushrooms and
    parsley

DIRECTIONS:
1. Preheat the oven to 425°F (225°C).
2. Mix the flour with half of the milk and all of the eggs. Whisk until you have a smooth batter. Add the rest of the milk and the salt.
3. Put the butter in a baking sheet and place it in the oven to melt the butter. Pour the batter into the baking sheet and bake the pancake in the center of the oven for about 30 minutes.
4. Cut the oven pancake into squares and serve with any of the above toppings.

Sweets & Treats

Evacuate the TV Studio!

I'M NOT KNOWN FOR HAVING a "sweet tooth," and I've never really been into cookies and candy. Maybe this is because I've always had easy access to them. If I was craving sugar as a kid, all I had to do was to walk into Manager Kerstin's refrigerator at Ramlösa Tavern and take my fill, which quickly took all the fun out of it.

Most of the time, simple things are the best. When I was young, I preferred Grandma's rosehip soup with a dollop of whipped cream and crushed cardamom cookies on top. Just mentioning that treat is enough to give me a craving for it! Or her everyday dessert "lingonberries with milk" served in a tall glass to be scooped up with a spoon.

When it comes to more sophisticated sweets, it's important to take your time and keep your tongue in your mouth—no nibbling! It is worth test-baking a cake a few times to get really familiar with the recipe. And never bake if you're stressed, because that's a recipe for disaster.

One time, I was preparing a surprise party for my colleague and editor Martin Sundborn during my "Food" days with Tomas Tengby. I was at the old TV station in Gothenburg, which was nicknamed "The Mirage." (To be honest, I never really understood the name. That the police station called "The Baton House" was more understandable to me.) Anyway, the TV station wasn't exactly housed in a pretty building. It looked like your typical large, public building and was very far removed from any of the glamour you might associate with TV. But I loved the TV station house and the people who worked there. There was

soft clatter of Birkenstocks in the hallways and celebrities standing in every corner. Most of my job before taping was to test dishes that we would prepare during the program, and I had an inconspicuous little kitchen in the basement to work

in. That was where I was preparing my surprise for Martin. I had just turned on the stove to caramelize the sugar and was standing there stirring, waiting for it to melt. Just then, someone knocked on the door, and outside was a cluster of twenty school children, all staring at me as if they had seen a ghost. I could just imagine what they were thinking: "Is THAT Food-Tina?" "Is that really her?" "She is so tall!" "How can she fit into my TV?" "I have to tell Daddy—she's his favorite chef!"

Then, one of the teachers asked, "Do you mind if we take a picture of you and the kids?"

"Of course not," I said.

And with that, I completely forgot the pot on the stove! Of course, it took some time for the kids to loosen up and for us to finally get one good shot. Slightly stressed, I said goodbye and ran back into the kitchen, where the caramel had passed through every stage of melted sugar and was now black and as molten as lava from an Icelandic volcano. The fire alarm was sounding at full volume, and to shut it off, I jumped up and smashed it into the floor—just as if I was at home.

Well, I had to start all over to make my dessert. When it was finally finished, someone knocked on the door once again. I opened up, assuming it would be Martin. It wasn't. Outside were five firefighters in full gear—with hoses and helmets and everything.

"Didn't you know the whole building has been evacuated? There are 300 people in the parking lot and all the radio signals are out!"

. . . All of this because of some burnt caramel . . . it turned out to be one very expensive dessert. . . .

I think it's important to use real butter and real sugar when baking desserts, as well as real vanilla and high-quality chocolate. Don't be stingy with the ingredients or the calories. If you're going to skimp, don't even bother. Rather, eat less or less often, because dessert is meant to be delicious and they're meant to be *real*! The cream should be *real* cream. The fruit should be *real* fruit. The chocolate cake should be sticky and the carrot cake moist. And they are all meant to look mouthwatering! Here are my favorites of the world of sweets. Cookies, pies, ice cream, desserts, and sweet juices.

299

THINK LIKE TINA

READ THE RECIPES CAREFULLY

Just as when you bake bread, you really have to follow the recipes carefully when baking cookies. The temperature, both of the ingredients and in the oven, are very important—if you're sloppy, you can ruin the whole treat.

DON'T KNEAD THE SHORTCRUST DOUGH

The so-called shortbread-dough and regular short-crust dough should be mixed quickly to avoid creating gluten threads. If a sweet pie-crust collapses in the oven, it's because the dough was worked for too long.

Sprinkle salt on the pound cake!

SALT ENHANCES THE FLAVORS

If you add a little bit of salt (about half a pinch) to the pound cake batter, it will enhance the flavor of the cake.

A FAILED CAKE? NOT AT ALL!

Don't ever throw away an unsuccessful cake! Just spread some whipped cream on top and throw on some berries and lots of powdered sugar.

DON'T MIX THE POUND CAKE BATTER FOR TOO LONG

If you want your pound cake to rise up big and tall, avoid mixing it for too long after adding the flour and baking powder.

300

GLAZED BAKERY BUNS

You probably have a great sweet bun recipe of your grandma's, and to make it even greater, I have a tip from our baker Magnus Johansson. Always glaze the buns with egg immediately *after* they come out of the oven, not *before*, as it says in most recipes. This is what gives the buns a shiny surface, and it keeps the moisture inside the bun longer. Mix one egg with a little bit of water and salt. Glaze the buns right after removing them from the oven. The results will be moist and shiny.

LEFTOVER EGG WHITES?

Egg whites can be frozen. They're great for making meringues (see the lemon meringue pie on page 336 or the ice cream cake on page 356).

DRYING FRESH BERRIES

If you have picked berries and your freezer is already full of them, you can always dry the berries instead. Place them on a baking sheet and bake in the oven at 125–140°F (50–60°C) for about 3 hours. Open the oven door to let the heat out, and leave the tray with the berries inside the oven to dry overnight. Dried berries intensify in flavor and consistency. Frozen berries *cannot* be dried!

BETTER TASTING ICE CREAM

When you freeze ice cream or parfaits that won't be eaten for a while, you should place the plastic wrap directly on the surface of the ice cream or parfait. This prevents that thick, unsavory skin from establishing itself on the surface. The same goes for vanilla sauce and creams.

QUICK DESSERT

Mix store-bought vanilla ice cream with chopped peppermints, chocolate, or nuts. Put in a nice bowl and set it on the table for all to enjoy.

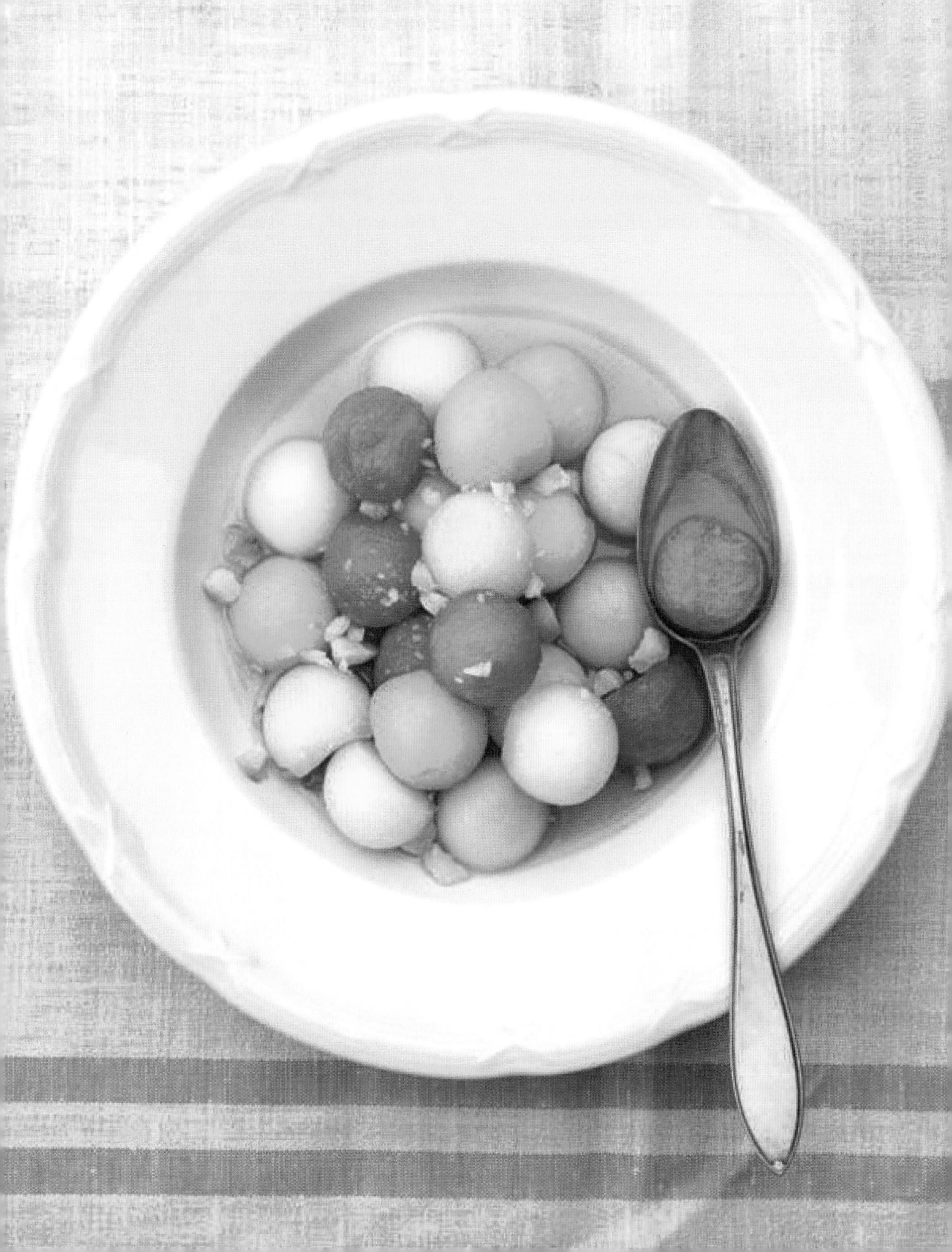

186. Fruit Salad with Spiced Syrup

I love this type of dessert, where you can just empty the fruit bowl and make syrup from the spices you have at home. And if you don't have oranges left, this dessert also is lovely spiced with anise and black pepper.

4 SERVINGS:

SPICED SYRUP:

> ½ cup (100 ml) maple syrup or honey
> ½ cup (100 ml) sugar
> 3½ tbsp (50 ml) water
> 1 tsp ground nutmeg
> 1 tsp anise
> 1 vanilla stick, scored lengthwise
> ¼ tsp salt
> ½ red chili, finely chopped
> ½ lemon, juice

FRUIT SUGGESTIONS:

> 2 bananas
> 3 oranges
> 4 clementines
> 1 pineapple
> 1 pomegranate
> ½ box gooseberries

DIRECTIONS:

1. Bring all ingredients for the syrup to a boil.
2. Cut the fruit into pieces and arrange them on a platter.
3. Remove the vanilla stick and pour the syrup on top of the fruit. Serve right away.

187. Melon Salad with Campari and Macadamia Nuts

The macadamia nut is an Australian hazelnut named after the botanist John Macadam—a fun and useless piece of knowledge if you're ever on Jeopardy! Use whatever type of melon you have on hand. It's completely fine if you only use one variety. This is a simple fruit salad to put on the table after a summer barbecue. Partner it with some Greek yogurt.

4 SERVINGS

> 1 small watermelon
> ½ honeydew
> ½ cantaloupe
> ½ galia melon
> ½ cup (100 ml) roasted and chopped macadamia nuts

CAMPARI MIX:

> ⅔ cup (150 ml) sugar
> 1⅔ cups (400 ml) water
> ½ lime, juice
> ½ cup (150 ml) Campari

FOR SERVING:

> Greek yogurt

DIRECTIONS:

1. Bring sugar, water, and lime juice to a boil. Let simmer for 3–5 minutes. Remove from the burner and let it cool. Add the Campari.
2. Scoop out balls of melon from all melons with a melon baller, or peel the melons and cut them into small pieces. Put the melon balls in the Campari mix. Let rest in the fridge for 2 hours.
3. Sprinkle macadamia nuts on top and serve.

MANGOS AND PEACHES

Mangos and peaches work just as well with the Campari mix. Try it and you'll see!

188. Orange Salad with Dates and Roasted Walnuts

It doesn't have to get any more complicated than this, so don't overdo it when you hear the word dessert. It doesn't have to be a grand affair. I think dessert is more about making an effort for your guests or family. Try this delicious orange salad and discover how you can surprise your guests with only simple ingredients.

4 SERVINGS
6 oranges
1¼ cups (300 ml) roasted walnuts (see page 28)
1 cup (200 ml) cored dates
1¼ cups (300 ml) natural yogurt
⅓ cup (75 ml) maple syrup or honey
freshly ground black pepper

DIRECTIONS:
1. Peel the oranges with a knife and slice them (see photo on next page). Spread them out on a large plate.
2. Coarsely chop the walnuts and dates. Sprinkle them over the oranges and drizzle half of the syrup on top.
3. Scoop the yogurt into a bowl and drizzle the remaining syrup on top.
4. Sprinkle a light helping of freshly ground pepper over both the yogurt and the oranges. Serve together.

189. Vanilla-poached Rhubarb with Mom's Soft-serve Ice Cream

Memorize this recipe! It's important to slice the rhubarb very thin in order for the vanilla syrup to penetrate each nook and make the rhubarb deliciously crispy.

4 SERVINGS
6 rhubarb stalks
VANILLA SYRUP:
1⅔ cups (400 ml) water
1¼ cups (300 ml) sugar
1 cup (200 ml) white wine
1 lemon, zest
1 vanilla stick, scored lengthwise
MOM'S SOFT-SERVE ICE CREAM:
1 pint (½ liter) vanilla ice cream
½ cup (100 ml) heavy cream

DIRECTIONS:
1. Rinse, clean, and cut the rhubarb diagonally as thin as possible. You'll only have to peel them if it's late in the summertime.
2. Bring water, sugar, wine, lemon juice, and vanilla stick to a boil. Let it simmer for 3–5 minutes. If the rhubarb is really sour, you may need to add more sugar. Pour the syrup over the rhubarb. Cover it and let it cool; this will allow the rhubarb to soften.
3. Combine the ice cream and heavy cream and serve right away with the rhubarb.

MAKE A SORBET INSTEAD
You can also put this delicacy in the freezer. Use a fork to loosen the frozen syrup and rhubarb before serving. Serve as a refreshing sorbet during the hot summer months.

189.

190. Mascarpone Gratin Blackberries with Grand Marnier

This dish was created for the TV series *Cook Along*, so you know it's a quick recipe. The secret is in the blackberries. They're supposed to be frozen when they're put in the oven and should be cold in the center when taken out. So, basically, cold berries and a hot oven! If you're having guests over for an elaborate dinner, prepare the cream in advance, since the berries are right there in the freezer. It can't get any quicker than that.

4 SERVINGS
9–11 oz (250–300 g) frozen berries
2 tbsp liqueur of choice, preferably
    Grand Marnier
1 lime, zest and juice
9 oz (250 g) mascarpone cheese
2 egg yolks
1 tsp vanilla sugar
4 leveled tsp of brown sugar

DIRECTIONS:
1. Preheat the oven to 475°F (250°C).
2. Put the frozen blackberries in a bowl and pour the liqueur over them. Add lime zest and juice.
3. Mix the mascarpone cheese, egg yolks, vanilla sugar, and half of the brown sugar.
4. Place the berries in individual serving bowls. Dollop some mascarpone mix onto the berries and sprinkle some brown sugar on top. Bake in the oven for about 5 minutes. The cheese and sugar are meant to bubble a little bit. Serve right away.

191. Raspberry Crumble with Almonds

You can replace the raspberries in this recipe with blackberries or apples. I'm childishly fond of the English word "crumble"—when you hear the Swedish word, you'll know why! Doesn't *crumble* sound so much more delicious than *smulpaj*? No matter what language you speak, this crumble tastes great with whichever berry you choose.

6 SERVINGS
FILLING:
1 lb (500 g) raspberries
2 tbsp sugar
1 tsp cornstarch
1 tsp vanilla sugar
CRUMB TOPPING:
¾ cup + 1½ tbsp (200 ml) flour
1 tsp baking powder
1 cup (250 ml) coarsely chopped almonds
½ cup (100 ml) sugar
5⅓ tbsp (75 g) butter, room temperature

DIRECTIONS:
1. Preheat the oven to 400°F (200°C).
2. Mix raspberries, sugar, cornstarch, and vanilla sugar for the filling. Place it in the bottom of a greased baking pan, 8–10 inches (22–24 cm) in diameter.
3. Combine all dry ingredients for the crumb topping, and use your fingers to mix it all together with the butter. Sprinkle the crumbs over the raspberries and bake in the oven for about 35 minutes, until the crumble has turned golden brown.
4. Serve with Mom's soft-serve ice cream (see page 305) or dessert cream (see page 322).

DELICIOUS WITH LIME

If you're using blueberries or blackberries, squeeze half of a lime over them for an out of this world taste.

192. Crème Brûlée with Warm Cloudberries

Everyone should taste crème brûlée at least once in their life. My husband and I served crème brûlée as our wedding dessert, but we used different berries. A neat little blow torch makes caramelizing it easier, but you can also bake it on broil with the oven door open. The secret to a really successful crème brûlée is that it must have a hot and hard surface with a cool interior. If you can't find cloudberries, try raspberries, blackberries, or even update some cloudberry jam from IKEA.

4 SERVINGS

   1⅔ cups (400 ml) heavy cream
   ½ cup (100 ml) milk
   1 vanilla stick, scored lengthwise
   5 egg yolks
   ½ cup (100 ml) sugar
   2 tbsp raw sugar

WARM CLOUDBERRIES:

   9 oz (250 g) cloudberries
   1 tbsp sugar
   2 tbsp liqueur, preferably Licor 43

DIRECTIONS:

1. Preheat the oven to 225°F (110°C).
2. Bring heavy cream, milk, and vanilla stick to a boil. Stir the egg yolks and sugar together—but don't whisk! Pour the cream mixture over the egg mixture and stir gently until the sugar has melted. Remove the vanilla stick and pour the batter into four individual ramekins.
3. Place the ramekins in a hot water bath in a baking tray (the water should reach about halfway up the ramekins) and bake for about 45 minutes to 1 hour until the surface of the brûlée has just solidified. Cool the crème brûlée in the fridge.
4. Heat up the cloudberries in a pot on the stove and carefully stir in the sugar and liqueur.
5. Sprinkle the raw sugar on top of the crème brûlée and burn the sugar with a blow torch or broil in the oven until the sugar has melted. Watch this step carefully!
6. Serve the crème brûlée with the warm cloudberries.

FLAVOR THE CRÈME BRÛLÉE

You can always try flavoring the crème brûlée. Substitute the vanilla with, for example, 1 tbsp lavender, 1 tbsp cacao, or ¼ tsp ground cardamom. It also tastes wonderful with ½ tsp lemon or orange zest or ½ cup (100 ml) blueberries or fresh raspberries.

193. Sweet Oven Pancake with Strawberries

This was a bit of an experiment gone right. And for all of you who like Austrian *Kaiserschmarrn*, you will dance with joy at your very first bite. Totally, absolutely, super-delicious! Any kind of berry will work with this masterpiece.

4–6 SERVINGS

5 eggs
4 tbsp sugar
1 cup (250 ml) flour
3 cups (700 ml) milk
2 tbsp (30 g) butter

FOR SERVING:

fresh strawberries
whipped cream

DIRECTIONS:

1. Preheat the oven to 425°F (225°C).
2. Divide the eggs into whites and yolks. Whisk the egg whites and the sugar into a stiff foam.
3. Mix the flour with half of the milk and all of the egg yolks. Whisk until the batter is smooth. Add the rest of the milk and then fold the egg white foam into the batter.
4. Put the butter on a baking sheet and place it in the oven until the butter has melted. Pour the batter into the baking sheet and bake the pancake in the center of the oven for about 25–30 minutes.
5. Serve with fresh strawberries and whipped cream. To make it extra special, sift powdered sugar on top.

194. Warm Cinnamon Apples with Digestive Biscuit Stuffing

An apple pie within an apple. Everything can be substituted, if need be. Use Marie tea biscuits instead of Digestive biscuits, or even chocolate cookies if you're so inclined. Shred some lemon zest into the butter, or dare to omit the cinnamon and use ground fennel and anise instead. But before you start experimenting, get familiar with this recipe. . . .

4 SERVINGS

8 apples, preferably Macoun
8 crumbled Digestive cookies
½ cup (100 ml) finely chopped hazelnuts
1 stick + 2½ tbsp (150 g) butter, room temperature
3 tbsp ground cinnamon
8 cinnamon sticks
maple syrup or honey

VANILLA SAUCE:

See recipe on page 318

DIRECTIONS:

1. Preheat the oven to 350°F (180°C).
2. Core the apples and slice off the tops. Place the apples in a baking pan.
3. Mix the cookie crumbs and hazelnuts with the butter, sugar, and cinnamon. Press the mixture into the opening in the apple that was left after coring, and place the "lid" on top. Push a cinnamon stick into each apple and drizzle some syrup on top. Bake in the oven for 20–30 minutes, until the apples have turned soft.
4. Serve the apples with vanilla sauce.

195. Apple Compote with Amaretti and Creamy Milk

This simple dish has a delicate edge to it, all because of the vanilla in the compote and the Amaretti macaroon. The apple compote is incredibly delicious! Serve it warm in a large bowl, with plenty of crushed Amaretti on top. If you're in a hurry you can substitute Amaretti for ready-made almond biscuits. They're not exactly the same thing, but it will do just fine.

4 SERVINGS

APPLE COMPOTE:

6 firm apples

1 vanilla stick, scored lengthwise

3½ tbsp water

½ lemon, juice

3½ tbsp sugar

4 tbsp honey

CREAMY MILK:

½ cup (100 ml) heavy cream

½ cup (100 ml) milk

1 tsp powdered sugar

AMARETTI:

1 oz (30 g) bitter almonds

6 oz (170 g) sweet almonds

2½ cups (600 ml) sugar

5 egg whites

1¼ cups (300 ml) powdered sugar

DIRECTIONS:

1. Grind the almonds for the Amaretti or run them in the food processor (or buy almond flour). Mix the ground almonds (or almond flour) with the sugar and egg whites. Dollop tablespoon-sized cookies onto a baking sheet lined with parchment paper. Let the surface of the cookies dry for about 24 hours at room temperature.

2. Preheat the oven to 475°F (250°C).

3. Using three fingers, pinch each cookie into points. Place the baking sheet in the oven and reduce the heat to 425°F (225°C). Bake the cookies for about 7 minutes until they are golden brown and their edges are dried out. Remove a cookie and put it on a cold surface; if it stiffens, it's ready and it's time to remove the baking sheet from the oven. Let the cookies cool on a cooling rack.

4. Peel and core the apples for the compote. Split each apple into 8 wedges. Simmer the apples, vanilla stick, water, lemon juice, sugar, and the honey in a covered pot for about 10 minutes, until it turns into a coarse compote.

5. Serve the compote warm or cold with some creamy milk and Amaretti.

AMARETTI GO WITH EVERYTHING

Amaretti macaroons will last for a long time if they're stored in a dry place. They actually complement most desserts quiet nicely.

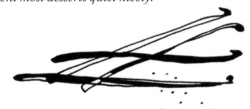

195.

196. Southern Swedish Apple Cake with Vanilla Sauce

This is a typical Southern Swedish apple cake, and it's simply delicious. I associate this dessert with black soup and goose. The texture of the cake is a bit different from most apple cakes, so you should really try it to understand just how unique it is! Try the apple cake with some dessert cream (see page 322).

4 SERVINGS

1 loaf dark rye bread (approx. 1 lb [500 g])
1 stick + 2½ tbsp (150 g) butter
¾ cup (200 ml) sugar
½ tbsp ground ginger
½ tbsp ground cinnamon
½ tbsp ground anise
½ tsp ground cardamom

APPLE PUREE:

10 apples (approx. 3 lbs [1½ kg])
1 cup (200 ml) sugar
1 lemon, zest and juice

VANILLA SAUCE:

1⅔ cups (400 ml) milk
½ vanilla stick, scored lengthwise with seeds removed
3 egg yolks
1½ tbsp sugar
2 tsp cornstarch
¾ cup (200 ml) whipped cream

DIRECTIONS:

1. Bring the milk and the vanilla stick to a boil and let simmer for 3–4 minutes. Set aside to rest for 10 minutes.
2. Whisk the egg yolks with sugar and cornstarch. Add the vanilla milk and stir. Pour the mixture back into the pot and simmer at low heat until the sauce has thickened. Let it cool in a cold water bath while stirring. Remove the vanilla stick. Keep the sauce chilled in the fridge until ready to serve.
3. Preheat the oven to 350°F (175°C).
4. Remove the crust from the rye bread and cut the bread into pieces. Grind them into crumbs in a food processor or by hand with a grater. Melt the butter in a large frying pan. Fry the bread crumbs, sugar, and all the spices over low heat for about 10 minutes.
5. Core the apples and cut them into pieces. Melt the butter in a pot. Add the apple pieces and stir until they turn into a coarse purée. Season with lemon zest and juice.
6. Line the bottom of a pie dish with half of the bread crumbs and press them lightly. Fill the dish with the apple purée and cover with the rest of the bread crumbs. Bake in the oven for 15 minutes.
7. Fold the whipped cream into the vanilla sauce and serve the apple cake.

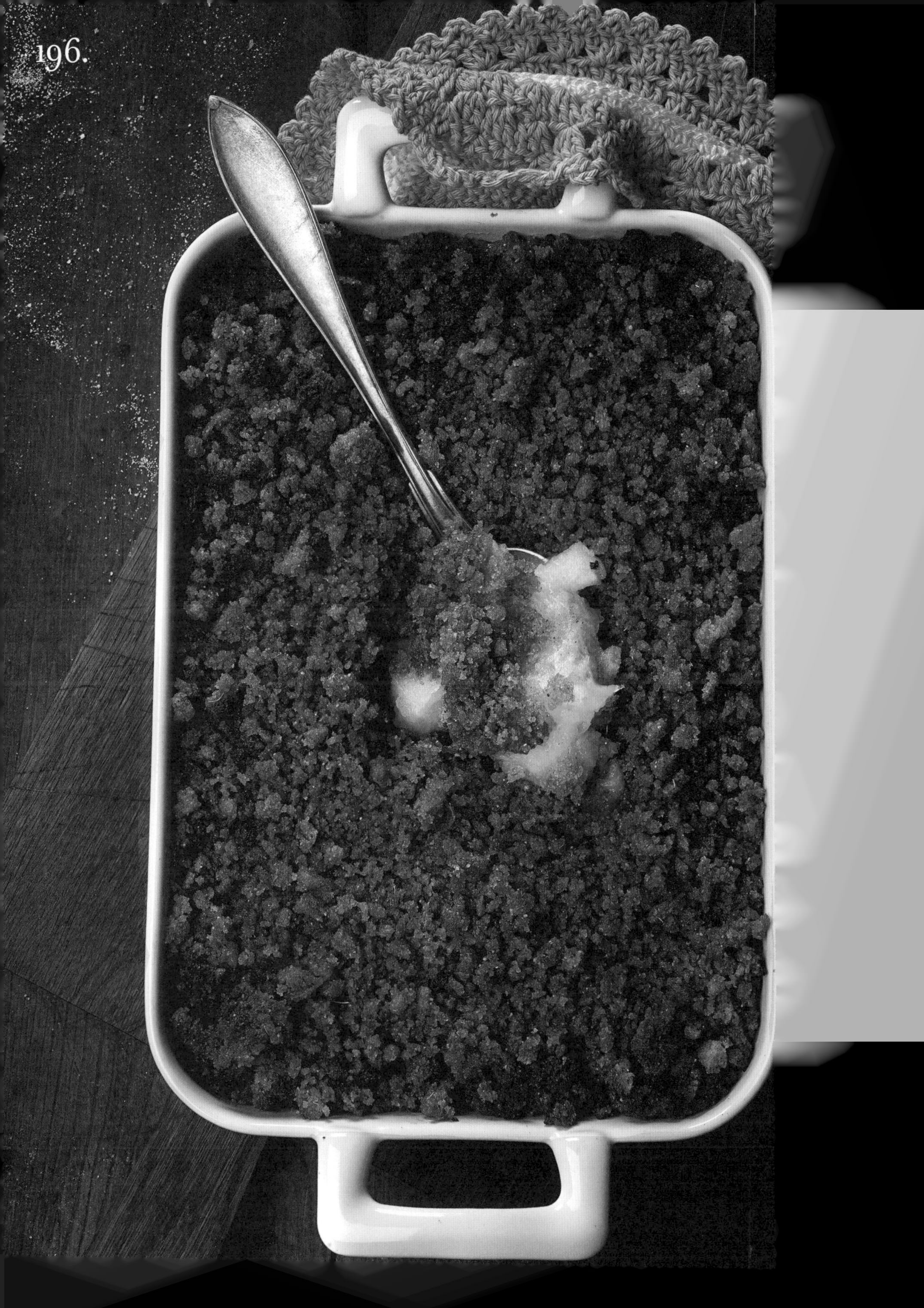

198.

197. Tarte Tatin

This dessert ended up costing Swedish Television quite a bit of money. . . . In one of my programs, I had recommended that the viewers place plastic wrap on the stove for easy clean-up if any caramelized sugar bubbled over. And although this does work for old-fashioned stoves with four burners, it evidently does not work on modern ceramic glass stovetops. The plastic wrap burns straight onto the stovetop! If only you could know how many viewers complained that they had plastic wrap fused to their new stoves! One or two stoves had to be replaced by Swedish Television, just because of my directions to the audience.

4 SERVINGS
    4 firm apples
    7 tbsp (100 g) butter, at room temperature
    1 cup (250 ml) sugar
    ½ lemon, juice
    2 frozen puff pastry sheets
FOR SERVING:
    Mom's soft-serve ice cream (see page 305)

DIRECTIONS:
1. Preheat the oven to 425°F (225°C).
2. Peel, core, and divide the apples.
3. Grease a cast iron pan. Sprinkle some sugar over it and put the apple halves round-side down into the pan. Squeeze the lemon juice on top.
4. Roll out the puff pastry and place half of a pastry sheet on top of each apple. Fold the edges under the apples. Put the cast iron pan in the oven and let it bake for 10–15 minutes, until the puff pastry turns golden brown. Let the apples cool down.
5. Place a large plate on top of the pan and flip the pan over so the tarts loosen from the pan and fall onto the plate. Sprinkle with powdered sugar just before serving.
6. Serve with Mom's ice cream.

198. Mint and Black Pepper Pickled Pears with Dessert Cream

Using preground black pepper versus grinding it yourself in a pepper mill is like night and day. This dessert cream is one of my favorite creams; I learned to make it during my days at restaurant Restaurationen in Copenhagen. It's a wonderful complement to any dessert, apple pie, or even fresh strawberries in the summertime. Make a jar and give it away as a present!

6–8 SERVINGS
    6 large pears
    water + ½ lemon, juice
MINT AND BLACK PEPPER SYRUP:
    ¾ cup (200 ml) sugar
    ¾ cup (200 ml) water
    2 limes, zest and juice
    1¾ oz (50 g) fresh mint (1 bunch)
    1 tsp freshly ground black pepper, coarsely ground
DESSERT CREAM:
    3 egg yolks
    3½ tbsp sugar
    ½ tsp vanilla sugar
    1 cup (250 ml) whipped cream

DIRECTIONS:
1. Peel the pears, but leave the stem on. Put the pears in a bowl with cold water and some lemon juice, so they don't brown. Bring all the ingredients for the syrup to a boil and add the pears. Let simmer for about 15 minutes or until the pears are soft all the way through. Let the pears cool down in the syrup.
2. Whisk the egg yolks, sugar, and vanilla sugar for the dessert cream. Add the whipped cream. The dessert cream will last for 3–4 days in the fridge.
3. Serve the pears with a little bit of the syrup and the dessert cream.

199. Spiced Pickled Pears

A flashback from the '70s. . . . The pears can be eaten either hot or cold. If you want to serve them hot, heat some of the stock and add a dollop of butter to it. Place a pear in the middle of a plate and pour the buttery stock on top.

4–6 SERVINGS
10–15 small pears
water + ½ lemon, juice
SPICED STOCK:
4 cups (1 liter) orange juice
¾ cup (200 ml) honey
½ cup (100 ml) sugar
2 cinnamon sticks
1 tbsp fennel seeds
1 tbsp whole cardamom
1 vanilla stick, scored lengthwise
8 cloves
4 star anise
½ orange, zest

DIRECTIONS:
1. Peel the pears, but leave the stem. Place the pears in a bowl of water and squeeze in some lemon juice to prevent them from browning.
2. Bring orange juice, honey, sugar, and all spices including the vanilla stick to a boil. Add the pears and cover them with parchment paper to prevent them from floating up and browning. Let simmer for 15 minutes. The cooking time might vary depending on what type of pear you use so check with a knife to see if they are soft. Place the pot somewhere cold and let the pears cool under a closed lid.
3. Pour the pears and stock into clean glass jars and store in the fridge.
4. Serve the pears with ice cream or whipped cream. Or use the dessert cream from the previous recipe.

200. Pear Flambé with After Eight

So delicious and so contemporary. The warm pear is remarkable contrasted with the chilled, shredded pear. The liquor is important for the flambé. If you don't have any at home, ask a neighbor. You only need a small amount. In exchange for 3½ tbsp of the liqueur, offer your neighbors a dinner at your house.

4 SERVINGS
6 pears
7 tbsp (100 g) butter
3 tbsp sugar
½ lemon, juice
3½ tbsp Xanté (pear cognac)
8 After Eight mints

DIRECTIONS:
1. Put two of the pears directly in the fridge; they will be used later. Peel the other four. Divide the peeled pears lengthwise, core and all.
2. Melt the butter and sugar in a frying pan and caramelize. Place the pears into the pan, core-side down. Squeeze the lemon juice on top. Put a lid on the pan and let it simmer over low heat for about 7 minutes. The pears should be soft by now, and will be lying in a cloudy, buttery, fudgy stock.
3. Add the pear cognac and light it up with a match. Let the flames burn out. You can add a little bit more cognac if you like.
4. Place the pears into four bowls. Place one After Eight onto each pear half and pour the sauce over them. Shred the frozen pears on top for garnish.

201. Apricot Compote with Maple Syrup Biscuits

If you like this recipe, you're bound to love the apple compote with Amaretti recipe on page 315. These maple syrup biscuits have a nutty flavor, and they're simply divine!

4 SERVINGS

APRICOT COMPOTE:

   10½ oz (300 g) fresh apricots, cored or dried apricots

   ¾ cup (200 ml) white wine

   ⅓ cup (75 ml) sugar

   ½ cup (100 ml) water

   ½ vanilla stick

   ½ lemon, zest and juice

CREAMY MILK:

   ½ cup (100 ml) heavy cream + 1/2 cup (100 ml) milk

   1 tsp powdered sugar

MAPLE SYRUP BISCUITS:

   3½ tbsp (50 g) butter

   ½ cup (100 ml) maple syrup

   3½ tbsp flour

   1 tbsp powdered sugar

   1 egg white

DIRECTIONS:

1. Bring all ingredients for the compote to a boil in a covered pot and let simmer for 5 minutes. Remove the lid and let simmer for another 5 minutes until it has turned into a chunky compote.
2. Preheat the oven to 350°F (180°C).
3. Melt the butter for the biscuits and set aside. Mix all the other biscuit ingredients together and add the butter. Dollop teaspoon-sized biscuits onto a baking sheet lined with parchment paper and use the back of a spoon to spread them out until they are flat and round. Bake the biscuits for 5–6 minutes.
4. Heat up the creamy milk carefully in a saucepan. Serve the compote with the biscuits and the warm creamy milk.

202. Warm Pineapple with Chili and Lime Cream

Melting sugar in stages means adding a little bit at a time—when some of the sugar has melted, add some more. Do not stir the sugar, but rather shake the pan to prevent the sugar from lumping. If this does happen, you can either sift them out or cook a little longer and see if they melt that way. It's a great dessert for a large party, as it looks great and is easy to prepare. Hot, cold, or warm: it looks good no matter how you serve it.

4 SERVINGS

   1 fresh pineapple

   1⅔ cups (400 ml) sugar

   1 cup (250 ml) water

   1 red chili

   1 vanilla stick, scored lengthwise

   1 lemon, juice

LIME CREAM:

   ½ cup (100 ml) sour cream

   ½ cup (100 ml) mascarpone cheese

   1 tbsp powdered sugar

   1 lime, zest and juice

DIRECTIONS:

1. Peel and cut the pineapple into wedges. Remove the core.
2. Melt the sugar in stages in a pot over low heat. Add the water, a little bit at a time while whisking, until it has turned into a light caramel mixture.
3. Core the chili and remove the white walls inside. Finely chop or cut it into thin strips. Add the pineapple, chili, and vanilla stick to the stock. Add the freshly squeezed lemon juice and let simmer over low heat for 10–15 minutes.
4. Mix the ingredients for the lime cream. Serve the pineapple with the stock and the lime cream.

201. 202.
203. 204.

203. Nutella Mousse with Mango and Coconut Soup

The mousse takes center stage in this dish. I've served it a number of times with raspberry baked rhubarb or with ice cream with sliced strawberries and whipped cream on top.

4 SERVINGS

NUTELLA MOUSSE:

   1¼ cups (300 ml) heavy cream
   ½ cup (100 ml) Nutella

COCONUT SOUP:

   1 can coconut milk (approx. 14 oz [400 g])
   1¼ cups (300 ml) powdered sugar
   1 lime, zest and juice

FOR SERVING:

   fresh mango slices
   freshly ground black pepper

DIRECTIONS:

1. Heat 3½ tbsp of heavy cream in a pot and mix it with the Nutella until the mixture is smooth. Whip the rest of the heavy cream and then fold the Nutella mixture into it. Place the mousse in the fridge and let it rest for at least 4 hours.
2. Heat up the coconut milk and stir in the sugar and lime zest. Add some lime juice and let it cool.
3. Whisk the mousse lightly with a balloon whisk right before serving. Serve with sliced mango and the cool coconut soup topped off with a sprinkling of freshly ground black pepper.

204. Grape Salad with White Chocolate Mousse

Easy peasy! White chocolate mousse and grape salad with a hint of high-quality olive oil—done deal! And of course, you can serve the mousse with any other fruit you like.

4 SERVINGS

WHITE CHOCOLATE MOUSSE:

   ¾ cup (200 ml) heavy cream
   3½ oz (100 g) white chocolate

GRAPE SALAD:

   1¼ cups (300 ml) grapes
   1 lime, zest and juice
   1 tbsp high-quality olive oil, preferably a peppery variety

DIRECTIONS:

1. Heat up the heavy cream in a pot. Coarsely chop the chocolate and melt in the heavy cream. Remove from the heat and let it cool. Cover the surface with plastic wrap and let the mousse rest in the fridge until it's thoroughly chilled; ideally, let it chill overnight.
2. Cut the grapes in half and remove any seeds. Place the grapes in a pot and add lime zest, lime juice, and olive oil. Cover with a lid and bring to a boil. Let simmer for 2 minutes. Place the grape salad in the fridge until it has cooled.
3. Whisk the mousse lightly with a balloon whisk until it is really fluffy and serve it with the grape salad.

205. Raspberry Mousse À La Napoleon

There are only two reasons I go to the bakery:– for the Napoleons and the Semla, Swedish buns stuffed with whipped cream and almond paste. This raspberry mousse isn't too sweet, and it's also quite delicious with dessert cream (see page 322) and some roasted hazelnuts on top.

4 SERVINGS
RASPBERRY MOUSSE:
1 lb (500 g) frozen raspberries, thawed
½ cup (100 ml) powdered sugar
2 gelatin sheets
1¼ cups (300 ml) heavy cream
CARAMELIZED PUFF PASTRY:
2 puff pastry sheets
1–2 tbsp powdered sugar per puff pastry sheet (optional)

DIRECTIONS:
1. Puree the raspberries and the powdered sugar. Sift away any seeds.
2. Place the gelatin sheets in water for about 5 minutes.
3. Heat ½ cup (100 ml) of the raspberry mixture in a pot, but do not let it boil. Squeeze the gelatin sheets and add them to the mixture. Stir until they dissolve. Mix the "raspberry gel" with the rest of the raspberry purée.
4. Whip the heavy cream and mix with a third of the raspberry creation. Mix in the rest of the whipped cream and stir until smooth. Let the mixture rest in the fridge until ready to serve. Preheat the oven to 400°F (200°C).
5. Sprinkle the powdered sugar over the puff pastry; let the dough absorb the sugar as you roll it out. Place the puff pastry sheets onto a baking sheet lined with parchment paper. Cover the puff pastry with another piece of parchment paper and place another baking sheet on top to press it all down. Stick all this in the oven and bake for about 15 minutes. Cut the puff pastry into individual rectangles and bake for another couple of minutes, until they are golden brown. Let them cool.
6. Spoon the raspberry mousse onto half of the puff pastry sheets and use the other half as lids. Sprinkle some powdered sugar on top and garnish with raspberries.

206. Dark Chocolate Mousse with Berry Soup

A quick recipe! But be careful not to make the portions too large—it's a heavy dessert. It's better to feel like you want more than to be begging, "please make this stop!"

4 SERVINGS
DARK CHOCOLATE MOUSSE:
4½ oz (125 g) dark chocolate (70%)
2 egg yolks
1 cup (250 ml) whipped cream
BERRY SOUP:
¾ cup (200 ml) water
½ cup (100 ml) sugar
2 star anise
½ vanilla stick, scored lengthwise
½ cup (100 ml) white wine
½ cup (100 ml) frozen raspberries
approx. 4½ oz (125 g) fresh, mixed red berries

DIRECTIONS:
1. Melt the chocolate over a water bath or in the microwave and let it cool down a little. Add the egg yolks and then fold in the whipped cream. Let it rest in a cool place for at least 4 hours.
2. Bring water, sugar, star anise, vanilla stick, wine, and frozen berries for the berry soup to a boil. Sift the soup. Put the mixed berries in a bowl and pour the soup over it. Let it cool.
3. Serve the berry soup in a bowl with the chocolate mousse.

206.

207. Apple Compote and Cognac Cream with Chocolate and Ginger Mousse

This dessert needs a bit of time to prepare. The walnuts and the crispy rice puffs should be made the day they are to be served, otherwise they go stale. The last time I made this dish, my colleague Benny and I got all dressed up. I found my old graduation dress, and Benny put on his aged tuxedo (although he had to suck in his gut to wear it!).

4 SERVINGS
CHOCOLATE MOUSSE:
3½ tbsp heavy cream
1 tsp shredded fresh ginger
1 tsp lemon zest
5⅔ oz (160 g) milk chocolate
1½ tbsp (20 g) butter
2 egg yolks
3 egg whites
1 tbsp sugar

COGNAC CREAM:
⅔ cup (150 ml) whipped cream
½ lemon, zest
1 tbsp cognac

WALNUTS AND CRISPY RICE PUFFS:
½ cup (100 ml) walnuts
1 tbsp powdered sugar
½ cup (100 ml) puffed rice

APPLE COMPOTE:
4 small apples, peeled and cut into small pieces
½ lemon, juice
½ vanilla stick
½ tbsp sugar

DIRECTIONS:

1. In a pot, heat up the heavy cream for the mousse with the ginger and the lemon zest. Do not let it boil. Chop the chocolate into pieces and melt it in a bowl over a water bath or carefully in the microwave. Remove the chocolate from the heat and stir in the butter, heated cream mixture, and then the egg yolks.

2. Whisk the egg whites with the sugar. Fold half of it into the chocolate mixture until it turns into a smooth cream. Let it rest in the fridge for at least 4 hours.

3. Put all ingredients for the apple compote in a pot and let it boil under a closed lid for about 5 minutes. Let it cool and put it in the fridge until ready to serve.

4. Mix the ingredients for the cognac cream and refrigerate.

5. Roast the walnuts in a frying pan. Add the puffed rice and sprinkle the sugar on top. Let it all caramelize. Spread the mixture on a piece of parchment paper to cool.

6. Layer the various components in tall glasses or out onto plates. Top with some extra walnuts and puffed rice.

208. Lemon Meringue Pie

I would always choose this pie for my birthday dessert when I was a child. I'll never forget the time my mother was supposed to bring the pies to my grandparents' house where we were having my birthday party. Our dog, Hamilton, got so excited when he saw me that he jumped up and put a paw in each pie. Of course, we still ate the pies—it was only our dog's paws after all!

Take your time to make the warm whipped meringue. It holds longer and doesn't release any moisture. Keep in mind to mix the short crust quickly. This prevents any gluten strands from forming and making the pie crust bread-like, which will happen if you work it for too long a period of time.

10–12 PIECES
SHORTCRUST:
4½ oz (125 g) almond paste
¼ tsp salt
1 stick + 1 tbsp (125 g) butter
1 egg
1½ cups (350 ml) flour
LEMON CURD:
See recipe on page 272
WARM WHIPPED MERINGUE:
4 egg whites (approx. 5⅓ oz [150 g])
1 cup (250 ml) sugar
½ lemon, zest

DIRECTIONS:
1. Make sure all ingredients are at room temperature. Mix the almond paste and salt in a food processor until the paste is really smooth (you can also mix it by hand). Add the butter in small pieces. Add the egg and, lastly, the flour. Make sure not to overwork the dough after adding the flour. Roll the dough in plastic wrap and let it rest in the fridge for about 2 hours.

2. Roll out the dough between floured sheets of plastic wrap. It's meant to be about an inch (2 cm) larger than the pie pan. Place the crust on top of the pan and press down gently. If the pie crust hangs over the edges, it will not sink down properly when it is baking. Cut off the edges and let the pie crust rest in the freezer for about 10 minutes.

3. Preheat the oven to 400°F (200°C).

4. Remove the pie crust from the freezer and prick it with a fork a few times before putting it in the oven. Reduce the temperature to 350°F (180°C) and bake the pie crust until it has some color, about 8–10 minutes.

5. In a small pot, bring the water for the water bath to a boil. Place a small bowl that can handle the heat into the water and add the egg white, sugar, and lemon zest. Whisk until the sugar has melted. The meringue should not be lumpy (feel it with your fingers). Remove the bowl from the water and whisk with a hand mixer until the meringue is firm. Put the meringue in the freezer while you prepare the pie—because it contains so much sugar, it will not freeze.

6. Set the oven to broil (525°F [275°C]).

7. Dollop the lemon curd into the pie crust and top it off with the meringue. Put the pie on the top oven rack and keep the oven door open. Burn the meringue until it has a nice color. This will take a few minutes.

209.

209. Soft Meringue with Cake Filling and Mojito Berries

I am childishly excited by the Sweden's Budapest cake, and this is my version of my goofy favorite. You can serve this cake with the lemon curd on page 272 or with just some whipped cream.

6 SERVINGS

> 6 egg whites
> 1¼ cups (300 ml) sugar
> ¾ cup (200 ml) puffed rice
> melted butter for glazing
> ¾ cup (200 ml) coconut flakes

CAKE FILLING:

> 10 egg yolks
> 5 tbsp cornstarch
> 2 cups (500 ml) milk
> 2 cups (500 ml) half and half
> ½ cup (125 ml) sugar
> 1 handful fresh mint leaves

MOJITO BERRIES:

> 8 cups (2 liters) fresh strawberries, cleaned and
>   cut into halves
> 1 box raspberries (approx. 4½ oz [125 g])
> 1 box blackberries (approx. 4½ oz [125 g])
> 1 box red currants (approx. 3½ oz [100 g])
> 1 lime, zest and juice
> dark rum to taste
> 1 handful fresh mint leaves

FOR GARNISH:

> berries and mint leaves

DIRECTIONS:

1. Preheat the oven to 275°F (130°C).
2. Whisk the egg whites and sugar into a fluffy mixture. Fold in the puffed rice.
3. Place a piece of parchment paper on a baking sheet and grease it with butter. Spread the meringue onto the baking sheet and sprinkle plenty of coconut flakes on top. Bake in the oven for about 45 minutes.
4. Remove the meringue from the oven and turn it upside-down onto a new sheet of parchment paper.
5. Mix the berries in a bowl with the lime juice, rum, chopped mint leaves, and lime zest. Let it marinate for about 10–15 minutes.
6. Mix egg yolks, cornstarch, and ½ cup (100 ml) milk in a bowl. Bring the rest of the milk, half and half, sugar, and mint leaves to a boil. Pour the hot mint syrup over the egg mixture and whisk it together.
7. Gently heat up the cream in a pot while stirring constantly, until it thickens and turns smooth. Remove the pot from the burner. Pour the cream into a new bowl and refrigerate. If you want a lighter filling, add some whipped cream when serving.
8. Spread a thick layer of filling onto the meringue and top with the berries. Carefully roll up the meringue and garnish with berries and mint leaves.

210. Carrot Cake with Cardamom and Walnuts

A tried and true recipe. The spices set the tone for the cake, and the oil makes the cake really moist. Follow the recipe to the letter, and I promise it will turn out incredible!

APPROX. 12 SLICES

3 eggs
1½ cups (350 ml) sugar
⅔ cup (150 ml) coarsely chopped walnuts
½ tsp salt
1½ tsp ground cardamom
1 tbsp ground cinnamon
1⅔ cups (400 ml) wheat flour
1½ tsp baking soda
1½ tsp baking powder
1⅔ cups (400 ml) shredded carrots
1 cup (250 ml) neutral oil
butter for greasing the pan

TOPPING:

¾ cup (200 ml) powdered sugar
2 sticks (200 g) butter, melted and cooled
7 oz (200 g) cream cheese
3 tsp vanilla sugar
1 lemon, zest and juice

FOR GARNISH:

10 small, delicate carrots
½ cup (100 ml) orange juice
3 passion fruits, halved and hollowed
2 tbsp sugar

DIRECTIONS:

1. Preheat the oven to 400°F (200°C).
2. Whisk eggs and sugar into a fluffy mixture. Add walnuts, salt, cardamom, cinnamon, and the flour mixed with the baking soda and baking powder. Mix everything together. Add the carrots and oil.
3. Pour the batter into a greased cake pan with a removable bottom. Bake the cake in the oven for about 30–40 minutes until it releases from the edges. Make sure that it is cooked all the way through by inserting a toothpick or knife into the cake. Let it cool.
4. Mix the powdered sugar, melted butter, and cream cheese into a cream. Add the vanilla sugar and the lemon zest and juice. Continue to mix and then spread the cream out on top of the cake. Let the cream settle before serving.
5. Boil the carrots with the orange juice, passion fruit, and sugar in a pot until the carrots are soft. It will take about 4–5 minutes over medium heat. Let them cool.
6. Garnish with the carrots and passion fruit as pictured.

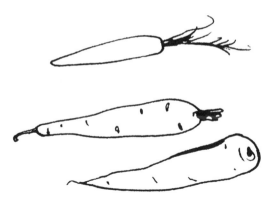

211. Chocolate and Soft Whey Butter Cake

These next two cake recipes are perfect to prepare in an empty milk carton.

10–12 SERVINGS

9 oz (250 g) dark chocolate, in pieces
7 tbsp (100 g) butter
½ cup (100 ml) soft whey butter
½ cup (125 ml) honey
4 eggs at room temperature
1¼ cups (300 ml) almond biscuits
6 Digestive biscuits
1 empty milk carton

DIRECTIONS:

1. Melt the chocolate, butter, soft whey butter, and honey in a bowl that can withstand the heat of a water bath. Let it cool a little.
2. Separate the egg yolks from the egg whites. Break the egg yolks in a bowl and in a separate bowl, whisk the egg whites into a foam. Stir the egg yolks into the chocolate mixture, and then stir in the egg white foam.
3. Crush the almond biscuits and Digestive biscuits. Wash the milk carton thoroughly and cut off the front panel so the carton resembles a loaf pan. Spread down a layer of the cookie crumbs and then cover with a layer of the chocolate mix. Alternate between cookie crumbs and chocolate mix until the carton has been filled up. Let it rest in the fridge for 24 hours. Slice and serve.

EGGS AT ROOM TEMPERATURE

It's important that the eggs are at room temperature before adding them to the warm chocolate mixture. Otherwise the batter will clump.

212. Radio Cake

They say a beloved child has many names, and this one is also known as "cookie cake" or "cellar cake." The radio cake has a ganache-like feel to it. I made this recipe with Tomas Tengby for a Christmas show one year—not for a radio program, but for TV. He absolutely loved it and I know you will too. The cake will keep for a long time. If you cut it into petit fours, you can have a piece with your coffee for each of the twelve days of Christmas.

10–12 SERVINGS

¾ cup (200 ml) almond flakes
½ cup (100 ml) sugar
1⅓ lbs (600 g) dark chocolate
1¼ cups (300 ml) heavy cream
5½ tbsp (75 g) butter

DIRECTIONS:

1. Roast the almond flakes in a dry frying pan. Add the sugar and let it caramelize, fusing the almond flakes together into a hard paste. Spread the almond paste out onto a baking sheet and when it has cooled, crush it coarsely.
2. Chop the chocolate and put it in a bowl. Bring the heavy cream to a boil and pour over the chocolate. Add the butter while stirring to create a smooth chocolate cream.
3. Line a loaf pan with plastic wrap. Then, layer the chocolate cream with the almond paste alternately until the pan is full. Refrigerate for 24 hours.
4. Cut it into slices or small cubes and serve as petit fours with coffee.

211.

212.

213. Date Cake with Warm Muscovado Sauce

A long time ago, I found this recipe in an American food magazine and changed a few ingredients in it. You might start hiccupping when you see the amount of cognac it calls for, but it's the cognac and dates that make the cake! This cake gives off a feeling of Christmas time, and it's great with a few slices of oranges instead of the blackberries. The muscovite sauce is a yummy dark fudge sauce that's also heavenly on top of the raspberry crumble on page 310, especially when complemented with whipped cream.

10–12 PIECES
10½ oz (300 g) whole dates, without pits
½ cup (100 ml) water
½ cup (100 ml) cognac
CAKE BATTER:
2 sticks + 1 tbsp (250 g) butter + butter to grease the pan
¾ cup (200 ml) brown sugar
4 eggs
1⅔ cups (400 ml) flour
2 tsp baking powder
MUSCOVADO SAUCE:
½ cup (100 ml) maple syrup or honey
½ cup (100 ml) dark brown muscovado sugar
¾ cup (200 ml) heavy cream
FOR GARNISH:
fresh berries

DIRECTIONS:
1. Preheat the oven to 350°F (175°C).
2. Mix the dates with water and cognac until you have a pretty smooth mixture. Be careful, because it can splash a lot, especially if you're using a food processor.
3. Whisk the butter and brown sugar into a fluffy mix. Add the eggs, one at a time. Fold in the flour combined with the baking powder and finish the mixture by adding the date paste.
4. Grease a bundt pan and pour the batter into it. Bake at the bottom of the oven for about 50 minutes.
5. Mix all of the ingredients for the muscovado sauce and bring to a boil. Let simmer for 10 minutes until it has reached a fudge-like consistency.
6. Pour the warm fudge sauce over the cake. Garnish with fresh berries.

214. Marble Cake with Cream Cheese

This is not your average marble cake. Because of the cream cheese, it's a little bit acidic in flavor, a lot creamier in texture, and it tastes so much better than regular marble cake. Try flavoring the cream with shredded orange zest. Combine the chocolate and cream cheese only very lightly to make sure the cake gets a proper marbled effect.

10–12 SLICES
7 oz (200 g) dark chocolate, in pieces
2 sticks (200 g) butter + butter for greasing the pan
1 cup (250 ml) sugar
3 eggs
¾ cup (200 ml) flour
CREAM CHEESE MIX:
14 oz (400 g) cream cheese
½ cup (125 ml) sugar
1 tsp vanilla sugar
2 eggs

DIRECTIONS:
1. Preheat the oven to 350°F (180°C).
2. Melt the chocolate and butter in a water bath.
3. Whisk the sugar and eggs until fluffy. Sift the flour into the mixture and then pour in the melted chocolate.
4. Whisk the cream cheese with sugar, vanilla sugar, and eggs. Pour ¼ of the chocolate batter into the baking pan. Add the cream cheese mix and then pour the rest of the chocolate mix on top. Create a beautiful marbled pattern by dragging a spoon lightly through the batter. Bake in the oven for 35–45 minutes.

215. American Pancakes with Maple Syrup Sauce

Make something special for breakfast over the weekend with these pancakes. Prepare the batter on Saturday night so you don't have to get so messy at the start of your day.

4 SERVINGS

¾ cup (200 ml) flour
1 tsp baking powder
½ tsp salt
2 tbsp sugar
1 egg
½ cup (125 ml) milk
2 tbsp butter, melted
butter for the pan
whipped cream (optional)

MAPLE SYRUP SAUCE:

1¾ oz (50 g) brown sugar
3½ tbsp (50 g) butter
½ cup (100 ml) heavy cream
⅔ cup (150 ml) maple syrup

DIRECTIONS:

1. Mix all ingredients for the maple syrup sauce in a pot and let it simmer for about 20 minutes.
2. In the meantime, mix flour, baking powder, salt, and sugar for the pancakes.
3. Lightly whisk the egg and the milk. Add the melted butter and mix in the dry ingredients. Stir until you have a smooth batter. Let it rest for a few minutes.
4. Heat up a frying pan and fry a couple of pancakes at a time over medium heat until they are golden brown. You'll know it's time to flip them when the surface bubbles.
5. Serve the pancakes with the sauce and add a dollop of whipped cream.

216. French Toast

I admit it's been a while since I've eaten French toast, but my brother still loves to eat it. The best French toast I ever had was when my mom would use white bread or just a simple wheat loaf without anything fancy to it. This French toast is supposed to be eaten as is, hot and fresh out of the pan. Try making French toast using spiced bread (see page 262) and Manitoba baguette (see page 268).

4 SERVINGS

2 eggs
½ cup (100 ml) milk
1 tbsp flour
¾ cup (200 ml) sugar
1 tbsp cinnamon
8 slices of sweet bread, preferably a little dry

DIRECTIONS:

1. Whisk eggs, milk, and flour. Mix the sugar with the cinnamon.
2. Turn the bread slices over in the egg mixture. Let them rest in the mixture for a few minutes until they soften and are saturated.
3. Pan-fry the French toast on both sides in butter. Remove them from the pan and flip them over in the sugar and cinnamon mix. Serve with ice cream or whipped cream.

215.

216. 217.

217. Warm Chocolate Pastry with Ice Cream and Peppermint Crumbs

Prepare the chocolate cake in advance and put it in the freezer. Take it out a few minutes before you're ready to bake it in the oven. Serve it warm. The oven time can vary depending on what type of baking pan you use. The cake is meant to be creamy in the middle and have a "baking bump" on top.

4 SERVINGS

1 stick + 2½ tbsp (150 g) butter + butter for
   greasing the pan
5⅓ oz (150 g) dark chocolate
½ cup (100 ml) powdered sugar
2 eggs
⅓ cup (75 ml) flour
1 container of vanilla ice cream (2 pints [½ liter])
crushed peppermint

DIRECTIONS:
1. Preheat the oven to 350°F (180°C).
2. Melt the butter, chocolate, and powdered sugar in a bowl over a water bath and let it cool.
3. Mix in the eggs, one at a time, and sift in the flour. Stir until you have a smooth batter.
4. Grease four baking pans or copper baking pans and divide the chocolate batter into them, leaving about an inch (2 cm) from the top unfilled. Bake in the oven for 10–12 minutes.
5. Cut the ice cream into cubes and dip them in crushed candy canes. Put a cube on each chocolate pastry and serve immediately.

218. South of Sweden Chocolate Cake with Raspberry Baked Rhubarb

I really don't know if this cake has anything to do with the south of Sweden at all, but it's always been called as such. Serve the rhubarb either with the cake or with simply a dollop of dessert cream (see page 322). A dollop of whipped crème fraîche (or sour cream) without any sugar is also a tasty option with this pie.

10–12 PIECES

9 oz (250 g) dark chocolate
2 sticks + 1 tbsp (250 g) butter + butter for
   greasing the pan
1⅔ cups (400 ml) powdered sugar
approx. ¾ cup (200 ml) flour
4 eggs

RASPBERRY BAKED RHUBARB:

6 stalks rhubarb
14 oz (400 g) frozen raspberries
¾ cup (200 ml) sugar

DIRECTIONS:
1. Preheat the oven to 300°F (150°C).
2. Clean the rhubarb and cut it into 4 inch (10 cm) sticks. Put them on a baking sheet. Add the raspberries and sugar. Cover it with aluminum foil and bake in the oven for 20–30 minutes, until the rhubarb has softened somewhat. Give the sheet a little shake at half-time. Let the rhubarb cool.
3. Increase the temperature to 350°F (180°C).
4. Melt the chocolate, butter, and powdered sugar in a bowl in a water bath. Remove the bowl from the water and sift the flour into the mix. Add the eggs and whisk the mixture until smooth. Pour into a greased baking pan and bake for 18–20 minutes or for 6–8 minutes if you use portion-sized pans.
5. Cut the rhubarb as you like and garnish the cake(s).

218.

220.

221.

219.

219. Raspberry Sorbet

So ridiculously scrumptious! The egg whites make the sorbet fluffy. If it gets hard as rock in the freezer, and the guests are getting impatient, I'll usually just run the sorbet or (even ice cream) through a food processor or blender. It becomes soft and luscious.

8–10 SERVINGS

1¼ cups (300 ml) sugar
1 cup (250 ml) cold water
1 lb (500 g) frozen raspberries
2 tbsp freshly squeezed lemon juice
1 egg white

DIRECTIONS:

1. Bring the sugar and water to a boil. Let it cool down.
2. Press the raspberries through a sieve and mix them with the sugar water. Add the lemon juice. Whisk the egg white with a fork and add it to the mixture.
3. Pour the mixture into the ice cream maker and run the machine until the sorbet is frozen.

Super Tasty

A MORE ICE CREAM-Y FEEL

Fold some lightly whipped cream into the sorbet and it will feel more like ice cream!

220. Chocolate Sorbet

This chocolate sorbet is really divine with the raspberry baked rhubarb on page 349. It's just as delicious in a cone.

8–10 SERVINGS

1 gelatin sheet
7 oz (200 g) dark chocolate
1⅔ cups (400 ml) water
approx. 2½ tbsp light molasses
3 tbsp brown sugar
⅔ cup (200 ml) cocoa powder

DIRECTIONS:

1. Lay the gelatin sheet in water for about 5 minutes.
2. Chop the chocolate finely. Boil the water, syrup, brown sugar, and cocoa powder. Pour it over the chocolate pieces and stir until you have a smooth cream.
3. Remove the gelatin sheet from the water and stir it into the chocolate cream.
4. Pour the mixture into an ice cream maker and run it until the sorbet is frozen.

ICE CREAM MAKER

If you don't already own an ice cream maker, you should go out and get one. Sorbet and ice cream both taste so much better when prepared in one.

221. Vanilla Ice Cream

This is the way vanilla ice cream is meant to be made—without gelatin. When it's made with gelatin, it feels almost like you're wearing a belt and suspenders at the same time. If you boil the ice cream mixture thoroughly with a thermometer at the ready, there's no need for any "just in case" gelatin sheets. And if you do make a mistake, throw it out and do it right—try try again! The half and half gives the ice cream a creamy consistency, but you can also use half-milk and half-half and half instead.

8–10 SERVINGS
4 cups (1 liter) half and half
1 vanilla stick, scored lengthwise
8 egg yolks
⅔ cup (150 ml) sugar

DIRECTIONS:
1. Pour the half and half into a pot. Scrape the vanilla beans into the pot and toss in the vanilla stick as well. Bring to a boil.
2. In a bowl, combine the egg yolks and sugar and stir.
3. Pour half of the vanilla cream mixture over the egg yolks and stir vigorously. Then pour the egg mixture back into the pot with the rest of the half and half. Simmer at a temperature of 180°F (82°C) (measure the temperature with a digital thermometer). Sift the mixture over a bowl and let it cool.
4. Pour the mixture into an ice cream machine and run it until the ice cream is frozen.

222. Simple Lemon Ice Cream

I made this ice cream in Barbro "Lill-Babs" Svensson's backyard. This ice cream is a perfect "someone-is-at-the-door-dessert"—all you have to do is spoon it onto a flat surface or into small cups to make it freeze more quickly. If you use ready-made lemon curd, the process will obviously will be much faster than if you make your own.

4 SERVINGS
2½ cups (600 ml) heavy cream
¾ cup (175 ml) sweetened condensed milk
½ lemon, zest and juice
¾ cup (200 ml) lemon curd (see page 272)

DIRECTIONS:
1. Whisk the heavy cream but don't make it too stiff. Fold in the condensed milk and flavor it with the lemon zest.
2. Squeeze the lemon juice into the lemon curd and stir. Using a fork, drizzle the lemon curd into the cream mixture.
3. Pour it into a bowl or a pan and let it rest in the freezer for about 5 hours until the ice cream has frozen. Or you can pour the ice cream onto a flat surface or into small coffee cups to reduce the freezing time. It's even quite tasty when it's only half frozen.
4. Serve the ice cream with any toppings you like. Peaches and roasted nuts make a great combination, and almond flakes are classic.

223. Glace Au Four—Ice Cream Cake

Great for big parties! You can make the cake part a few days in advance, and prepare the meringue topping the day before. Just put it in the freezer overnight. When it's time to serve it up, just spread the meringue on top of the cake (the meringue doesn't freeze in the freezer) and broil it with the oven door open—this is if you don't have a blow torch. If you do, use that instead, as the results are so much better. The hard chocolate covered toffee can be exchanged for chocolate of your choice or with nuts or dried strawberries.

8–10 SERVINGS

2 meringue bottoms
3½ oz (100 g) Daim bars or Heath bars
*   (chocolate covered toffee bars)*
2 quarts (2 liters) vanilla ice cream
½ quart (½ liter) strawberry sorbet

MERINGUE TOPPING:

4 egg whites
1 lemon, zest
½ tsp freshly squeezed lemon juice
¾ cup (200 ml) sugar

DIRECTIONS:

1. Line a cake pan with a removable bottom with plastic wrap and place in one of the meringue bottoms. Place the pan in the freezer.
2. Crush the toffee bars coarsely. Stir or whisk the vanilla ice cream until it's soft and add the crushed toffee bars. Pour the ice cream into the pan and cover it with the sorbet. Place the second meringue bottom on top. Cover the pan with plastic wrap and place it back in the freezer. Let it rest for 4–5 hours or even overnight.
3. Bring a small pot of water to a boil for a water bath. Put the egg whites, lemon zest, juice, and sugar in a stainless steel bowl with a thick bottom. Place the bowl in the pot of water and whisk with an electric whisk until the meringue is thick without being grainy (feel with your fingers). Remove the bowl from the water bath and continue whisking until the mixture has cooled.
4. Spread or pipe the meringue onto the cake and place it in the freezer for about 30 minutes.
5. Remove the cake from the freezer and burn the top with a kitchen blow torch until it becomes a lovely golden color. Serve right away.

223.

225.

224. Citrus Salad with Passion Fruit Parfait

Citrus salad with maple syrup is super easy to make. Just dollop some Greek yogurt on top and sprinkle with some freshly ground black pepper. Save the egg whites to make a meringue, for the ice cream cake on page 356, perhaps.

8–10 SERVINGS

¾ cup (200 ml) powdered sugar
10 egg yolks
8 passion fruits
½ lemon, zest and juice
2 cups (500 ml) light whipped cream

CITRUS SALAD:

2 grapefruits
2 oranges
2 passion fruits
1–2 tbsp maple syrup

DIRECTIONS:

1. Whisk the sugar and egg yolks until fluffy.
2. Scrape the pulp from the eight passion fruits and mix the pulp with the lemon zest and juice. Add the whipped cream. Put the parfait in a container and let it rest in the fridge for about 3 hours or overnight.
3. Cut the grapefruit and oranges into fillets and put them in a bowl. Scrape the pulp from the two passion fruits and add to the bowl. Drizzle maple syrup on top. Store in a cool place until ready to serve.
4. Serve the salad with the parfait.

225. Spette Cake with Rum Raisin Parfait

Whenever I buy an ice cream cone, I always opt for rum raisin. I love when the raisins have been soaked in the rum for a very long time and have hardened. So delicious! Spette cake is fun and is about as Swedish as you can get, but it's not easy to find. If your local IKEA doesn't have it, use meringue instead or just omit the cake completely—it's not what makes this dish. Just substitute with some crushed, dark chocolate.

6 SERVINGS

¾ cup (200 ml) raisins
½ cup (125 ml) dark rum
2 cups (500 ml) heavy cream
5 egg yolks
1 tsp vanilla sugar
½ cup (125 ml) sugar
1⅔ cups (400 ml) spette cake or meringue, coarsely crushed

DIRECTIONS:

1. Let the raisins soak in the rum until the rum is completely absorbed. This will take about 24 hours.
2. Lightly whip the heavy cream in a bowl. In a separate bowl, whisk the egg yolks with the vanilla sugar and add in the regular sugar a little bit at a time. Whisk the mixture until it is fluffy. Stir in the raisins. Fold the whipped cream and the crushed cake into the egg mixture.
3. Line a baking pan with plastic wrap and pour in the parfait mixture. Put the parfait in the freezer for at least 24 hours.
4. Remove the parfait from the freezer and let it rest in the fridge for 30 minutes before serving. Remove the plastic wrap and garnish with some additional crumbled cake.

226. Raspberry-Peach Popsicle

The perfect popsicle for kids. The neighborhood ice cream truck will have big competition this summer!

10 SERVINGS/POPSICLES

1 lb frozen raspberries
1 can peaches + the syrup
1 tbsp freshly squeezed lemon juice
3 tbsp powdered sugar

DIRECTIONS:

1. Combine the raspberries with the peaches and syrup. Flavor with lemon juice and powdered sugar.
2. Pour into popsicle molds and freeze for a few hours until the popsicle has solidified. Serve on hot summer days.

SEEDS WITH CHARACTER

If you want, you can always sift out the raspberry seeds, but I think it gives the popsicle character.

227. Coconut-Lime Popsicle

Try freezing the popsicle mix in a large pan and serving it as is for guests to scrape up with their forks. It's great as a palate cleanser between courses during dinner.

10 SERVINGS/POPSICLES

½ cup (100 ml) water
2 tbsp coconut flakes
¾ cup (200 ml) sugar
2 limes, zest + 3½ tbsp lime juice
2½ cups (600 ml) coconut milk

DIRECTIONS:

1. Bring the water, coconut flakes, and sugar to a boil and let simmer until the sugar has melted. Let it cool down. Add the lime zest and juice. Mix it all together with the coconut milk.
2. Pour into popsicle molds and freeze for a few hours until it has solidified.

Super Tasty

ROAST THE COCONUT FLAKES

If you lightly roast the coconut flakes in a frying pan, it will provide a more mature flavor.

228. Old-fashioned Vanilla Popsicle with Sprinkles

Every Swede has had one of these popsicles one time or another. But this simple treat can also be dressed up fancy! Fun to make with the kids.

4 SERVINGS
½ quart (½ liter) vanilla ice cream
sprinkles of choice
wooden popsicle sticks

DIRECTIONS:
Divide the ice cream into four squares. Insert a popsicle stick into each ice cream square and dip it into the sprinkles. Dip as many times as you like and eat them quickly!

229. Homemade Magnum Bars

You have to try this! Serve in style with the carton and all on the table.

4 SERVINGS
7 oz (200 g) dark chocolate (70%)
½ cup (100 ml) heavy cream
2 tbsp strong coffee
½ quart (½ liter) vanilla ice cream
½ cup (100 ml) roasted, chopped hazelnuts
  (see page 28)
wooden ice cream sticks

DIRECTIONS:
1. Finely chop the chocolate and place it in a bowl. Bring the heavy cream and the coffee to a boil. Pour it over the chocolate and stir until you have a smooth cream.
2. Divide the ice cream into four squares (or fewer, depending on how big your craving is) and insert a popsicle stick into each square. Drizzle chocolate sauce on top and sprinkle with hazelnuts. Let the popsicles rest in the freezer for about 15 minutes before serving.

230. Frozen Chocolate-dipped Bananas

I used to buy these in Båstad every time I got off the ferry. I wouldn't be surprised if it's the only place on Earth that sells them. Healthiest treats in the world!

8 SERVINGS
4 peeled bananas, cut in half across the middle
4½ oz (250 g) dark chocolate (70%)
1 tbsp coconut oil
wooden popsicle sticks

DIRECTIONS:
1. Melt the chocolate and the coconut oil in a water bath over a pot on the stove or in the microwave. Let the mixture cool a little. Insert the wooden sticks in the bananas.
2. Dip the bananas into the chocolate and place them on a baking sheet lined with parchment paper. Place it in the freezer for at least 4 hours until the chocolate has solidified.

MAKE IT HEALTHIER WITH HAZELNUTS
Chop some hazelnuts finely and sprinkle them on the bananas before freezing them. If any popsicle can be healthy, this is it. The bananas last about a week in the freezer.

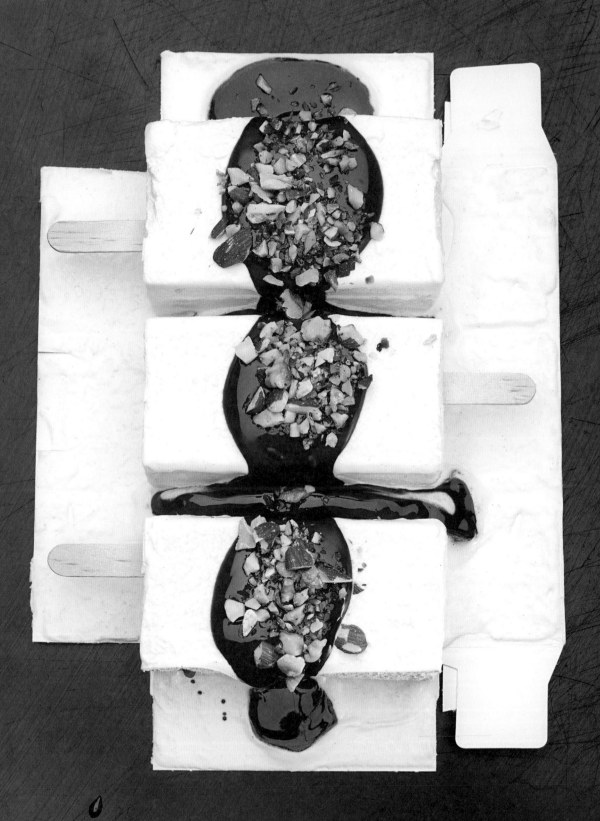

230.

231.

232.

233.

231. Raspberry Juice

This juice has a fresh and genuine raspberry flavor. It really tastes organic. The trick here is the tartaric acid, in combination with the gentle preparation, which makes for a very aromatic juice. Try this recipe with really ripe strawberries.

APPROX. 1½ QUARTS (1½ liters)
CONCENTRATED JUICE

8 cups (2 liters) raspberries (frozen is fine)
3 cups (700 ml) water
¾ oz (20 g) tartaric acid
4 cups (1 liter) sugar per 4 cups (liter) juice

DIRECTIONS:

1. Mix all the ingredients and stir. Let rest overnight at room temperature and then stir again until all raspberries are mashed.
2. Sift through a cheese cloth.
3. Measure the juice and pour it into a food processor. Add the sugar slowly and blend the juice and sugar for about 30 minutes, until the sugar has dissolved. Skim the top and pour into bottles. Store in the fridge. When ready to serve, pour the concentrated raspberry juice into a glass and dilute with water to your liking.

232. Lemon Juice

This is one of my grandmother's recipes. It's a sour juice that's long-lasting and is exactly how a lemon juice should taste.

APPROX. 1 QUART (1 liter)
CONCENTRATED JUICE

4 lemons, zest and juice
4 cups (1 liter) sugar
4 tbsp citric acid
4 cups (1 liter) water

DIRECTIONS:

1. Wash the lemons in room temperature water. Zest them with a potato peeler but be sure not to include the bitter white skin under the surface. Mix the lemon zest, juice, sugar, and citric acid in a bowl.
2. Bring the water to a boil and pour it into the bowl. Stir until the sugar has dissolved.
3. Squeeze the lemons and let some of the pulp and seeds fall through into the bowl, as this will give more flavor to the juice. Let it rest for at least 24 hours in the fridge.
4. Sift the juice and pour it into clean bottles. Freeze the bottles, but make sure they're only ¾ full; otherwise, they can explode in the freezer. You can also freeze the juice in ice cube trays. If you would like to drink the juice straight, pour the concentrated lemon juice into a glass and dilute with water to your liking.

233. Rhubarb Juice

I still have rhubarb juice in the fridge. When it starts getting cold outside, I'll have a glass of rhubarb juice and reminisce about the summer. You can also make this juice with frozen rhubarb.

APPROX. 1½ QUARTS (1½ liters)
CONCENTRATED JUICE
4½ lbs (4 kg) rhubarb
3 cups (700 ml) water
1 lemon, juice
1⅓ lbs (600 g) sugar per 4 cups (1 liter) juice

DIRECTIONS:

1. Clean the rhubarb and cut it into pieces. Put the pieces in a pot with cold water and add the lemon juice. Bring to a boil and let it simmer for about 20 minutes.
2. Let the rhubarb drain through a cheese cloth. Measure the juice and pour it into a clean pot with the correct amount of sugar and boil for about 20 more minutes. Skim the top of the juice thoroughly.
3. Pour the juice into clean bottles. Store in the fridge or in the freezer. When ready to serve, pour the concentrated rhubarb juice into a glass and dilute with water to your liking.

234. Elderflower Lemonade

I usually make elderberry juice every other year. Most years, by the time I remember to make it, it's already too late, but luckily my girlfriends always have extra. For adults, gin and elderflower is a delightful combination. But be sure not to pick the elderflowers off the side of the road because the taste of car exhaust does not go well in juice. If you want to preserve it for a longer period of time in either the fridge or at room temperature, you can add sodium benzoate.

APPROX. 3 QUARTS (3 liters)
CONCENTRATED JUICE
8 cups (2 liters) water
4½ lbs (2 kg) sugar
approx. 40 large elderflowers, cleaned
3 lemons
1¾ oz (50 g) citric acid
½ tsp sodium benzoate

DIRECTIONS:

1. Boil the water and sugar in a large pot.
2. Shake the water from the elderflowers and put them in a large stainless steel pot that can handle hot water. Cover it with a lid or plastic wrap.
3. Wash the lemons and cut them into pieces. Add them to the pot with elderflowers. Add the citric acid and the hot sugar water while stirring. Let cool somewhat and cover once again with the lid or plastic wrap. Let the juice rest for at least 24 hours; ideally it should rest for 5 days.
4. Sift the juice using a sieve or a linen towel and a colander.
5. Dilute the sodium benzoate in a glass with a small amount of juice, then add it to the rest of the juice. You don't need the sodium benzoate if you intend to freeze the juice.
6. Pour the juice into clean glass bottles, plastic soda bottles, or jars. Before serving, dilute with water to taste. You can also freeze the juice in jars or ice cube trays (just be sure not to fill them up to the top, since the juice expands when frozen).

We're taking the last photographs for the book. Next to me is Benny and our photographer, Charlie. The photos are being taken by our assistant, Marysia Klim.

Index

377

Acknowledgments!

It has been such an incredible journey to make this book! A huge thank you to my colleague and partner in crime, Benny Cederberg, and to the very talented photographer, Charlie Drevstam, for coming along on this journey. We had such a wonderful time taking all the photos for this book!

Thank you to the beautiful Stina Wirsén, who in her very unique way framed this book so beautifully with her drawings. I am awed.

Also, a great big thank you to my Swedish publisher, Bonnier Fakta, for its wonderful staff with the capability and patience to understand the thought processes of an author with a chaotic mind. Big hug to Lisa Ydring, Anna Paljak, and Annika Lyth.

And thank you Bibbi Ringqvist. You and Benny are my anchors. I'm so happy that I have you. It's because of you that I stay grounded.

And last but not least, a great big thanks to our sweet assistant, Marysia Klim. Without you, we would simply have too many cookies in the fridge!